D0866915

ART AND EDUCATION

BOOKS WRITTEN BY STAFF MEMBERS OF THE BARNES FOUNDATION

THE ART IN PAINTING
Albert C. Barnes

THE AESTHETIC EXPERIENCE
Laurence Buermeyer

AN APPROACH TO ART
Mary Mullen

ART AND EDUCATION
Dewey, Barnes, Buermeyer, Mullen, de Mazia

ART AS EXPERIENCE
John Dewey

PRIMITIVE NEGRO SCULPTURE
Paul Guillaume and Thomas Munro

THE FRENCH PRIMITIVES AND THEIR FORMS
Albert C. Barnes and Violette de Mazia

THE ART OF RENOIR
Albert C. Barnes and Violette de Mazia

THE ART OF HENRI-MATISSE
Albert C. Barnes and Violette de Mazia

THE ART OF CÉZANNE
Albert C. Barnes and Violette de Mazia

Art and Education

A COLLECTION OF ESSAYS

by

JOHN DEWEY, ALBERT C. BARNES,
LAURENCE BUERMEYER, MARY MULLEN,
VIOLETTE DE MAZIA

Published by
THE BARNES FOUNDATION PRESS
MERION, PENNA.

Third Edition

First Printing, 1954
Second Printing, 1960
Third Printing, 1969

Copyright, 1929, 1947, 1954

THE BARNES FOUNDATION

Library of Congress Catalogue Card Number: 54–13256

Printed in the United States of America

BY WILLIAM J. DORNAN, INC.
Collingdale, Pennsylvania

PREFACE TO THIRD EDITION

FOR this preface to the latest edition of *Art and Education*, the Trustees of The Barnes Foundation have selected the following passages from the writings of the late Albert C. Barnes. These were chosen for their direct bearing upon the basic ideas developed by contributors to this collection of essays.

"The value of scientific method, in brief, resides not in any assurance of its infallibility in use, but in its service in making cumulatively effective the investigations of many different observers. It is to this systematic application of method that we must look for deliverance from the aesthetic chaos of our own day."[1]

"Nor does the program pretend to furnish the student with a foot-rule by which to measure artistic greatness: the value of every artist, like the value of every individual, is in some degree unique, and there are no scales in which to weigh it. What the method does seek to do is to make experience and judgment relevant to the object ostensibly experienced and judged."[1]

". . . every artist's career is an adventure in

[1] *Method in Aesthetics*, The Philosopher of the Common Man, G. P. Putnam's Sons, New York, N. Y.—Copyright 1940.

v

perception, and the education of the student will end when the last artist has ceased to paint."[2]

Readers familiar with the attitudes of Professor Dewey and Dr. Barnes towards the applicability of the scientific method to a study of the arts will note in the quoted excerpts a similarity in their views regarding methods of education, on occasion arrived at independently by each. Their mutual interest in the problems of education and philosophy brought the two men together into a lifelong friendship and exchange of views, and led to a close collaboration for the purpose of putting their educational theories into practice at The Barnes Foundation.

MERION, 1954.

[2] *Ibid.*

PREFACE TO SECOND EDITION

In the twenty years that have elapsed since most of the articles included in the first edition of *Art and Education* were first published, The Barnes Foundation has carried on its program of giving instruction in its gallery and of conducting research in esthetics, scientific method, and the objective analysis of plastic art. It has published volumes on the French Primitives, on Henri-Matisse, on Renoir and on Cézanne, together with a completely revised edition, the third, of *The Art in Painting*. Now that a new edition of the present work is called for, it is possible to present once more a general outline of what has been accomplished by the Foundation since its establishment, to restate its general principles and methods, and to illustrate by specific examples the fruitfulness of the methods and the wide range of their application.

From the very beginning, the program of the Foundation has been based upon the philosophy of John Dewey, and it is fitting that the opening statement here should be made by Professor Dewey. The four chapters reprinted here, from *The Art of Renoir*, offer further testimony to the parallel between his views and ours, as does his Foreword to that volume, which we present with deep satisfaction. In these same chapters will be found a fuller statement of method, of psychological principles and of the nature of form, than was available in 1929. Taken together, they present a compact summary of the logic, psychology, and esthetics which are fundamental to the work of the Foundation, and which may serve as the background against which all the other essays in the book should be read. The chapters reprinted from *The Art in Painting* appear here in the 1937 version, and have thus been kept abreast of the Foundation's progress in research. Additional chapters are added from *The Art of Henri-Matisse* and *The Art of Cézanne* to illustrate applications of method not foreshadowed in the first edition of the present volume.

Gradual supersession or abandonment of errors in courses in art education in universities, colleges and schools, that were rife in 1929, has permitted some abridgment of the polemical part of the book. Unfortunately, not all confusion and superstition are dead or even moribund, even in high places, and conditions in the educational world have necessitated the addition of other articles not part of the original collection.

ALBERT C. BARNES

MERION, 1947.

PREFACE TO FIRST EDITION

THIS book owes its existence to the widespread demand for information about the purposes, activities and educational program of The Barnes Foundation. Painters, critics, teachers and many other persons interested in art or in education have requested such information in order to learn of the precise character of the Foundation's work. It seems advisable, therefore, to give in the present volume a conspectus of the work done.

The Foundation from the start was intended not only to offer instruction to individual students enrolled in its own classes or in those of allied institutions, but also to put before the public a tried and tested method for education in art, and an outline of what such education should be. To the latter end were issued various books written by members of its staff and also the *Journal of The Barnes Foundation*. This *Journal* was begun as an instrument both of construction and of controversy, for there was an obvious and long-existing need for putting before the public a statement of the living issues both in art and in education in art. The *Journal* itself ceased publication when its primary work was done, and is now out of print; but the insistent demand, from every part of the country, for copies of its issues, seems to indicate that its contents still have a function to fulfill.

Most of the articles in the *Journal* are republished here, together with other material elsewhere printed, for which credit is duly given. There has been a slight amount of revision in some of the articles for the purpose of bringing out more clearly the thread of connection running through the whole. Since, however, some appearance of disjointedness may remain, it has seemed advantageous to have here a very brief statement of the general position of The Barnes Foundation. In everything published under its auspices, the prime and unwavering contention has been that art is no trivial matter, no device for the entertainment of dilettantes, or upholstery for the houses of the wealthy, but a source of insight into the world, for which there is and can be no substitute, and in which all persons who have the necessary insight may share. This insight, however, is impossible except by the aid of others' insight, especially of the insight of the past, for which another word is "tradition." At the same time, tradition merely imitated, carried on inertly, is worthless: there is no art unless tradition is used freely, freshly and personally, as a means of individual expression. To the establishment of these fundamentals, with illustrations of their application, Section I is devoted.

In Section II, the same principles appear, combined with the educational principles of which the original and classic expression is found in the published works of Professor Dewey and more especially in his book, *Democracy and Education.* The stress here is upon method rather than upon any precise application, although a general type of application is indicated.

In Section III, social and institutional questions are treated because education in art is unfortunately carried on in large measure under conditions which fore-ordain its futility. Politics, mere prestige, and the activities of those who have wealth without intelligence or discrimination, or good intentions without discernment, are largely in control in existing institutions and academies, and their hand is fatal to any real aesthetic cultivation. Any work which did not deal with them, and mention them by name, would be false to the cause of education in art.

ALBERT C. BARNES

MERION, 1929.

CONTENTS

Section II

CONSTRUCTION AND CONTROVERSY

Section III

COMPARATIVE STUDIES:
RENOIR, CEZANNE, MATISSE, STRAVINSKY

Section I

ART AND EDUCATION

FOREWORD[1]

JOHN DEWEY

THE authors have covered in this volume [*The Art of Renoir*] the artistic work of Renoir and the method that must be used in any intelligent approach to the understanding and appreciation of art in all its forms. Their treatment of these topics leaves nothing for me to add, and contains nothing that I should wish to change.

The Barnes Foundation, however, is an educational institution, and this volume, like those which preceded it, is a fruit of educational activities. The method and material of the present work have a definite bearing not only upon education in the plastic arts, but upon education in general. Although this implication will be evident to the book's intelligent readers, there is perhaps some reason for underscoring it. At all events, in responding to the honor of an invitation to write some introductory words, it is of the educational phase of this work and of The Barnes Foundation that I shall speak.

For many years, I have thought and taught that experience is an interaction between the self and some aspect of its environment. Purposeful, intelligent action is the means by which this interaction is rendered significant. In the course of such action, objects acquire meaning and the self becomes aware of its own powers, since, by intelligent control of the environment, it directs and consolidates its own capacities. Purposeful action is thus the goal of all that is truly educative, and

[1] From Albert C. Barnes and Violette de Mazia, *The Art of Renoir*, The Barnes Foundation Press, Merion, Pa., 1944.

3

2

it is the means by which the goal is reached and its
content remade. Such activity is of necessity a growth
and a growing. It begins when an infant makes his first
purposeful adaptions to his surroundings; as he makes
them, he acquires attitudes and habits which enable
him to widen his purposes and to discover and use the
means and methods of achieving larger purposes. In
this process of intelligent living there is no inherent
limit. It should go on from infancy to death. Arrest of
continuous growth is a form of premature decay and
death.

In intelligent living, in directed interaction of the self
and its world, action (in the limited sense of the word),
emotion, and understanding are all involved. Intelligent adaption of self to surrounding objects and events
brings these functions into balance. Thought then
becomes knowledge and insight; emotion becomes interest; motor responses become mastery of things and
qualities about us and of the human potentialities relevant to them. Arrest of the process of growth is really
the arrest of intelligent living, of education. Growth,
intelligent living, education have many enemies. These
enemies are powerful. They are, unfortunately, re-en-
forced by the practices which dominate the professed
agencies of education, the schools and the institutions
called educational.

Every one-sided emphasis upon routine and mechanical habit is such an enemy. At the outset, impulses
which have not yet been ordered into effective modes of
action predominate because of the absence of any purpose or meaning. The problem is to secure the intelligent direction of such impulses. But the schools—in
the name of efficiency and under the pressure of those
mechanical forces that are so strong in the present social
environment—substitute for intelligent direction the

formation of rigid and thoughtless habits. Through such inadequacies, the acquisition of knowledge is transformed into the amassing of mere information; memory, instead of being the ally of judgment, is converted into a substitute for it. Facts and principles are "learned" in isolation, whereas *in intelligent living* they are so intimately connected with each other that they are active agencies for grasping meaning and enhancing values. A conformity that restricts then takes the place of what otherwise could have been a never-ending voyage of discovery. Emotions which, when connected with the meaning of objects and with purposeful action, are *interests* attaching the self to the changing world, are left free-floating. Instead of giving secure anchorage, they dissolve into reveries that come between the self and the world. All of these breaks and arrests in growth, in intelligent living, in education, characterize traditional learning as practiced in the educational institutions of today.

The method employed in the volume to which these words are prefixed avoids the disorder just noted, a disorder which has permeated current ways of appreciating and understanding art. For, quite apart from set courses in the production and understanding of painting and other art forms (where the disorder is not unknown), the effects of the institution of traditional learning have deeply influenced attitudes in all modes of experience. I know of no statement of the relation of scientific method to intelligent living—the real meaning of science—equal to that found in the early pages of the first chapter of the present volume. Yet, since the material of science is itself often taught in our institutions of learning with little regard to science *as the method of observation and of interpretation of what is observed*, there is small cause for wonder that the scientific method has as yet found little recognition in other phases of human experience, and especially in art. We need not be surprised that, in the teaching of the arts, there has grown up the idea that the fine arts and the method of intelligence—for that is what scientific method is—are polar opposites in any study and understanding that is objectively grounded. In the artistic range of experience, more than in any other, the habit of separating mind (active in observation and reflection) and emotion is deep-seated. In this range, the evils of this habit are most conspicuous. Education, essentially a training of perception, is abandoned. Private emotion, and judgment that is also private, because they are not based on an awakened perception of objects and their relations to one another, come between the self and the perceptible world.

It makes little difference whether the teacher engages chiefly in giving instructions about "facts" or endeavors to stir what is usually called "appreciation." The former concerns biographies of artists, the history of schools, the technique of handling materials—whether the subject be painting or literature. But facts are something *about* objects; they are used instead of the direct perception of objects. Appreciation becomes an effort to stir the emotions. Emotions *are* involved in all genuine perception. But they are a factor in appreciation only when they are responses to objectively perceived elements and relationships progressively discovered in the object itself—whether a painting, a poem, a symphony or a so-called scientific object.

The teacher, if gifted with imagination, can engage in poetic utterance about the work of art and charm the pupil. This process has elements of value lacking in the accumulation of dry facts about the work. But while the teacher's flight of fancy may have a basis in the background of his own experience, the pupil, who lacks this basis, will let his imagination work along the lines of his own private desires and feeling, and, in the end, will be still further removed from the ability to direct his emotions to the object as an object. The result is that his possible interest in increasing his perception of works of art is diverted into interest in pursuing his own lines of reverie. When the method of the teacher leads the pupil to *see* in the object features and relations he had not seen before, both teacher and pupil come into intellectual and emotional control of the situation. Then the habit of objective seeing is formed, and the habit operates in subsequent seeing. The information acquired, instead of being put into dead storage, becomes an active resource. Experience is immediately enriched, and the capacity for growth, for continuing experience, is expanded and directed.

To learn to see anything well is a difficult undertaking. It requires the activity of the whole personality. Learning to perceive demands the interaction of the whole personality with things about it. This is true whether one is seeing a picture or painting it, mastering golf, building a new type of bridge, or reading the poetry of Keats.

Since my educational ideas have been criticized for undue emphasis upon intelligence and the use of the method of thinking that has its best exemplification in science, I take profound, if somewhat melancholy, ironic, satisfaction in the fact that the most thoroughgoing embodiment of what I have tried to say about education is, as far as I am aware, found in an educational institution that is concerned with art. I do not know whether it is matter for surprise that education in the esthetic field should be the first to do the obvious and simple thing. But I do know that hardly a week —

certainly not a month—passes that I do not receive a letter, sometimes from a teacher, sometimes from a student, which asks why there is such a gap between educational theory and educational practice; that does not ask, in effect, why teachers and students who wish to do productive work—work productive in experience, intelligence and interest—should be so hampered and harassed. I have ventured, therefore, into this brief summary of educational theory because this volume of The Barnes Foundation is so adequate an exemplification of what that theory means in practice. It is a reward, as well as an honor, to be associated with an educational institution that is engaged in vital education.

JOHN DEWEY'S PHILOSOPHY OF EDUCATION[1]

Albert C. Barnes

John Dewey's philosophy of education rests on the axiom that the indispensable elements of the democratic way of life—scientific method as intelligence in operation, art, education—are all bound together in a single organic whole. To put the matter in other terms, all genuine experience is intelligent experience, experience guided by insight derived from science, illuminated by art, and made a common possession through education. This conception has implications of the most far-reaching import. When the common experience which ought to be the birthright of all human beings is broken by barriers of ignorance, class-prejudice, or economic status, the individual thus isolated loses his status as a civilized human being, and the restoration of his wholeness is possible only by reestablishment of the broken linkage.

Applied to the field of education, this conception implies that the prevailing academic methods of instruction in art are misdirected from the very beginning. What the student needs to know is not how men of genius produced immortal masterpieces long ago, but how in the world that his own eyes show him he can discover more and more of what lends color and zest to what he does from day to day. The masterpieces have their indispensable function, but it is the function of guiding and training the student's own perception, not of standing in remote isolation as objects of worship or occasions for gush.

[1] From *The Humanist*, Winter, 1946.

The misconception which identifies art with what is remote, high-flown or artificial is paralleled by another which confines science to the laboratory or lecture-hall. If the chemist is thought of as operating exclusively with balances and test-tubes, the astronomer as helpless without a telescope, or the historian as a reader of volumes or manuscripts in a library, the essential factor of scientific procedure is lost sight of. Science is science not because laboratory apparatus or words of a technical vocabulary are employed, but because observation and reflection are joined and correlated by methods that have proved themselves to be illuminating and fruitful. The problems with which science is concerned originate outside the laboratory—in the fields which must be tilled, the swamps that must be drained, the epidemics that must be controlled, the refractory human beings whose acts and purposes must be harmonized for the sake of a good social order. As the problems crystallize, possible solutions take form in the realm of hypothesis, and it is in the laboratory that these receive their first experimental test; but the testing is never complete until the course of reflection has flowed out into the world again, and human activities there have been given a wider scope and a richer meaning.

Education is growth, the development of the faculties with which every normal child is born. Growth is gradual, fostered only by means of communication between the individual and his world. Education provides an orderly progression of the means by which the avenues of communication are gradually widened in scope. It is a never-ending process that extends from the cradle to the grave. "Gradual" means proceeding by a succession of steps or stages. If the learner attemps to vault over the stages through which natural growth inevitably proceeds, the result is pretense or self-deception, sham erudition masquerading as "culture." It is a view only too widely prevalent that what is "common" is commonplace, and hence contemptible; that distinction consists in avoiding and despising the common; and this is the view that inevitably leads in practice to the gentility which is only another name for vulgarity. In contrast, any work which proceeds from real living has its own integrity and dignity and whether it succeeds or fails never sinks into the meretricious or tawdry.

The interconnection of science and art becomes more fully apparent when we consider them both as means of communication, as indispensable factors in every stage and aspect of education. Born, as we all are, helpless and speechless and dependent upon others for all the necessities of life, we must acquire slowly and gradually the capacities which make life more than a sum of vegetative and animal processes. As the utterly self-centered and uncomprehending infant develops, the chaos which is his world begins to take on order and to mirror the objective world which lies about him. He learns to relate his cries, wails and random movements to what the things, and especially the persons, in his environment *do* to him. At some point in his growth he grasps the difference between things, which simply affect him, and persons who communicate with him. Throughout the rest of his life he elaborates the distinction. He learns that he must not treat persons as things: this is the dawn of morality. He learns that a more penetrating, a more comprehensive grasp of things enables him to do with them what he could never do by his untutored impulses: this is the dawn of science. He learns, for example, that with particular tones of his voice, gestures, combinations of words, he can make others aware of what he sees with his mind's eye: this is the dawn of art.

Morality, science, art, all alike, are forms of communication, possible only through the sharing of experience which constitutes civilized living. In its widest sense, education includes all of them; but only if education is conceived, not in the conventional sense, as preparation for life, but as living itself. To have conceived education thus, and to have developed the conception until it covers the whole field of human experience, has been the supreme achievement of John Dewey—an achievement rarely paralleled in scope in the entire history of education.

METHOD[1]

Albert C. Barnes and Violette de Mazia

It is a familiar fact that the appreciation of art is vitiated by every sort of whim, fancy and superstition. The average person, lacking any understanding of what the painter aimed to do, looks at a painting with the expectation of being given information, told a story, moved to the same sort of emotion that the thing in actual life would incite, or perhaps of being inspired to elevated and edifying sentiments. Even if he disavows any knowledge of art, he is probably under the impression that what he does *not* know is a set of arbitrary rules, comparable to those of tennis or chess. If he turns for enlightenment to what usually passes for education in art, he is only too likely to be confirmed in his error or to be led to the additional error of supposing that the biography of the artist, and the technical means of putting paint on canvas, are the key to the understanding he seeks. The result is that he comes away with no impression specifically relevant to what he has looked at, and that there are as many opinions about a work of art as there are persons who have observed it. He presumes that the only alternative to chaos, under these circumstances, is authority, and consequently it is frequently supposed that good art is that which qualified critics pronounce to be such, though of course what qualifies the critics remains a mystery.

A parallel state of affairs formerly prevailed in the understanding of Nature. Many natural scenes and

---

[1] From Albert C. Barnes and Violette de Mazia, *The Art of Renoir*, The Barnes Foundation Press, Merion, Pa., 1944.

processes, storms and sunsets, deserts and fields with blooming flowers have an obvious appeal to feelings either unpleasant or pleasant, and all primitive peoples consequently conceived Nature as controlled by powers friendly or hostile to human beings, and to be controlled by direct personal appeals. This was the period of animism and magic, which humanity outgrew only as it learned to disregard its own immediate emotions about Nature, and to seek verifiable information about objective physical processes. No such information, however, is possible to any one who relies upon his untutored senses, upon habits of interpretation which remain chaotic and infected by subjectivity; hence, animism was at first superseded merely by alchemy and astrology.

The change merely continued the conception of natural processes as intrinsically characterized by their effect upon our own welfare—metals are in themselves base or precious, for example, and the positions of the stars are directly related to human welfare. No real science was possible until a method of investigation was discovered, a method which wholly eliminated the idiosyncrasies of the particular observer from the object to be understood, and hence something which made the observations and interpretations of one individual verifiable by another. The scientific ideal, in other words, is that of complete objectivity, and its justification is found in the fact that by science, and by science alone, has the course of natural processes been brought under control. Science, in short, by excluding the individual's whims and fancies from the determination of what objectively exists, has made the physical world infinitely more amenable to the individual's enlightened purposes. The satisfactions denied him have been imaginary, those provided have been real.

A similar passage from dreams to reality in the world of art can be made only by the same means—the use of method based upon objective fact. The possibilities inherent in a painting reveal themselves to the un-tutored eye as little as do those of a piece of coal. Art, like science, involves a departure from the ways of activity and seeing things which the experiences of practical life impose; and the appreciation of art, like the understanding of science, requires a grasp of the artist's specific purpose. No activity, no perception of anything, is possible except by virtue of a set of meanings and habits, qualities to be identified in the objects about us, and dispositions to perform specific acts when the identification has been made. The habits common to eating, dressing and undressing, getting about safely and expeditiously, using the necessary minimum of language are so familiar, the process of their acquisition is usually so completely forgotten, that they are likely to seem as natural as breathing, and to require no method. This means only that the method has been wholly absorbed by the mind and needs no conscious attention; it exists, however, in our readiness to notice the objective facts in a situation which sets off the familiar response.

Every perception, as we shall see in detail in the essay *Learning to See*[2], involves selection from among the many qualities of an object, of those relevant to our interests, and the amplification of such qualities by appropriate meanings stored up in our minds by past experience. This selection and supplementation, which are automatic in our most familiar activities, emerge into consciousness whenever a new form of action has to be acquired. Learning to sail a boat, drive an auto-mobile, play tennis, speak a foreign language involves, in addition to new muscular coördinations, sensitivity

[2] Page 145 of present Volume.

to a new set of stimuli and a grasp of the meanings that attach to them. The sensitivity and set of meanings are correlative: we notice only the characteristic things that point to consequences to be sought or avoided, and the only sort of meanings which we need or can consider are those which have objective indications in an existing situation.

Our interests, our general purposes, determine what we shall notice, how we shall interpret it, and what we shall do about it; and conversely, our ways of seeing, interpreting and doing, constitute our general interests, which are real and efficacious only in so far as they have taken form in definitely organized habits. Such organized habits, though rarely formulated in words, constitute methods without which we cannot perceive, think or act.

Just as the chauffeur, the tennis-player, the physician and the engineer have their individual sensitivity and corresponding store of meanings, so also has the artist. The dramatist or novelist is interested in human experiences, individual and collective; he seeks to portray character, depict situation or incident, and to accomplish this he requires a sensitive responsiveness to every aspect of personal and social relationships, the complication of human motives and the molding of individuality by convention and environment. His medium is that of language, and his command of his medium is shown in his sensitiveness to the use of words, his ability to characterize his subject-matter precisely, vividly, and effectively by the meanings, images and feelings which speech embodies. The painter is likewise interested in objective things and situations, but not in their causes or consequences, and not in the stream of consciousness of the persons who may appear in his pictures. What his eye is trained to see and his mind to organize and enrich, is the visible appearance of things, their shape and color, their texture and the manner in which they are composed in groups. These discoveries he embodies in colored pigments applied to canvas, and his command of his medium appears in his ability to make his paintings a true record of what his senses and imagination have grasped in the objective world. The driving force of his activity is the emotion which the world, in its visible aspect, arouses in him; but unlike the ordinary man, whose feelings spur him to produce practical changes in the things he sees, the artist expends his energy in sharpening his vision, refining and deepening his perceptions, discovering a richer plastic and human significance in the object of his interest.

In the essay *Expression and Form*[3] the way in which this process of expression goes on and its outcome in the creation of form will be described in detail; what is important for the present is the objective reference of any work of art, the fact that it records a discovery and that the discovery can be verified, the artist's experience shared, only by one who has himself learned to see.

From the fact that meanings are indispensable to seeing, it follows that art and intelligence are inseparably connected. Intelligence, as we shall see in the essay *Experience and Growth*,[4] is nothing but the use of meanings to illuminate existing situations, to bring to bear upon present problems the results of past experience. The scientist sees largely by means of instruments, microscope, spectroscope, thermometer, and the like, which reveal qualities which his unaided senses are not acute enough to discover; these instruments embody the results of past reflection, and make present reflec-

[3] Page 160 of present Volume.
[4] Page 177 of present Volume.

tion possible. The artist needs no mechanical aids to perception, but he too requires instruments and these are found in the traditions of painting. The traditions of art constitute the working capital of every artist; they are the records of what painters have in the past discovered and revealed as significant; and the ultimate test of any painter's importance is his ability to add contributions of his own, by means of which his successors may carry further the work of discovery. The intelligence of the painter manifests itself in his use of the traditions to illuminate for him the world which he seeks to depict; of the Venetian, for example, to open his eyes to the rich colorfulness of things, and to the function of color in building up forms, composing masses and welding together the picture as a whole.

Every tradition may be regarded as a way of seeing and a manner of organizing; by extracting from the whole body of traditions the elements which serve best the purpose of his individual vision, the painter displays his intelligence in creating his individual form. This intelligent use of traditions constitutes his method; without it he could do nothing, he would have no esthetic personality to express.

The parallel between art and science in their common objective reference, and their reliance upon method freed from personal idiosyncrasy, involves no derogation to the personality of the artist. We have already noted that objective science yields human values wholly inaccessible to hit-or-miss observation and guesswork colored by desire or prejudice; it does so because it is not a mechanical registration of brute force, but an intelligent search for significant fact. Similarly, the artist does not put down indiscriminately on canvas whatever is before him: he selects and rejects in accordance with the requirements of his design.

Design in the artist corresponds to the specific purpose which makes each science select from concrete things only the qualities or aspects which are relevant to its problems. There is no single formula which describes physical things truly for the purposes of all sciences, and no one way of envisaging the color, mass, line and illumination of an object which is prescriptive for all painters. No two men ever view anything from precisely the same point of view: every true individual, because of his natural endowment, his experience, the influences which have shaped him, the force of his individual personality, sees his world in his own unique way. The objectivity of the artist does not consist in an attempt to be like everybody else, to submit himself to a standard set by the average. What it does consist in is giving a definite form, recognizable by others, to his own vision; in reshaping what he sees, eliminating what is adventitious and supplying what his raw material may not itself display at all, until the form finally achieved is a fully objective expression of his individual reaction to the world.

In defining the conditions of success in art, we have also by implication defined those of failure. An artist who has not mastered tradition can see nothing significant or important; if he attempts to paint he can only tell a story, produce a document, or enter into a losing competition with the camera. Mere acquiescence in tradition, however, is equally futile; it qualifies a painter only as an academician. Since he exercises no initiative or individuality, he remains a copyist; he is a parasite upon tradition, his esthetic status is the same as the scientific status of someone who has read in a textbook that water is H_2O but has no idea how the fact is known or what implications it carries with it. To the academician tradition is a means not to reflection

3

and vision but to the avoidance of either: it takes him not toward but away from the real world. Far from contributing to the advance of artistic insight, he hinders it by adding the weight of his example to the inertia against which all progress has to struggle.

This sketch of the distinctive purpose of art and the conditions of success in it, in defining the method of the artist, has indicated also the only possible method for the understanding of the work of art. The artist is interested in seeing an object in its full significance, not merely in noting in it the indications of its practical bearing in our welfare. To acquire this more comprehensive interest of the artist is thus the first step to be taken in grasping the record of his experience. What he sees is not only more finely differentiated in its detail, it is more comprehensively ordered, more organically unified, than what we are ordinarily capable of perceiving. The principle of its unification is that of *plastic form*, the balanced union of color, line, light and space, by which an object is created which has an imaginative reality denied to the world of literal fact, and also incomparably greater human significance. Any method for the proper study of plastic art must therefore be based upon the conception of plastic form, which defines the only relevant aim of all painting.

Since the artist's ability to see and organize, to create form, depends upon the meanings supplied by the traditions, understanding of his accomplishment depends equally upon possession of these meanings; in their absence no differentiation between the artist and the academician is possible. Since the individual design, the specific purpose which governed the painting of a particular picture, determines the extent and manner in which each of the plastic means is used, their organization also must be grasped and entered into. To suppose that all painters have identical purposes is merely academicism carried to its final conclusion. Since the achievement of a profound esthetic vision, a distinctive personal form, is gradual and involves accumulative growth and enrichment of experience, the artist's work can be fully grasped only if the progress of his development is traced, together with the progressive incorporation in his form of more and more material both from the traditions and from the actual world.

A study of art based upon such a method promises results of the same verifiable objectivity as those of science. Since it does not appeal at any point to mere emotion, it eliminates an otherwise ineradicable source of confusion and blindness; since it can be applied only by the constant exercise of personal observation and intelligent applications of meanings, it eliminates also the appeal to dogmatic authority which is no less fatal than mere emotionalism to real understanding. It obviously provides no rule of thumb, applicable by every one; but no more does science: none of the significant results of science can be tested and judged except by the highly trained and specially qualified.

Since personality remains essential in art, and a measure of personal incompatibility seems to be inherent in experience, the enjoyment of a particular artist's work as distinguished from a judgment of its value, will probably always vary with the individual observer. The variations which actually exist at present, however, are the outcome chiefly of confusion or distraction, such as irrelevant preferences in matter of subject; with the shift of interest to plastic essentials, these may be more and more uprooted. From the intelligent use of objective method, in a word, may be expected a personal response as completely relevant to the work of art as are the judgments of a chemist or biologist to the processes of the physical world.

EXPERIENCE, NATURE AND ART[1]

John Dewey

Contemporary theories of art generally suffer from inconsistency. They are only in part interpretations of art and of experience as these are to be observed today; in part, they represent a survival of opinions and assumptions inherited from the Greeks. According to Greek theory, art is a form of practice, and so incurs the reproach of being concerned with a merely subjective, changing and imperfect world. This was true of all arts, of those now classified as "fine" as well as of the useful crafts practised by the artisan. In contrast with both, science was regarded as a revelation—in fact, the only true revelation—of reality. It was thought to be through science alone that access is provided to the world as it is in itself, not colored or distorted by human wants or preferences. Art corresponded to production, science to "contemplation," and the productive was branded as inferior, an activity proper only to mechanics and slaves.

This view was a reflection in theory of the Greek social system, in which a menial class performed all necessary labor, and freeman and citizens alone enjoyed the fruits of that labor. Since the leisure class held the position of power and honor, its part in life was regarded as intrinsically superior, and the artist, who by the labor of his hands shaped the objects which were the food of contemplation, belonged to the lower realm of nature and experience.

[1] From *Journal of The Barnes Foundation*, October, 1925. Adapted from Professor Dewey's book, *Experience and Nature*, Open Court Publishing Company, Chicago, 1925.

Contemporary opinion accepts, in the main, the Greek view that knowledge is contemplation, and that it alone reveals nature as nature is. The Greek disparagement of art, it partly accepts and partly rejects; accepts it as regards the useful arts, which are clearly modes of practice, but rejects it as regards the fine arts. In fine art it makes a distinction between the experience of the artist, which is considered to be creative, and the experience of the beholder or connoisseur, which is regarded as passive. Of these, it ranks the artist above the connoisseur, the producer above the consumer. At the same time, although it regards knowledge as contemplation, it recognizes that science, the systematic pursuit of knowledge, is active, an affair of making experiments, and so belongs to the realm of practice.

These notions are consistent neither with each other nor, as a whole, with experience. The Greek view was sound in recognizing the continuity of "useful" with "fine" art; it erred in neglecting the connection of knowledge with experiment, and so in isolating knowledge from practice. If knowledge is truly contemplation, and is on that account superior to mere practice, then all arts, that of the painter no less than that of the carpenter, are inferior to science, and the painter stands in rank below the dilettante who looks at paintings. If, however, not knowledge but art is the final flowering of experience, the crown and consummation of nature, and knowledge is only the means by which art, which includes all practice, is enabled to attain its richest development, then it is the artist who represents nature and life at their best.

Current discussion of esthetics and art falls into inconsistency about the active and passive rôles of art largely because it confuses art as a process of execution, of creation of a type of material things, and art as the enjoyable appreciation of things so created. To avoid this inconsistency it is advantageous to use the word "artistic" to designate the activities by which works of art are brought into being, and to reserve the term "esthetic" for the appreciation of them when created, the enhanced or heightened perceptions in which they result.

Although the view here defended asserts that there is no ultimate difference between the artist and the artisan, there is an obvious empirical difference between the activities and experience of the artist, as we actually find him, and those of the artisan. That the artist's life is the more humanly desirable, that it is the richer, more self-rewarding, more humane, none would deny. The difference, however, is not one between esthetic contemplation and mere labor, but between those activities which are charged with intrinsic significance—which are both instrumental, means to more remote ends, and consummatory, immediately enjoyable—and those forms which are *merely* instrumental, and in themselves nothing but drudgery. This fact is due to nothing in the nature of experience or practice, but only to defects in the present economic and social order. To call the greater part of the productive activities now carried on "useful arts" is mere euphemism, by which the essential irrationality of the existing régime is concealed. Innumerable commodities which are manufactured by the "useful arts" are only apparently and superficially useful; their employment results not in satisfaction of intelligent desire, but in confusion and extravagance, bought at the price of a narrowed and embittered experience. There can be no true understanding of either practice or esthetic appreciation while practice is in large measure slavery, and while "esthetic appreciation" is merely one of the forms of distraction by which intervals of respite from slavery are whiled away.

The degradation of labor is paralleled by a degradation of art. Most of what passes for art at present falls under three captions:

First, there is mere indulgence in emotional outpouring, without reference to the conditions of intelligibility. Such "expression of emotion" is largely futile—futile partly because of its arbitrary and willfully eccentric character, but partly also because the channels of expression currently accepted as permissible are so rigidly laid down that novelty can find acceptance only with the aid of violence.

In addition to this type—and frequently mingled with it—there is experimentation in new modes of craftsmanship, cases where the seemingly bizarre and over-individualistic character of the products is due to discontent with existing technique, and is associated with an attempt to find new modes of expression. It is aside from the point to treat these manifestations as if they constituted art for the first time in human history, or to condemn them as not art because of their violent departure from received canons and methods. Some movement in this direction has always been a condition of growth of new forms, a condition of salvation from that mortal arrest and decay called academic art.

Then there is that which in quantity bulks most largely as fine art: the production of buildings in the name of the art of architecture; of pictures in the name of painting; cf novels, dramas, etc., in the name of literary art; a production which in reality is largely a form of commercialized industry in production of a class of commodities that find their sale among well-to-do persons desirous of maintaining a conventionally approved status. As the first two modes carry to disproportionate excess that factor of difference, particularity and contingency, which is indispensable in all art, deliberately flaunting avoidance of the repetitions and order of nature, so this mode celebrates the regular and finished. It is reminiscent rather than commemorative of the meanings of things. Its products remind their owner of things pleasant in memory though hard in direct undergoing, and remind others that their owner has achieved an economic standard which makes possible cultivation and decoration of leisure.

Obviously no one of these classes of activity and products, or all of them put together, mark off anything that can be called distinctively fine art. They share their qualities and defects with many other activities and objects. But, fortunately, there may be mixed with any of them, and, still more fortunately, there may occur without mixture, process and product which are characteristically excellent. *This occurs when activity is productive of an object which affords continuously renewed delight.* This condition requires that the object be, with its successive consequences, indefinitely instrumental to *new* satisfying events. For otherwise the object is quickly exhausted and satiety sets in. Anyone who reflects upon the commonplace that a measure of artistic products is their capacity to attract and retain observation with satisfaction under whatever conditions they are approached, has a sure demonstration that a genuinely esthetic object is not exclusively consummatory, but is causally productive as well. A consummatory object that is not also instrumental turns in time to the dust and ashes of boredom. The "eternal" quality of great art is its renewed instrumentality for further consummatory experiences.

When this fact is noted it is also seen that limitation of fineness of art to paintings, statues, poems, songs and symphonies is conventional, or even verbal. Any activity that is productive of objects whose perception is an immediate good, and whose operation is a continual source of enjoyable perception of other events, exhibits fineness of art. There are acts of all kinds that directly refresh and enlarge the spirit and that are instrumental to the production of new objects and dispositions which are in turn productive of further refinements and replenishments. Frequently moralists make the acts *they* find excellent or virtuous wholly final, and treat art and affection as mere means. Estheticians reverse the performance, and see in good *acts* means to an ulterior external happiness, while esthetic appreciation is called a good in itself, or that strange thing, an end in itself. But on both sides it is true that in being predominantly fructifying, the things designated means are immediately satisfying. They are their own excuses for being just because they are charged with an office in quickening apprehension, enlarging the horizon of vision, refining discrimination, creating standards of appreciation which are confirmed and deepened by further experiences. It would almost seem that when their non-instrumental character is insisted on, what is meant were an indefinitely expansive and radiating instrumental efficacy.

It is the fact that art, so far as it is truly art, is a union of the serviceable and the immediately enjoyable, of the instrumental and the consummatory, that makes it impossible to institute a difference in kind between useful and fine art. Many things are termed useful for reasons of social status, implying depreciation and contempt. Things are sometimes said to belong to the menial arts merely because they are cheap and used familiarly by common people. These things of daily use for ordinary ends may survive in later periods, or be transported to another culture, as from Japan and China to America, and being rare and sought by connoisseurs, rank forthwith as works of fine art. Other things may be called fine because their manner of use is decorative or socially ostentatious. It is tempting to make a distinction of degree and say that a thing belongs to the sphere of use when perception of its meaning is instrumental to something else; and that a thing belongs to fine art when its other uses are subordinate to its use in perception. The distinction has a rough practical value, but cannot be pressed too far. For in production of a painting or poem, as well as in making a vase or temple, a perception is also employed as a means for something beyond itself. Moreover, the perception of urns, pots and pans as commodities may be intrinsically enjoyable, although these things are primarily perceived with reference to some use to which they are put. The only *basic* distinction is that between bad art and good art, and this distinction between things that meet the requirements of art and those that do not applies equally to things of use and of beauty. Capacity to offer to perception meaning in which fruition and efficacy interpenetrate is met by different products in various degrees of fulness; it may be missed altogether by pans and poems alike. The difference between the ugliness of a meretriciously conceived and executed utensil and a meretricious and pretentious painting is one only of content or material; in form, both are articles, and bad articles.

The relation of the esthetic and the artistic, as above defined, may now be stated more precisely. Both are incidental to practice, to performance, but in the esthetic the attained vision with which the artist presents us releases energies which remain diffuse and inchoate, which raise the whole level of our existence, but do not find issue in any single or specific form. In the artistic the existing consummation is utilized to bring into existence further analogous perceptions. A painter, for example, uses a picture not only to guide his perception of the world, but as a source of suggestions for painting additional pictures. Art in being, the active productive process, may thus be defined as an esthetic perception, together with an *operative* perception of the efficiencies of the esthetic object. A parallel contrast is to be found in scientific experience. The layman may by his knowledge of science understand the world about him much more clearly, and regulate his actions more effectively, than he could without it, but he is not called a scientist until he is able to utilize his knowledge to make fresh scientific discoveries. As to the scientist, knowledge is a means to more knowledge, so to the artist esthetic insight is a means to further esthetic insight, and not merely to enhancement of life in general. The distinction between the esthetic and the artistic, important as it is, is thus, in the last analysis, a matter of degree.

The meaning of the view accepted here may be made clearer if it is contrasted with the theory of art prevalent today in one school of critics, that esthetic qualities in works of fine art are unique, separate not only from everything that is existential in nature but from all other forms of good. In proclaiming that such arts as music, poetry, painting, have characteristics unshared by any natural things whatever, such critics carry to its conclusion the isolation of fine art from the useful, of the final from the efficacious.

As an example, we may consider that theory of art which makes the distinguishing quality of the esthetic object its possession of what is called "significant form." Unless the meaning of the term is so isolated as to be wholly occult, it denotes a selection, for the sake of emphasis, purity, subtlety, of those forms which give consummatory significance to everyday subject-matters of experience. "Forms" are not the peculiar property or creation of the esthetic and artistic; they are characters in virtue of which anything meets the requirements of an enjoyable perception. "Art" does not create the forms; it is their selection and organ-ization in such ways as to enhance, prolong and purify the perceptual experience. It is not by accident that some objects and situations afford marked perceptual satisfactions; they do so because of their structural properties and relations. An artist may work with a minimum of analytic recognition of these structures or "forms;" he may select them chiefly by a kind of sym-pathetic vibration. But they may also be discrimi-natively ascertained; and an artist may utilize his deliberate awareness of them to create works of art that are more formal and abstract than those to which the public is accustomed. Tendency to composition in terms of the formal characters marks much contempo-rary art, in poetry, painting, music, even sculpture and architecture. At their worst, these products are "sci-entific" rather than artistic; technical exercises, and of a new kind of pedantry. At their best, they assist in ushering in new modes of art and by education of the organs of perception in new modes of consummatory objects, they enlarge and enrich the world of human vision. But they do this, not by discarding altogether connection with the real world, but by a highly funded and generalized representation of the formal sources of ordinary emotional experience.

Thus we reach a conclusion regarding the relations

of instrumental and fine art which is precisely the opposite of that intended by selective estheticians; namely,
that fine art consciously undertaken as such is peculiarly
instrumental in quality. It is a device in experimentation carried on for the sake of education. It exists for
a specialized use, use being a new training of modes
of perception. The creators of such works of art are
entitled, when successful, to the gratitude that we give
to inventors of microscopes and microphones; in the
end, they open new objects to be observed and enjoyed.
This is a genuine service; but only an age of combined
confusion and conceit will arrogate to works that perform this special utility the exclusive name of fine art.

Art is great in proportion as it is universal, that is,
in proportion as the uniformities of nature which it
reveals and utilizes are extensive and profound—provided, however, that they are freshly applied in concrete objects or situations. The only objects, insights,
perceptions, which remain perennially unwithered and
unstaled are those which sharpen our vision for new
and unforeseen embodiments of the truth they convey.
The "magic" of poetry—and pregnant experience has
poetic quality—is precisely the revelation of meaning
in the old effected by its presentation of the new. It
radiates the light that never was on sea or land but
that is henceforth an abiding illumination of objects.

INDIVIDUALITY AND EXPERIENCE[1]

John Dewey

The methods of picture-making employed in the classes of Professor Cizek in Vienna raise a question that has to be dealt with in every branch of instruction. The question develops in two directions, one suggested by his statement that it is impossible to exclude outside influences, and the other by his report that upon the whole the more original constructions are those of younger pupils, that older students seem gradually to lose interest, so that no prominent artist has been produced. The problem thus defined consists in the relation of individuality and its adequate development to the work and responsibilities of the teacher, representing accumulated experience of the past.

Unfortunately, the history of schools not only in art but in all lines shows a swing of the pendulum between extremes, though it must be admitted that the simile of the pendulum is not a good one, for the schools remain, most of them, most of the time, near one extreme, instead of swinging periodically and evenly between the two. Anyway, the two extremes are external imposition and dictation, and "free-expression." Revolt from the costly, nerve-taxing and inadequate results of mechanical control from without creates an enthusiasm for spontaneity and "development from within," as it is often phrased. It is found that children at first are then much happier in their work—anyone who has seen Cizek's class will testify to the wholesome air of cheerfulness, even of joy, which pervades

From *Journal of The Barnes Foundation*, January, 1926.

the room—but gradually tend to become listless and finally bored, while there is an absence of cumulative, progressive development of power and of actual achievement in results. Then the pendulum swings back to regulation by the ideas, rules and orders of someone else, who being maturer, better informed and more experienced is supposed to know what should be done and how to do it.

The metaphor of the pendulum is faulty in another respect. It seems to suggest that the solution lies in finding a mid-point between the two extremes which would be at rest. But what is really wanted is a change in the direction of movement. As a general proposition no one would deny that personal mental growth is furthered in any branch of human undertaking by contact with the accumulated and sifted experience of others in that line. No one would seriously propose that all future carpenters should be trained by actually starting with a clean sheet, wiping out everything that the past has discovered about mechanics, about tools and their uses, and so on. It would not be thought likely that this knowledge would "cramp their style," limit their individuality, etc. But neither, on the other hand, have carpenters been formed by the methods often used in manual training shops where dinky tasks of a minute and technical nature are set, wholly independent of really making anything, having only specialized skill as their aim. As a rule carpenters are educated in their calling by working with others who have experience and skill, sharing in the simpler portions of the real undertakings, assisting in ways which enable them to observe methods and to see what results they are adapted to accomplish.

Such learning is controlled by two great principles: one is participation in something inherently worth while, or undertaken on its own account; the other is perception of the relation of means to consequences. When these two conditions are met, a third consideration usually follows as a matter of course. Having had an experience of the meaning of certain technical processes and forms of skill there develops an interest in skill and "technique:" the meaning of the result is "transferred" to the means of its attainment. Boys interested in baseball as a game thus submit themselves voluntarily to continued practice in throwing, catching, batting, the separate elements of the game. Or boys, who get interested in the game of marbles, will practice to increase their skill in shooting and hitting. Just imagine, however, what would happen if they set these exercises as tasks in school, with no prior activity in the games and with no sense of what they were about or for, and without any such appeal to the social, or participating, impulses as takes place in games!

If we generalize from such a commonplace case as the education of artisans through their work, we may say that the customs, methods and *working* standards of the calling constitute a "tradition," and that initiation into the tradition is the means by which the powers of learners are released and directed. But we should also have to say that the urge or need of an individual to join in an undertaking is a necessary prerequisite of the tradition's being a factor in his personal growth in power and freedom; and also that he has to *see* on his own behalf and in his own way the relations between means and methods employed and results achieved. Nobody else can see for him, and he can't see just by being "told," although the right kind of telling may guide his seeing and thus help him see what he needs to see. And if he has no impelling desire of his own to

become a carpenter, if his interest in being one is perfunctory, if it is not an interest in *being* a carpenter at
all, but only in getting a pecuniary reward by doing
jobs, the tradition will never of course really enter into
and integrate with his own powers. It will remain,
then, a mere set of mechanical and more or less meaningless rules that he is obliged to follow if he is to hold
his job and draw his pay.

Supposing, again, that our imaginary pupil works
for and with a master carpenter who believes in only
one kind of house with a fixed design, and his aim is
not only to teach his apprentice to make just that one
kind of house, but to accept it with all his soul, heart
and mind as the only kind of house that should ever
be built, the very type and standard model of all houses.
Then it is easy to see that limitation of personal powers
will surely result, not merely, moreover, limitation of
technical skill, but, what is more important, of his powers of observation, imagination, judgment, and even
his emotions, since his appreciations will be warped
to conform to the one preferred style. The imaginary case illustrates what often happens when we
pass from the education of artisans to that of artists.
As a rule a carpenter has to keep more or less open;
he is exposed to many demands and must be flexible
enough to meet them. He is in no position to set up
a final authority about ends and models and standards,
no matter how expert he may be in methods and means.
But an architect in distinction from a builder is likely
to be an "authority;" he can dictate and lay down what
is right and wrong, and thus prescribe certain ends and
proscribe others. Here is a case where tradition is
not enhancing and liberating, but is restrictive and en-
slaving. If he has pupils, he is a "master" and not an
advanced fellow worker; his students are disciples

4

rather than learners. Tradition is no longer tradition but a fixed and absolute convention.

In short, the practical difficulty does not reside in any antagonism of methods and rules and results worked out in past experience to individual desire, capacity and freedom. It lies rather in the hard and narrow and, we may truly say, uneducated habits and attitudes of teachers who set up as authorities, as rulers and judges in Israel. As a matter of course they know that as bare individuals they are not "authorities" and will not be accepted by others as such. So they clothe themselves with some tradition as a mantle, and henceforth it is not just "I" who speaks, but some Lord speaks through me. The teacher then offers himself as the organ of the voice of a whole school, of a *finished* classic tradition, and arrogates to himself the prestige that comes from what he is the spokesman for. Suppression of the emotional and intellectual integrity of pupils is the result; their freedom is repressed and the growth of their own personalities stunted. But it is not because of any opposition between the wisdom and skill of the past and the individual capacities of learners; the trouble lies in the habits, standards and ideas of the teacher. It is analogous to another case. There is no inherent opposition between theory and practice; the former enlarges, releases and gives significance to the latter; while practice supplies theory with its materials and with the test and check which keep it sincere and vital. But there is a whole lot of opposition between human beings who set themselves up as practical and those who set themselves up as theorists, an irresolvable conflict because both have put themselves into a wrong position.

This suggests that the proponents of freedom are in a false position as well as the would-be masters and dictators. There is a present tendency in so-called advanced schools of educational thought (by no means confined to art classes like those of Cizek) to say, in effect, let us surround pupils with certain materials, tools, appliances, etc., and then let pupils respond to these things according to their own desires. Above all let us not suggest any end or plan to the students; let us not suggest to them what they shall do, for that is an unwarranted trespass upon their sacred intellectual individuality since the essence of such individuality is to set up ends and aims.

Now such a method is really stupid. For it attempts the impossible, which is always stupid; and it misconceives the conditions of independent thinking. There are a multitude of ways of reacting to surrounding conditions, and without some guidance from experience these reactions are almost sure to be casual, sporadic and ultimately fatiguing, accompanied by nervous strain. Since the teacher has presumably a greater background of experience, there is the same presumption of the right of a teacher to make suggestions as to what to do, as there is on the part of the head carpenter to suggest to apprentices something of what they are to do. Moreover, the theory literally carried out would be obliged to banish all artificial materials, tools and appliances. Being the product of the skill, thought and matured experience of others, they would also, by the theory, "interfere" with personal freedom.

Moreover, when the child proposes or suggests what to do, some consequence to be attained, whence is the suggestion supposed to spring? There is no spontaneous germination in the mental life. If he does not get the suggestion from the teacher, he gets it from somebody or something in the home or the street or from what some more vigorous fellow pupil is doing. Hence the chances are great of its being a passing and superficial suggestion, without much depth and range—in other words, not specially conducive to the developing of freedom. If the teacher is really a teacher, and not just a master or "authority," he should know enough about his pupils, their needs, experiences, degrees of skill and knowledge, etc., to be able (not to dictate aims and plans) to share in a discussion regarding what is to be done and be as free to make suggestions as anyone else. (The implication that the teacher is the one and only person who has no "individuality" or "freedom" to "express" would be funny if it were not often so sad in its outworkings.) And his contribution, given the conditions stated, will presumably do more to getting something started which will really secure and increase the development of strictly individual capacities than will suggestions springing from uncontrolled haphazard sources.

The point is also worth dwelling upon, that the method of leaving the response entirely to pupils, the teacher supplying, in the language of the day, only the "stimuli," misconceives the nature of thinking. Any so-called "end" or "aim" or "project" which the average immature person can suggest in advance is likely to be highly vague and unformed, a mere outline sketch, not a suggestion of a definite result or consequence but rather a gesture which roughly indicates a field within which activities might be carried on. It hardly represents thought at all: it is a suggestion. The real intellectual shaping of the "end" or purpose comes during and because of the operations subsequently performed. This is as true of the suggestion which proceeds from the teacher as of those which "spontaneously" spring from the pupils, so that the former does not restrict thought. The advantage on the side of the teacher—if he or she has any business to be in that position—is the greater probability that it will be a suggestion which will permit and require thought in the subsequent activity which builds up a clear and organized conception of an end. There is no more fatal flaw in psychology than that which takes the original vague fore-feeling of some consequence to be realized as the equivalent of a *thought* of an end, a true purpose and directive plan. The thought of an end is strictly correlative to perception of means and methods. Only when, and as the latter becomes clear during the serial process of execution does the project and guiding aim and plan become evident and articulated. In the full sense of the word, a person becomes aware of what he wants to do and what he is about only when the work is actually complete.

The adjective "serial" is important in connection with the process of performance or execution. Each step forward, each "means" used, is a partial attainment of an "end." It makes clearer the character of that end, and hence suggests to an observing mind the next step to be taken, or the means and methods to be next employed. Originality and independence of thinking are therefore connected with the intervening process of execution rather than with the source of the initial suggestion. Indeed, genuinely fruitful and original suggestions are themselves usually the results of experience in the carrying out of undertakings. The "end" is not, in other words, an end or finality in the literal sense, but is in turn the starting point of new desires, aims and plans. By means of the process the mind gets power to make suggestions which are significant. There is now a past experience from which they can spring with an increased probability of their being worth while and articulate.

It goes without saying that a teacher may interfere and impose alien standards and methods during the operation. But as we have previously seen, this is not because of bringing to bear the results of previous experience, but because the habits of the teacher are so narrow and fixed, his imagination and sympathies so limited, his own intellectual horizon so bounded, that he brings them to bear in a wrong way. The fuller and richer the experience of the teacher, the more adequate his own knowledge of "traditions," the more likely is he, given the attitude of participator instead of that of master, to use them in a liberating way.

Freedom or individuality, in short, is not an original possession or gift. It is something to be achieved, to be wrought out. Suggestions as to things which may advantageously be taken, as to skill, as to methods of operation, are indispensable conditions of its achievement. These by the nature of the case must come from a sympathetic and discriminating knowledge of what has been done in the past and how it has been done.

THE PROBLEM OF APPRECIATION[1]

Albert C. Barnes

THE object of this book is to endeavor to correlate in the simplest possible form the main principles that underlie the intelligent appreciation of the paintings of all periods of time. We shall seek to show, briefly, what is involved in esthetic experience in general; after that, to give an account of the principles by which painting may be judged and so intelligently enjoyed; finally, to illustrate these principles by applying them to particular painters and tendencies in painting.

The approach to the problem of appreciation of art is made difficult by the unconscious habits and preconceptions which come to us from contact with a society which is but little interested in art. When other interests, such as those of a practical, sentimental, or moral nature, directly affect the esthetic interest, they are more likely than not to lead it astray, and the result is what may be called a confusion of values. Before trying to tell what the proper excellence in a painting is, we must make clear what it undeniably is *not*.

We miss the function of a painting if we look to it either for literal reproduction of subject or for information of a documentary character. Mere imitation knows nothing of what is essential or characteristic, and documentary information always has an ulterior practical purpose. The camera records physical characteristics but can show nothing of what is beneath

[1] From Albert C. Barnes, *The Art in Painting*, Harcourt, Brace & Co., New York, N. Y., 1937.

the surface. We ask of a work of art that it reveal to us the qualities in objects and situations which are significant, which have the power to move us esthetically. The artist must open our eyes to what unaided we could not see, and in order to do so he often needs to modify the familiar appearance of things and so make something which is, in the photographic sense, a bad likeness. What we ask of a painter is that, for example, in a landscape, he should catch the spirit of the scene; in a portrait, that he should discover what is essential or characteristic of the sitter. And these are obviously matters for judgment, not for photographic reproduction or documentary cataloguing.

By a common popular misconception, a painter is often expected to tell a story and is judged by his ability to make the story edifying or entertaining. This is not unnatural, since we are all ordinarily interested in real things because of the part they play in the story which is life. A work of art may, incidentally, tell a story, but error arises when we try to judge it by the narrative, or the moral pointed, instead of by the manner in which the artist has used his materials to produce a work of plastic art; when, in other words, a literary or moral value is mistaken for a plastic value.

Scarcely less destructive to genuine esthetic appreciation is the confusion of technical proficiency with artistic significance. Art is not only an expression of the artist's creative spirit, but also a kind of handicraft, a skill in employing a special technique. As in other handicrafts, some natural ability combined with instruction and practice may enable a person to handle a paintbrush; for one real artist there are hundreds of capable craftsmen in paint. It is not especially difficult to learn to recognize these technical devices; but it *is* difficult to recognize greatness in the effects obtained, to distinguish between professional competence and artistic genius. To look merely for professional competence in painting is academicism; it is to mistake the husk for the kernel, the shadow for the substance.

This error is really more serious than the novice's confusion of plastic art with narrative, sentiment, or photographic likeness, because the novice usually knows that he is such and is willing to learn, but the academician supposes himself to have learned already, and his mind is usually closed to the existence of anything but technique. With his eyes fixed upon the forms in which the living spirit of the past has embodied itself, he neglects the contemporary manifestations of that spirit, and often refuses to see or acknowledge them when they are pointed out to him. This is the reason why the most formidable enemy of new movements in art has always been, not the indifferent public, but the hostile academician. The public does not know that what he says applies only to technique and not to art itself, and is correspondingly impressed. His motive need not, of course, be a conscious motive, and doubtless often is not. The mere fact of novelty, to one who has systematically addressed himself to the old and familiar things, is an irritation. It challenges precious habits, it threatens to overturn judgments with which the academician has identified himself, and which are in consequence dear to him. Pride joins hands with natural human inertia to oppose what is living in the interest of what is dead.

These errors and confusions arise because the ordinary observer has never really learned to see. He can recognize familiar objects, and the traits in them which would be of practical importance or sentimental concern in real things, but such recognition is in no proper sense perception or vision. It identifies the object only for the purpose of passing on to something else—uses, consequences, or private fancies which are no part of its intrinsic character. People often suppose that there is some secret about art, some password which must be divulged before they can discover its purpose or meaning. Absurd as such an idea is, it contains the important truth that seeing is something which must be learned, and not something which we all do as naturally as we breathe.

To make apparent in more detail the necessity for learning to see, we shall consider briefly the psychology of perception. The obvious instruments of perception are our sense-organs, by which impressions reach us from the external world. Such impressions, however, convey nothing to us unless we can interpret them, attach meaning to them, and interpretation is possible only to one who can bring the residue or record of past experience to bear on any particular situation with which he may be confronted. At any moment, the sum total of our actual sensations is a chaos: we are besieged by a medley of sights, sounds, feelings of warmth or coolness, of bodily comfort or discomfort, by far the greater part of which have no connection with one another, and could not possibly enter into any single experience. To be conscious of anything in particular, to retain our sanity, we must disregard nearly all of them, fixing our attention upon those which fit into some intelligible scheme or picture. But the connections which bring about intelligibility, which "make sense," have all been learned from past experience; this experience, retained in memory, is called forth as occasion for it arises. It then directs our attention to the significant aspects of the existing situation, to which it gives form and meaning—which, in a word, it enables us to perceive.

We have all had the experience of being in an unfamiliar situation, and finding ourselves unable to see more than a fraction of what is going on in it. The machinery in the hold of a steamship, the babel of voices when many people are speaking in a foreign language, the actions of those with whose manners, customs and traditions we are unfamiliar—all these things are likely to appear to us as so much confusion and blur. Our difficulty is both that we do not see and that we do not comprehend. We see and hear something, and we can at least recognize wheels and shafts in the machinery, vowel sounds and consonant sounds in the words spoken, gestures and goings to and fro in the actions of the strange people. But we perceive vaguely, and much of what is happening escapes us altogether. It is only after, and by means of, understanding, that we can perceive with any precision, or notice more than a small part of the details in the scene before us. What we do see is hazy, scanty, and without perspective. We overlook the important and significant, and the odds and ends that come to our attention are jumbled together without rhyme or reason. Our senses, meanwhile, may be as acute as those of another who misses nothing in the picture; but we have not learned to use them, and he has.

The expression "to use our senses" is an indication that seeing or hearing is an active process, not a mere registration of impressions. After we have learned the purpose and the general plan of the machinery, we know how to look for the parts and the connections of which we were at first oblivious. When we have learned the vocabulary of a foreign language and know what to listen for, the finer shades of sound begin to stand out. We have acquired by experience a background which enables us to comprehend the machinery or the foreign language.

These are only outstanding examples of a process which is going on all the time. As long as we are really alive, we continue to grow by extending the application of our funded experience, perceiving things more and more precisely and discriminately, and at the same time investing them with constantly enriched meanings. The process is exemplified in every activity of life, from playing tennis or driving a motor car to practicing medicine or engaging in scientific research. As the system of meanings which makes up our minds is amplified and organized, our perceptions become correspondingly richer and more comprehensive. Vision and intelligence, in other words, are co-implicative, neither is possible without the other, and all growth involves their interaction.

This general principle furnishes us with the clue to esthetic education. We perceive only what we have learned to look for, both in life and in art. The artist, whether in paint, words or musical tones, has embodied an experience in his work, and to appreciate his painting or poem or symphony, we must reconstruct his experience, so far as we are able, in ourselves. There is no essential difference in kind between the experience of the artist and that of the observer of his work, whatever may be the difference in their respective abilities. The experience of the artist arises out of a particular background, a set of interests and habits of perception, which, like the scientist's habits of thought, are potentially sharable by other individuals. They are only sharable, however, if one is willing to make the effort involved in acquiring a comparable background and set of habits. To see as the artist sees is an accomplishment to which there is no short cut, which cannot be acquired by any magic formula or trick; it requires not only the best energies of which we are capable, but a methodical direction of those energies, based upon scientific understanding of the meaning of art and its relation to human nature.   The artist illuminates the objective world for us exactly as does the scientist, different as the terms are in which he envisages it; art is as little a plaything, a matter of caprice or uncontrolled subjectivity, as is physics or chemistry.   What has made the study of science valuable and fruitful is method, and, without a corresponding method of learning to see, the study of art can lead only to futility. We must understand, in other words, what the distinctive aspects of reality are in which the artist is interested, how he organizes his work to reveal and organize those aspects, the means which he employs, and the kind of satisfaction which rewards his efforts when they are successful.   Only in the light of such an understanding can any one build up in himself the background and habits of perception which will give him admission to the world of esthetic experience.

THE ROOTS OF ART[1]

Albert C. Barnes

ART, like every other human activity, has its roots in the fundamental needs of our nature, and provides one of the ways in which these needs find satisfaction. It was formerly believed that "beauty" is something which exists independently in nature, like magnetism or gravitation, and that it can be defined without reference to human wants and interest. Innumerable attempts to find such a definition have proved futile, and it is now recognized that the understanding of art must be sought in psychological principles.

Everything that human beings do is ultimately dependent upon the feelings that things and acts arouse in them. Some experiences are immediately felt as satisfactory, others as unsatisfactory, and life consists in an effort to secure the former and avoid the latter. This is a fact which requires no justification: human beings are so constituted as to have preferences, and behind preferences, in the last analysis, we cannot go. Reason or intelligence can show that one particular preference conflicts with another, and often guides us by making clear which of the two represents the more comprehensive good, but it can never prove anything a good which does not lead, directly or indirectly, to some experience valued for its own sake. We are often compelled to accept privation and pain, but only for the sake of a positive value, which outweighs their unpleasantness.

[1] From Albert C. Barnes, *The Art in Painting*, Harcourt, Brace & Co., New York, N. Y., 1937.

To say that an experience is of positive value, that it is worth having for its own sake, is to say that in it an instinctive prompting finds fulfilment.[2] To eat when we are hungry, to turn away from what disgusts us, to be victorious when our will is pitted against that of another, are things felt to be good in their own right; they are satisfactions of instincts and are enjoyed immediately, for their own sake. Of course, the enjoyment is greater as the range of instinctive gratification is broadened. Victory means the immediate experience of triumph; it may also mean the accomplishment of remoter ends which have an instinctive appeal of their own; and the confluence of these separate satisfactions heightens our enjoyment in the experience of victory. In general, the ideal is approached as our instinctive promptings are harmoniously united in every act. Then every experience gains value from all the resources of our nature, and suffers loss from no sense of desire thwarted or damage done to any of the interests which we have at heart.

The enjoyment of art is one of the experiences which are desirable for their own sake. It is, of course, capable of acquiring other values also. It may enable us to make a living; it may improve our morals or quicken our religious faith; but if we attempt to judge a work of art directly by its contribution to these ends, we have abandoned the track. A work of art presents to the spectator an opportunity to live through an experience which by its own quality vouches for its right to existence, and whatever other value it has depends upon this value. If it lacks this, it is a counterfeit.

Art, in other words, is one of the ways in which instinct finds satisfaction. It differs from the ordinary

[2] See Mary Mullen, *An Approach to Art*, pp. 13–14, The Barnes Foundation Press, Merion, Pa., 1923.

manifestations of instinct, however, in that it does not take the form of a course of practical action. We read the poem, look at the picture, listen to the symphony, but we are not thereupon prompted to do anything further, as we are when we are moved by some actual object to fear, anger or affection. This does not mean that the experience is passive, that we simply allow the esthetic object to do something to us while we do nothing in response—a suggestion conveyed by the definition of esthetic experience as contemplative. To hear the symphony, to see the picture, if the hearing and seeing are genuine, is the antithesis of idle reverie; it requires the energetic coöperation of all our powers, and nothing is more fatal to it than an attitude of relaxed and diffused attention. What distinguishes the response to works of art is that it takes the form of understanding, not merely intellectually but with our whole personality; of re-creating in ourselves, so far as we are able, the experience which the work of art records and embodies. This is an intensely active process, and often requires a much greater expenditure of energy than would overt action aiming at some practical end. It is, however, a different kind of activity from that ordinarily associated with instinct, and our next problem is to see wherein the difference lies.

Instincts and emotions are closely connected; indeed, an emotion may be defined as the immediate experience of an instinctive reaction. Hence esthetic experience may be regarded as an emotional response to an object or situation; but the conception of emotion popularly held is likely to make this statement misleading unless the term "emotion" is more accurately defined. In ordinary speech an "emotional" person is usually understood to be at the mercy of his feelings: his reactions are characteristically precipitate, violent and irrational. The popular conception of the artist as being "temperamental"—that is to say, lacking in balance and self-control—because he is exclusively swayed by emotion, has its roots in the same mistaken view. It is not emotion which results in instability and irrationality, just as it is not the artist but the person for whom art is a pose, who indulges in the sort of temperament in question. The "emotionalist" is the sentimentalist, "whose physiological complexion," as Santayana says, "involves more poignant emotion than his ideas can absorb." In a well-coördinated personality, feelings do not float in a vacuum and solicit attention for their own sake; they are fully absorbed by objective things, and there is no consciousness of the emotion apart from the situation that calls it forth. Rationality does not consist in the absence of emotion—that would be apathy or torpor—but in control of emotion by identification of the self with the situation as it objectively exists. So controlled, emotion impels us toward adequate perception, grasp of reality; otherwise, it leads to phantasy and illusion.

A much less ambiguous word than "emotion" is "interest." "Interest" implies concern, not with ourselves, but with objective things, and concern which is permanent. A real interest is an identification of ourselves with something which is real independently of us, as when we speak of interest in music, in the work of Beethoven, or in another individual. It is, furthermore, comparatively enduring. Its essential characteristic is that it induces him who has it to take pains, to make efforts, and so to order his activities that the object of his interest takes form in his mind and becomes the propelling force of his activities. Persistence of effort is the indispensable condition of real interest. When this is lacking, we say that a professed interest is

5

a sham or at least a delusion. A man who believes that
he is interested in paintings, but who takes no pains to
acquaint himself with the problems to be solved, who
will not study the methods of presentation proposed,
form some judgment through actual experience of their
adequacy, is a mere dilettante.

That in which we have no real interest passes before
our eyes without entering the range of our attention
or leaving any traces in our memory. What has value
for us—and this is an alternative expression for "what
interests us"—is attended to in detail, and remembered.
In general, the object of an interest has distinctness
in its parts and coherence as a whole, and in consequence it arouses a specific emotion, appropriate to it
as an individual thing, and not a mere mood, a vague,
undistinguished sense of exhilaration, languor, lachry-
mosity, ineffability, or what not. One who goes to a
symphony orchestra concert to pass the time, or for
social reasons, comes away with only the haziest ideas
of what was played. But for one with a genuine interest
in music, the concert means a series of intricate relationships between chords, melodies and movements, all
woven into a unified whole which reveals the spirit of
the composer. In other words, art is an expression of
interest, and that interest depends upon the sensibility
which makes us alive in the real world to things that
to one not sensitive would not exist.

The foregoing statements indicate that instincts become effective realities only as they become organized
interests. Such interests center about and develop real
things; they also make up the individual self. The self
is shadowy, insubstantial, futile, except in so far as it
has objective interests; but it is also true that the
objective world is a conglomeration of meaningless facts

except as it is organized by the interests of living beings. The artist does what no camera, no mere imitation, no mere document, can do; he selects aspects for emphasis and gives significant order; that is, his work is a creation. But it is appeal to feeling that confers significance and establishes a principle by which the essential can be distinguished from the trivial or irrelevant. Things are important not in themselves but by virtue of their relation to feeling or interest, and since men differ in their interests, no single set of things or qualities in the real world is important in general or without qualification. A conflagration interests various people differently: to the chemist it means, chiefly, a process of oxidation; to an owner, it may mean loss of money; to an artist, it means line, color, mass, in a series of relationships which he enjoys.

So to draw out and make clear the true character of anything is the task of the artist. Feeling is involved, since *what* is brought out depends upon the individual and his interests; and the satisfaction which instinct finds in comprehension, in imaginative realization, is one which is intrinsic to the process of bringing out, not something added afterwards: the person who comprehends and appreciates the work of art shares the emotions which prompted the artist to create. The artist gives us satisfaction by seeing for us more clearly than we could see for ourselves, and showing us what an experience more sensitive and profound than our own has shown him.

We all take some pleasure in seeing how things look, in observing their color, their contour, their movement, whether they are moving in our direction or not. In so far as we are successful in finding what is characteristic, appealing or significant in the world about us,

we are, in a small impromptu way, ourselves artists.[3]
But the man who is an artist because the interest in
understanding and depicting things is a master passion
with him, sees more deeply and more penetratingly
than we do, and, seeing better, can also show better.
His interests compel him to grasp certain significant
aspects of persons and things of the real world which
our blindness and preoccupation with personal and
practical concerns ordinarily hide from us.

[3] See Mary Mullen, *An Approach to Art*, page 23, The Barnes Foundation Press, Merion, Pa., 1923.

ART AS CREATIVE[1]

Laurence Buermeyer

We have urged and illustrated the point that esthetic experience in all its forms is an active process, that it enters into many activities other than those ordinarily associated with the word "art," and that when fine art itself is in question we can most fully understand it by conceiving it as a type of doing rather than as something undergone. Our problem now is to analyze the actual process of creation, to see how what is given at the start of the artist's labors is transmuted into the achieved result.

Art in general, as we have said, is an expression of emotion, an expression which consists not, as with ordinary expressions, in gestures, exclamations, or physically efficacious acts, but in an envisagement of the moving object in the terms or qualities that the emotion has seized upon and laid bare as significant. The object, so envisaged, is never identical with the object as it exists independently, either as a physical thing or as it is conventionally perceived. Rather, the esthetic object is such a reorganization of conventional impressions, a reinterpretation of familiar fact, as will reveal their distinctive significance for feeling or emotion. It is this principle which outlaws both photographic and academic art, in both of which absence of individuality on the artists' part, of personal creative force, is obvious from the meaningless or stereotyped version of the thing seen. Expression of emotion by interpreta-

[1] Adapted from Laurence Buermeyer, *The Aesthetic Experience*, The Barnes Foundation Press, Merion, Pa., 1929.

tion of what has moved us is always and everywhere the essence of the esthetic experience, and the esthetic experience is present wherever we find such interpretation, in the world of affairs and personal relations as well as in the world of "art" ordinarily so called.

Emotions are in the first instance aroused by objects which have a practical relation to our welfare, and art, if it is to offer a foothold for feeling, must in some degree possess an affinity with such objects. The version of natural things which art gives may be far removed from the original, for emotions contain the possibility of almost infinite transformation, and may travel far afield from the occasion of their first or "natural" appearance. This is true in ordinary life, as well as in the passage from ordinary life to art. What we love, hate, despise, admire, does not remain the same as our sensibilities develop and become refined. Between disgust at a bad smell or at a swarm of vermin, and disgust at a contemptible act or vulgar jest, there is a wide gulf, though in important psychological respects the emotion is the same in both. By what bridge, we must ask, does feeling cross the gulf between objects so disparate in kind?

The answer is clear. Our feelings respond, or may be taught to respond, to objects *analogous* to those which originally excited them, and analogy is community of form. The community of form, the resemblance, may be slight, and then the analogy is said to be subtle, but some formal identity there must be if feeling is to be relevant at all. The passage of emotion to art, in other words, depends upon form: art as a whole is creative by virtue of its selection, transformation, and reorganization of the forms of nature; within art, the process of creation is one of reorganization of the forms employed by previous art, and their diversification and enrichment by forms freshly borrowed from nature.

The meaning of form is essentially the same, whether applied to natural objects or to the things of art. All things possess characteristic quality or individuality chiefly through their form. It is by virtue of this that they are recognized for what they are, and increasingly so as recognition becomes penetrating or assured. We may say that a chair or a table or a human face gives us a sensation, but this is a loose and colloquial manner of speaking. It is the arrangement, and not, except incidentally, the particular quality of the sensations, that confers individuality upon any perception. A face is just the face it is because of the disposition of the features, the size of the eyes and the distance between them, the proportions of the forehead. Even what seems a matter of simple sensation, for example, the complexion, is formal, in that it depends upon color-contrast and not upon mere color. What we have merely an "impression" of, we know vaguely, superficially, uncertainly. In other words, nothing really known or grasped is a mere blur of qualities; its qualities are organized into a network of relations, and this organized network constitutes its form.

It is obvious from the above that whenever experience presents us with recognizable objects, whenever it is intelligible, it presents us with such forms. In ordinary personal life, these forms are organizations of events, relations of changes in one object to changes in another. Every impulse or instinct picks out of the chaos of our impressions such as are indicative of other impressions to be anticipated, sees in some of the things going on about us signs, warnings, or promises of things not yet seen, and correlates with them appropriate acts of coöperation or opposition on our part. To be angry is to observe a sign of obstruction to our will, to look for means of overcoming the obstruction, and to be prepared to take action accordingly. It is to see all these things in relation, so that they compose into a single plot or drama: indeed, most of the plots or dramas in literature are variations on a few simple formulas outlining the normal causes and courses of our more primitive instincts. This illustrates the characteristic passage of forms from life into art, and as art becomes great art, it increasingly makes such a selection of forms that human desire is freed, so far as possible, from the meaningless distraction, the obstructions without significance, that dog its steps in the real world.

Of course, the desires which art satisfies, even symbolically or impersonally, need not be those springing from such obvious and practically important instincts as fear, sex or pugnacity. They may be as central and pervasive as our fondness for rhythm or as incidental and trivial, in themselves, as our liking for a particular combination of colors. But of all the literally innumerable combinations of sensation which the artist can cause us to experience, only those have value which specifically appeal to something in our native constitution.

The creativeness of art, in summary, resides in its extraction, from the vast number of forms given in experience, of those which are peculiarly significant for emotion, and its reworking of these forms into what we may call a single coherent design. This design or form or vision is a grasp or understanding of the world, an illustration of what *is*, but it is creative in that the illumination is one which nature, unassisted by the artist, is powerless to provide.

These generalities may be illustrated by a brief sketch of some important episodes in the history of painting. Such a sketch will make it clear how in the evolution of forms, in which the creative aspect of art emerges, the artist is constantly drawing both on nature and on the traditions of art, the funded accomplishments of his predecessors. In the course of the development as personal expressiveness increases, truth increases also—a paradox if we think of art as a bare addition to experience or embellishment of nature, but a natural and inevitable consequence when we have understood the truth that art is a revelation of nature, though to be sure a revelation possible only through the agency of conscious human beings.

At the very beginning of modern art, we find painting subordinated to the end of illustration, especially illustration of religious themes. It was, in the main, almost flat, and its figures and background were almost entirely conventional in form. Drawing was exclusively line-drawing, and though the objects were colored, they were constructed by means of line and shading. To the shapes so drawn, color was added as though by an after-thought.

Later the Florentine painters conceived their pictures in three dimensions, and the objects in them were made to seem as tangible as possible. With this achievement, a new set of resources was put at the painter's disposal. He was encouraged to look for more in the real world, since he was able to provide new relationships between the elements in his compositions, and to endow his world with more of the fulness of reality. His new and more pregnant form enabled him to unify a greater variety of material, and he was both more true to nature and more free to modify nature in the interests of his individual conception.

The Venetians lent to their pictures a much greater splendor by enriching their palette and adding to the formal arrangement in space the effects of color-harmony. In addition, they used color as a constituent of objects with such effects that the objects appear more truly solid than in the Florentines. The freshness, depth and glow of swimming, harmonious, unifying color thus achieved, represented an enrichment of nature as it exists and a new instrument for lending it esthetic significance. It represented a new form. In the Florentines generally, color and shape remained distinct and the effect of three-dimensional solidity which appears in the majority of their work is attained by the contrast of light and shadow rather than by color incorporated into the structure of objects. In many instances, that method of using light to the comparative exclusion of structural color gives to the work of many of the Florentines, even Leonardo, the effect of deficiency of plastic means and leads to a somewhat stereotyped form which degenerated into an academic formula in some of the lesser men, Luini for example. With Rubens appeared a combination of the rich color of the Venetians with some of the technical devices of the Florentines for achieving the solidity of objects, and at the same time a heightened sense of movement and rhythm, a suggestion of forces acting in three dimensions, and of tumultuous activity. In his form, as in Titian's, the sharp contrast between line and color disappeared; color itself became more an instrument of draughtsmanship and one of the principal means of rendering solidity and of unifying the picture. Here as elsewhere, each new form makes available a new set of natural resources, and enables the painter so to modify and reshape this material that the result not only more truly grasps but more greatly glorifies the real world.

In Velásquez, though color, space-organization and movement show no further advance, an additional motif, realism, makes its appearance. Rubens made all that he touched grandiose, tempestuous; his pictures seem almost like the cataclysms of nature. Velásquez painted in a much more restrained style. He advanced upon all his predecessors, however, in his unimpassioned yet penetrating eye for the secret of his subject, in his ability to find in it that which lent itself to plastic representation and at the same time had characteristic significance. His concern was thus partly for the subject itself, yet not at all for "literary" subject-matter. He gave to all that he reproduced its plastic equivalent, and so promoted a real synthesis between color and shape, on the one hand, and the theme which they embodied. This of course had in some degree been done before, but in Velásquez there is far less reliance upon chance associations such as the "nobility" of classic scenes, the religious feeling which springs from ecclesiastical subjects, the power that depends upon magnitude and indication of great objective forces.

In the Nineteenth Century there was a development of forms not unlike the development during the Renaissance. Starting with David and Ingres, we find a rather stilted conventionality of theme, a sharp division between line and color, with the color dull in David, brighter but still superficial in Ingres. With Delacroix comes a great access of richness in color accompanied by an almost equal gain in movement and force. These latter, however, depended in part upon comparatively adventitious means, upon the suggestions provided by romantic and melodramatic subjects; but his more vivid color is an integral part of the shapes he painted.

Daumier scarcely used color at all, but he revealed the possibilities of organization, of solid reality, in tone, and recovered much of the formal power of Rembrandt.

Courbet introduced again the realism of Velásquez, added an earth-born force and pungency to his paintings, and thus stripped away the conventionality of vision which kept Ingres and Delacroix at arm's length from their world. Manet carried realism to completion, achieved a degree of fidelity to factual essentials worthy of Velásquez, and increased the repertoire which in Courbet had been restricted to comparatively few aspects. Degas employed Ingres' line to express movement, and so aided in restoring to plastic art that type of organization. The impressionists were in the main satisfied to use the forms already current in their time, except that by studying minutely the variations in color under varying illumination, they added new richness to the harmonies and contrasts which color presents, and in that sense augmented painting's armory of forms. Cézanne achieved a solidity of objects by a new method of modeling in color and by the aid of intentional distortions.

In Renoir the achievements of Nineteenth Century painting reached their consummation. In him, color and line and solidity fuse. Shapes are not drawn and modeled and then colored: color, combined with light, is the material out of which they are made up, and the color itself is of greater richness, variety and brilliance than in any of his predecessors. Not only is color used for drawing and the rendering of solidity, but the color-relations themselves are a formal and unifying element in a high degree. His composition unites balance, rhythm and movement, and the whole conveys perfectly the spirit of what is portrayed. In him, in a word, the forms of his predecessors are united.

However, the development of new forms is not the same as progress towards an absolute goal. No doubt new values are revealed as painting goes on its way, but there is loss as well as gain. This is true of progress of all sorts. In life in general we have paid for our increased command over nature, our more humane disposition towards our fellows, and our more complete self-consciousness by a loss of the simplicity and directness that cannot survive in a time of many and variously conflicting aims. Just how we have lost, we may see by comparing George Meredith with Homer. So in painting, as new effects become possible, old effects, not necessarily less valuable, become impossible. The naturalness of Manet may seem a great advance over the artificiality of David; but when we compare Manet with Titian or Tintoretto we are less certain that his style is the better. The stateliness, the magnificence, of the Renaissance portraits is something which our age cannot match, much as it may have surpassed the Renaissance in other respects. Progress, to repeat, is partial, and is always accompanied by retrogression. It is therefore futile to ask whether in any absolute sense Renoir and Cézanne represent an advance upon Giorgione and Rubens.

If we turn to literature we find the same gradual disentanglement of what is characteristic or essential in experience from the adventitious or irrelevant material in which, for primitive apprehension, it is set.

The form of a drama may be regarded as the working-out of a situation, the episode or series of episodes which follow from the interaction of a set of characters who are brought together under particular conditions. It is the revelation of what such a situation does to such characters, and the situation and characters are chosen with reference to a single effect. In *Othello*, for example, we have the state of affairs created by a misalliance, a marriage between two persons of antecedents so diverse that any understanding between them is precarious, and the condition is complicated, and given tragic import, by the presence of a third person who wishes and is able to foment discord. Iago is able to persuade Othello that Desdemona is false to him; Othello thereupon kills Desdemona, and on finding that he has been misled and that Desdemona is innocent, kills himself. Upon Othello's suicide, that is to say his pronouncement and execution of judgment upon himself, hangs the moving and tragic effect of the whole play, since it vindicates his essential nobility, his power of acting as judge in his own case no less justly than in his wife's. If he were a lesser man, his ruin might be pathetic but it would not be tragic. Just that issue, in other words, is essential to a form in which the tragic emotion can be adequately embodied.

It is impossible, however, to avoid asking the question whether the same situation and its issue would have the same emotional force today. We may observe that its force depends essentially upon acceptance by the reader or spectator of a set of conventions about jealousy, "honor," and retributive justice. But if we no longer regard retributive justice as divinely ordained, if it has come to appear as a barbarous, or at least a medieval superstition, Othello appears at the end pathetic, doubtless, as the victim of an illusion, but fundamentally stupid, and so not fully tragic. The form of the play, that is to say, no longer seems adequate to Shakespeare's purpose: it has ceased to be of universal human significance, and becomes essentially a document in Elizabethan conventionality.

The same sort of decay in a literary form or motif is seen in Mr. D. H. Lawrence's *Sons and Lovers.* It was once the fashion to make marriage the climax of love stories, and to represent the difficulties to be surmounted as residing in external circumstances, such as parental objections, the machinations of rivals, or any of the familiar causes of slips between cup and lip. But modern writers, with a more adequate sense of what is likely to come between individuals, reverse the order of events. Marriage is not necessarily or even usually the consummation of this particular relationship: it may be merely the prelude to it; and the really significant events may come after the ground is clear and the persons thus set free from irrelevant hindrances begin to discover whether or not they can enjoy a richer experience together than either could find in isolation. In this instance, as in the preceding, a form has been shown by experience to lack true expressiveness, to be inadequate to the purpose it is expected to fulfill.

These examples indicate that the value or finality of a form cannot be judged by any formula which can be abstractly stated and applied infallibly. Its expressiveness must be judged by the reaction of an individual as a complete personality, by its appeal to feeling. This reaction, this feeling, are the outgrowth of a multitude of habits, convictions and preferences, of which many, and those not the least important, cannot be brought into consciousness by their possessor. Absolute finality, in a word, is impossible in esthetic judgment or appreciation. But absolute finality has already taken flight from science, it seems to be abandoning morals and its persistence in dogmatic religion is a fact which lends itself to various interpretations. If no creation in art is final, we may find solace in the thought that future artists will not be reduced to a traffic in conventionalities.

ART AND THE IVORY TOWER[1]

Laurence Buermeyer

In the minds of many the terms "art" and "the ivory tower" mean the same thing. Not every one, it is true, would use words so figurative or so high-flown as "the ivory tower" to describe what he means by art, but there are many equivalent expressions for the abstractness, the remoteness, conceived to be characteristic of it. What is near at hand, a part of our ordinary concerns, is not thought to be art: to encounter art we must go to the museum, the opera-house, the "classical" work of literature. When we do meet it we are a little uncomfortable, and also a little proud, for we are improving our minds, cultivating our sensibilities. Incidentally, we are challenging an investigation of our sincerity, and courting ridicule if the investigation goes against us. We are attempting to be better than our fellows, and if we fail the result is ignominy. In any case, we are setting ourselves apart, for better or for worse.

Along with this view goes usually a readiness to deplore the indifference to art, on the part of the public, which is said to be characteristic of our time as it was not of the Periclean Age, or of the Thirteenth Century in Western Europe. The ugliness of a great part of our material surroundings, the present low estate of the artist, and the general sordidness of much of our life, need not be disputed. But it is a question whether responsibility for this lamentable state of affairs is to be laid wholly at the door of those who are deaf to the

[1] From *Journal of The Barnes Foundation*, May, 1925.

gospel of art as that is ordinarily preached. So long as art is considered to be, by its nature, removed from the world in which we live and the things which naturally interest us there, the "swinish multitude" is perhaps not too severely to be castigated if it prefers the sty to the walled garden.

There is, however, a view of art which does not look to the ivory tower or the walled garden for its ideal. To distinguish this view from that usually held, we may begin with a point apparently trivial. In popular speech, the terms "artist" and "painter" are used interchangeably. The same is true of "sculptor," "composer," or "poet," and "artist:" in each case the artist is regarded as someone who can do something that we ordinary mortals cannot. Expression in ordinary prose, however, is not considered an art, since all of us are capable of that. Art and a specialized skill thus become one and the same thing. Whatever else the artist is or is not, he is in a class apart from his fellows, and the connoisseur or the esthete in a measure shares his distinction. This, roughly, is the popular equivalent of the ivory-tower view.

In contrast, an opinion has gained ground in recent years that art is primarily not a kind of technique or skill, like the ability to play chess, but that it is identical with all individual perception of the world and the things about us. Those familiar with recent discussion of esthetics will at once recognize this as the view of Benedetto Croce. For Croce, the most immediate clue to the meaning of art is to be found, not in the things that most of us cannot do, such as the composition of symphonies or the carving of statues, but in what, more or less, everyone can do. We can all talk, he says; therefore, if we would know what the artist does, we need only consider what we do when we use words to make our ideas or impressions communicable. All expression is art: we express ourselves whenever we look at the world, listen to the sounds there, and give to our fellowmen an intimation of what we have seen and heard. Really, the heart of expression is to be found in the immediate experience of apprehending. Words, like chisel or brush, serve merely as a means of communication.

Croce's view, which has gained a considerable vogue, suffers as much from excessive catholicity (at least in the hands of its interpreters) as does the traditional view from excessive exclusiveness. If we are all artists, the degrees of artistry become relatively unimportant, and attempted education in art is an impertinence. Complacency is no less fatal to growth than blind idolatry; however, the Crocean view does bring us closer to realities than the opposed opinion that art is inseparable from craftsmanship, and until it is understood a true esthetics can scarcely be begun.

We ordinarily suppose, when looking at an object, that we see all of it that is there to be seen. We think of our mind as like a camera, faithfully reproducing whatever is before it. If we are unable to describe what we see, or paint a picture of it, that is merely because of our deficient mastery of words or paintbrush. The artist is thus the man who can reproduce his experiences, while we too have the experiences in spite of the fact that we cannot coin them into works of art. A very rudimentary knowledge of psychology suffices to destroy this error. What we ordinarily see in any object is a mere blur of qualities, from which only such traits as are practically important stand out. We may notice, in looking at a tree, whether it bears fruit, or whether it casts enough shade to make a cool resting-place; we may see that it is a hard-wood tree, and therefore commercially valuable, or that it is infested with parasites, and so in need of spraying. But these are only a fraction of its qualities, and the rest of them, the texture of its bark, the set of its branches, the precise shape and color of its leaves, the symmetry of its total form, are likely to be disregarded. So with all things. We notice a house far away, and if we are in need of shelter we estimate the distance to it and the chances of our gaining admittance. The arrangement of doors and windows, on the other hand, the harmony between color of stone and color of roof, the number of chimneys, and so on, may be entirely disregarded. So too of the signs by which we judge of its distance: its apparent size, its relation to intervening objects, the clarity of its outline. Our perceptions, in brief, are very vague indeed, and it is because of this vagueness, and not of any mere lack of technique, that we cannot describe or reproduce what we see.

Of course, this is not true only of things literally *seen*. The persons about us are equally hazy. We usually want to know only what we need fear or what we may hope from them, and so we detect only the signs of friendly or hostile intent, of trustworthiness or dishonesty. The result is that we can tell little about them. We can indicate how they entertain or bore us, whether they are kindly or malicious in disposition, but how their lives feel to them, how the world appears in their eyes, is something of which we can say little. As our understanding of a man grows, the sense of our ignorance of him grows also, and we become aware that we shall never fully grasp the springs of his action, the hidden sources of his thoughts, his hopes and his fears.

The artist's problem is thus revealed. It is not, primarily, to put upon canvas or paper a vision which may be had merely by turning the eye in a particular direction. After the gaze has been fixed, and before the pen or paintbrush is used, comes the most significant part of the artist's work. "The person to be painted stands before the artist like a world to discover." The seeing, the interpretation—it is this that exacts the labor and, when done, attests the triumph. He who can do it is the artist because he has something to say; he who cannot, whatever the skill with which he can repeat what others have said, is not an artist but an artisan, a tradesman; and since his pictures or his books, considered merely as material objects, are less useful than food or shelter, he stands in rank with the purveyor of cosmetics, and below the mason or the husbandman.

If to see and to interpret are art, then, it is true, we are all artists. But if, priding ourselves on the distinction, we forget that seeing and interpreting are the most arduous of human undertakings, we cannot be too quickly reminded of the debt we owe to those who have preëminently succeeded in the task, and who are artists in the distinctive sense. For most of us, and for all of us most of the time, seeing is a mechanical registration of pitiably meagre impressions, and "interpretation" is a hasty consignment to pigeon-holes made for us by others long ago. "Man lives not by bread alone, but chiefly by catchwords"—if we doubt this we need only ask ourselves how often we really judge an individual case on its merits, without recourse to some table of virtues and crimes, some set catalogue of things to be admired and things to be reprobated. Our world is ordinarily one of abstractions, of "shadow-shapes that come and go;" it is bloodless and lifeless.

The proof of this is our attitude toward the new, toward anything that will not fit easily into one of the pigeon-holes of our mind. In interpreting the familiar we are simply living on accumulated intellectual capital, chiefly that bequeathed us as children of our particular time and people. It is as little an esthetic achievement to see what everyone else sees as it is a scientific achievement, at the present date, to think of water as H_2O. It is the new which we really judge, which we truly *see*, and by which, in turn, we are judged; yet whenever our feelings are concerned we are comfortable only in the presence of what is familiar and well worn. What is really novel rarely challenges a desire to understand and render justice, but almost always an impulse to disregard, to condemn, to destroy. Of course, what is new does not necessarily mean what was produced in the current year; what is old may be new to *us*, or what is remote in space; but the closed mind is as reluctant to see in a new light what belongs to the time of Cheops as to revise its ideas of contemporary events. To see as we have always seen, to think as we have always thought—this is dear to the unregenerate nature of all of us.

An immovable conservatism, however, is no more destructive to the perception of fresh and living aspects in the world about us than is the absence of any traditions whatever. If we have eyes to see at all, it is not merely because Nature has given them to us, but also because other men have found out how to use *their* eyes, and so have taught us. Temperament unguided by tradition yields not originality but eccentricity—a meaningless eccentricity, because it is only by modification and enrichment of a tradition already in existence that the contributions of individuals can be added to the general store of culture. Between rigid habit and centrifugal dispersion of energies the artist, like the scientist, must steer a middle course: his success depends upon avoiding the extremes of mechanism and anarchy. Only so can he see and, in seeing, create a world distinctively his own. Distinctively, yet not exclusively, for when he has fashioned his world in a form which others can see, it becomes their world also, and he becomes, in so far forth, one of the creators of the human mind.

We are so accustomed to think of the human mind, like the human body, as having taken form when the race reached human estate, that an expression implying that the mind is still in process of creation may seem merely paradoxical, or at least figurative. But the mind is not an organ, like the heart or lungs; it properly includes the whole world of which we can be conscious; and this is built up gradually, through the labor of everyone who receives, transmits, and especially enriches our entire cultural tradition. Since the artist plays a distinctive and irreplaceable rôle in this cultural development, we can only judge his true importance by seeing how the development takes place.

The savage, doubtless, as he looks at the material world about him, can recognize the practically important features of the scene. He can identify the path through the wilderness, the way to his hunting-ground and the way home again. He can detect the color of the tiger's skin, and the cloud that presages rain or the lightning-flash. But, so far as we can judge, the tiger is merely a competitor for his food-supply, and on occasions a dangerous enemy to himself—never a being of whom he would ask the question,

> "In what distant deeps or skies
> Burned the fire of thine eyes?"

or

> "Did he who made the lamb make thee?"

If *we* can see the tiger as something other than a large predacious feline of nocturnal habits, with an occasional fondness for human flesh, if we can think of him as a particularly vivid embodiment of the fire of life, and marvel at the inexhaustible variety in which that life clothes itself—if we can do this, it is through no virtue of our own, but because our imagination has been quickened by a poet's touch.

Not the savage only, but many an ancestor much nearer us, perceived a world poor, mean and drab compared with ours. The Greeks, as their language indicates, could discriminate only a small number of separate colors, and there is little or no sense of landscape in their literature. If "the mountains look on Marathon," it was not a Greek poet who informed us of it; indeed, the sense of Nature as something with a life of its own, apart from the life of humanity, is distinctively modern, and but for the naturalistic bent of mind that came with and after the Renaissance we should probably be almost destitute of it. This bent of mind was scientific as well as esthetic; but if it is true to say, "The heavens declare the glory of Kepler and Newton," it is no less true to say, "The heavens declare the glory of Tintoretto and Claude Lorrain."

It is not only in giving color and spaciousness to the visible world, animating it with its own soul and setting our imagination free in its presence, that art does its work. No less than material things are our fellow-men transfigured when we see them in the light of art. Even without the aid of art we can, it is true, observe our fellows' actions as they go about their business, marry, bring up their children, grow old and die. Our weal and woe are too closely intertwined with theirs to permit us to be forgetful of them: we must in any case study their wishes, observe the rules that make a common life endurable, and offer them inducements for services desired. For that infinitesimal minority of them who are interesting to us as persons, we instinctively strive to do more, to offer kindnesses without expectation of reward, and to share the joys and sorrows that lend significance to experience. But while we trust to utility and instinct to guide our human associations, how halting the coöperation, how feeble the insight! Rites celebrated together, song and story embodying common delights and aspirations, are what make shared experience, in any pregnant sense, possible, and these things, whatever their ostensible purpose, are esthetic in quality.

Perhaps no better example of this could be found than in the rôle that the Homeric poems played in Greek civilization. It is sometimes said that the greatness of that civilization was partly due to the fact that the Greeks had no sacred books, in the sense that the Jews had; that is, that they had no rigid and binding code of laws which everyone was expected to obey in every detail. This is not quite true, since Homer was almost an oracle for them; it is true, however, that the *Iliad* and the *Odyssey* were less a prescription of a precise way of life than an embodiment of ideals, which owed their authority in no small degree to the glamour lent by the Homeric manner to the experiences reflected in them. In thus providing ideals which were embodied in exceedingly vivid and moving imagery, the poems gave to the Greeks a fund of vicariously enjoyed experiences, which shaped the purposes and crystallized the feelings of the Greek race as a whole, and at the same time did not so entirely fix them as to make variation impossible. Hence the possibility both of individualism in thought and feeling, and of communication between individuals, and consequently the birth of genuine reflection and personal distinction.

In modern times the development of the novel is perhaps the best illustration of the work of the artist in making individuals intelligible to each other. The novel is the form of art at present most universally enjoyed, and it is from novels, at least as much as from association with other individuals, that many of us derive our conceptions of human nature and of its possibilities. Furthermore, it is from these conceptions that our ideals for ourselves chiefly arise. Not that the novelist should directly indicate or recommend ideals: if he does that he becomes a moralist pure and simple. His contribution to life, to morals, is less direct but not less essential. Unless we are content to take all our moral laws on authority, we are obliged to judge of the goodness or badness of our acts by their effects on others, by the contribution they make to human welfare generally. To do this, we must enter imaginatively into the purposes of others, and it is in literature that human purposes are most effectively set forth. Law, custom and instinctive sympathy are of little use when we are dealing with the manifestations of human nature that are new or that lie outside the familiar circle of our acquaintanceship: universal human nature becomes intelligible only through art.

To make human nature intelligible to itself—that is the real purpose of art, that, and not any construction of a sanctuary for those who find the world of practical affairs too much for them. The artist makes human nature intelligible, not, like the psychologist, by analysis of it in the abstract, but by showing imaginatively the objects and activities in which it can find satisfaction. His command of a recognized medium, paint, words, musical sound, is necessary if he is to make what he imaginatively divines common coin, but it is in the divination, the vision, that he really exercises his vocation. This, and this only, is what makes him not a purveyor of amusement but a creator of life.

MYSTICISM AND ART[1]

Laurence Buermeyer

Mysticism means, psychologically, a sense of profound and moving identification with something not ourselves. It means also that the identity felt is not demonstrable, in the sense that a man's legal nationality is demonstrable, or his membership in a club or other organization. In mystical states of mind, in other words, we are conscious of an expansion of our personality through union with something not ourselves, but this union is felt and not seen. The mystic feels that the dissolution of the boundaries which ordinarily separate him from the world is not merely fanciful or illusory, but represents a truth deeper than the facts which meet the eye. If, however, he is challenged to exhibit evidence for his conviction, he cannot do so. His feeling is not a conclusion drawn from verifiable premises, and it can never be made an intelligible or moving reality to the non-mystic.

The fact that the validity of mystical states is not demonstrable logically is what William James means by calling such states "ineffable." But this is not a fact characteristic of mysticism only. "No one," James writes, "can make clear to one who has never had a certain feeling, in what the worth or quality of it consists. One must have musical ears to know the value of a symphony; one must have been in love one's self to understand the lover's frame of mind. Lacking the heart or the ear, we cannot interpret the musician or the lover justly, and we are even likely to consider

[1] Based on Albert C. Barnes, *Art and Mysticism*, The Art in Painting, Harcourt, Brace & Co., New York, N.Y., 1925.

76

them weak-minded or absurd. The mystic finds that most of us accord to his experiences an equally incompetent treatment."

Mysticism is thus no isolated phenomenon. It is only a high degree of something which enters into all our experiences, so far as they are concerned with ultimate values. All these are incommunicable to anyone of radically different temperament. We may illustrate its nature, first, by contrasting it with its opposite; second, by indicating some of the types of experience which are tinged with mysticism, but are not mystical in the fullest sense.

The complete antithesis of mysticism is the sense of isolation, of solitude in an alien and uncomprehending world. A world in which there is nothing, human or non-human, to answer and coöperate with our powers, to take cognizance of our feelings, is what we find most difficult to endure. All our instincts look to help, of some sort, from our environment. The child's cry of pain or anger, which depends upon parental solicitude for its efficacy, is only the most obvious instance of this. In our more mature years, when we no longer expect to have our wishes granted as by a miracle, but take thought about means as well as about ends, we only make the miracle one step more remote. We offer inducements to others to do as we wish, but there would be no inducements to offer if others were not in some degree responsive to our acts. When either human beings or natural objects behave in a way we do not foresee and cannot control, when they disappoint our expectations, we are frustrated, at a loss: it is then that the sense of ourselves as limited, impotent and alone, is brought home to us with painful force.

It is obvious that the sense of union is always a relative matter. Since it is pain, grief, any frustration of our desires by the independent course of events, which makes us feel alienated from our world, the sense of union depends upon accord between ourselves and our environment. Some coöperation from the world we must have if we are to live at all. But so long as this coöperation is secured only by deliberate forethought and execution of plans, people or things may not seem hostile or intractable, but they give us no actual sense of identification. Expansion of the self, in the mystical sense, occurs only when we divine an actual sympathy, when our wills are answered by an immediate, unpurchased responsiveness. The difference is that between dealing with a stranger, who must receive a *quid pro quo* for everything he does, and a friend, who is directly moved by perception of our wants to try to gratify them. Whenever what we desire is immediately presented to us, without any need of driving a bargain or paying a price, the resulting sense of harmony is an approach to the mystical experience.

Of course, the mixture of responsiveness and indifference in things which we ordinarily encounter is not provocative of any intense mystical feelings. Patriotism at its height, however, in which we are overwhelmingly impressed by the unity in thought, feeling and purpose between our fellow-countrymen and ourselves, is a genuinely mystical feeling. For the patriot, as for every other human being, the union is incomplete, differences remain; but the differences with the foreigner are so much greater that the former sink into insignificance. So also with the man in love. The extent to which another individual meets and satisfies his desires, his imagination, makes the inevitable residuary discords too trivial to hold his attention: the sense of union, temporarily at least, abolishes the sense of otherness, and mystical expansion is realized.

Unfortunately, this mystical expansion is often illusory. It is only too well known that love constantly attributes to its object virtues which do not exist, and that there are visions—for example, those of the drug-addict—which are merely visionary. "The sway of alcohol over mankind is unquestionably due to its ability to stimulate the mystical faculties of human nature, usually crushed to earth by the cold facts and dry criticisms of the sober hour. Sobriety diminishes, discriminates and says no; drunkenness expands, unites and says yes. It is in fact the great exciter of the Yes-function in man. It brings its votary from the chill periphery of things to the radiant core. It makes him for the moment one with truth. Not through mere perversity do men run after it. To the poor and unlettered it stands in the place of symphony-concerts and literature; and it is a part of the deeper mystery and tragedy of life that whiffs and gleams of something which we immediately recognize as excellent should be vouchsafed to so many of us only in the fleeting earlier phases of what in its totality is so degrading a poisoning. The drunken consciousness is one bit of the mystical consciousness."[2] The frequent tendency of mystical states of mind to sink into mere illusion and emotionalism makes it necessary, therefore, in considering the relation of art to mysticism, to consider also the false esthetic mysticism which corresponds to the patriotism which is jingoism, the love which is infatuation, the religion which is superstition.

The first and most obvious affinity between art and mysticism arises from the fact that art provides us with a world which is made by human beings for the direct satisfaction of their desires. This is true also

[2] James, *Varieties of Religious Experience*, page 387, Longmans, Green & Co., London, 1902.

of the material apparatus of life; but art, unlike the things which minister to our physical necessities, appeals immediately to personality. The artist puts his whole self into his work, as the engineer or manufacturer does not. The world he presents us with is a more humanized world than that of the man of business or the industrialist. Art without personality is nothing, but in the sphere of the merely useful, personality is a vanishing fringe around the borders of the mechanical.

Art, in other words, directly enlarges our vision by showing us the vision of our fellows, and in this sense it necessarily and always has some of the essential quality of mysticism. In a less specific manner, also, it contributes to the outgoing of the self into the world, by suggesting that the frustration of our desires by things over which we have no control is not final and absolute. How far the things of the world are really alien and hostile is always a problem. That they may be in a measure controlled materially, science and technology have made clear, but the actual command over "this sorry scheme of things entire" which either individuals or the race can exert, is infinitesimal. Art, in showing a peculiar sort of responsiveness in matter, its capacity for assuming forms which immediately satisfy our human desires, provides a presumption if not a promise that the unexplored remainder of the world may not be wholly alien or indifferent to us. In this again it joins hands with the mystical experience.

This is true even of the art of a writer like Lytton Strachey, or of a painter like Degas, both of whom seem essentially detached and ironical. It is only, however, as we approach artists whose interpretation of the world as a whole is colored by personal feeling, who seek to make the totality of things a living reality, that we come to art which is in the fullest sense mystical. We have mysticism at its height, in other words, when the harmony between the self and the world, realized in ordinary life only now and then, is taken to be the key to all experience. Then what is hostile or indifferent is regarded as essentially illusory or transient, everything is felt to be full of life, and at heart akin to ourselves. Union with the world is not a casual or momentary episode but the ultimate truth of things, and the responsive spirit is everywhere. The artists who give us this sense of all-pervasive life are the mystics *par excellence*. Dante, Milton and, in a somewhat different sense, Goethe, are essentially mystics; Beethoven and César Franck have more of the mystical quality than Mozart or Debussy, Giotto than Piero della Francesca, Rembrandt than Rubens.

In painting, the first and most obvious expansion of the self comes simply from the discovery of a wealth of relationships, harmonies and contrasts of color, linear rhythms, patterns of light and shadow, harmonious spatial intervals, which we find in real objects only occasionally, or in a comparatively degraded form. These relationships, once pointed out, often appear with the force of a revelation: the actual appearance of things—not of pictures only, but also of the things of nature—assumes a colorfulness, a richness, an arresting interest, which make the world seem transfigured. But although the eye, once opened, sees the beauty of line, of color, of far-reaching space, in a whole world which was formerly drab and lifeless, it is in works of art that these qualities appear at their best. Always, or nearly always, in the realm of fact, the colors are imperfectly harmonious, the spaces are too empty or else they are overcrowded, the lines are in some degree stiff and awkward. The desire for a satisfying order in things, in other words, is thwarted as often as it is satisfied, and the mind seeking to be thoroughly at home in the world must either turn to art, or else so select, simplify and rearrange its perceptions that they become in effect creative and esthetic.

Just so, in our dealings with persons, we constantly find that actual people fall short in complete expressiveness, mar as well as make the living drama in which they play their part, and for the adequate satisfaction of our imagination we must project into them a set of qualities, of passionate attitudes, which our actual perceptions do not fully warrant; that or else turn to the personalities presented to us in literature.

The highest range of mysticism, the vision of the world as a manifestation of indwelling life or spirit, is best illustrated by Giotto, El Greco, Rembrandt or Claude Lorrain. In Giotto, medievalism reaches the summit of its pictorial expression. The profoundly religious quality of his pictures is not due to their employment of Christian subjects or symbolism. Such subjects appear *ad nauseam* in the tedious and insipid altarpieces with which Catholic churches everywhere are filled. Upturned eyes, folded hands, a rapt and sanctified expression of face, only too often give the effect of mere sanctimoniousness, and the Biblical narratives which cover the walls of so many churches all over Europe are often no more mystical than the pictures in our own cinematograph theaters. It is the dignity, expressiveness and restraint of Giotto's line, the clear, luminous color in which his frescoes are bathed, the amplitude of his subtly indicated but convincing space, the whole effect of a transfigured but deeply real world, which make us feel that the universe as he saw it is really more exalted, more glorified, than that which our own unaided eyes can show us.

In El Greco we have not the Olympian calm of Giotto, but tortured sensibility, a perfervid, almost feverish, imagination. Again, however, there is no reliance upon mere facial expression, upon literal imitation of terror, agony, transports. The ecstatic vision of El Greco appears in the use of the plastic means themselves, in the writhing serpentine line, the distorted figures, the iridescent, shimmering color, the eerie and ghastly light, the movement which flows through every area of the canvas. The whole world appears to be in a turmoil, a turmoil animated by hopes and fears akin to those of human beings, but otherworldly, unearthly, transported.

These painters represent what may be called a supernatural mysticism. We find the mysticism of Nature, at least of romantic Nature, in Claude; of human beings, in Rembrandt. Nature, in Claude, is of course not the Nature of mechanical science or of material things in their individuality. What Claude shows is the majestic peace of the larger groupings of natural objects, of meadow, river, mountain and sea. This he renders largely through designs of space, in which the use of perspective and the arrangement of the masses give us an overwhelming effect of extensity, of infinity of distance. These vast spaces are filled with a glowing, colorful light, which makes them not merely indefinitely extended, but alive throughout the whole of their extension. From his pictures we get much the same effect that we do when, on a clear night, we not only see the stars but actually have some realization, however inadequate, of the magnitude of the stellar universe: the sense of a spaciousness by which our minds and feelings are carried outward forever further and further.

The mysticism of Rembrandt is different from any

7

of these. It is the realization of personality, a making manifest the unplumbed depths of human quality which lie all about us, but which we are ordinarily too dull to realize for ourselves. There is not in him, as there is in Goya or Degas, an actual portrayal of psychological states of mind; there is neither irony nor sentiment; the persons portrayed are perfectly natural, composed, even — superficially — prosaic; but we have the impression that their flesh is opaque no longer, that we see through it to the living human being of whom it is only the visible sign. This mystery of personality is conveyed by the use of chiaroscuro, the dramatic contrast between light and shadow, by which the effect of an illumination of what seemed commonplace is perfectly realized.

Another example, again quite distinctive in kind, is that of Cézanne. Cézanne, living after Manet and Monet, had an interest in the apparently commonplace which resembles Rembrandt's; but the life he depicts is that of things as well as of persons, and his means are color, much more than light. He had Manet's ability to see the essential, that which makes a thing what it is; but the things are far more solid and substantial, they have a more moving reality, than Manet's. This sense of solidity and substance in individual things is conjoined with a much greater command of space-composition than Manet's, so that he gives us a sense of life in Nature which has much of the epic power of Claude, but is realistic rather than romantic. His mysticism becomes apparent the moment we compare his work with that of a not altogether dissimilar painter, Matisse, also a great artist, but one whose work is much more superficial, much less powerful, much nearer mere decoration.

We must now consider the work of painters who

aimed at mystical effects but failed to achieve them. Such painting is on the way to the ineffable raptures of the alcoholic, the drug-addict, the sentimentalist. Or —to take the familiar examples—it corresponds to the illumination provided by the word "abracadabra," or by long-continued contemplation of the navel. Like all painting which descends from the plastic to the merely illustrative, it is characterized by reliance upon adventitious or conventional associations. We see an analogue to it in the patriotism which is merely flag-waving, or in the cheap fiction and balladry which rely on the stage-worn properties of romance—moonlit nights, weeping skies, sunsets over the sea. The paint-ers who are spurious mystics, lacking the penetration of eye which can catch an independent view of the liv-ing world, and the command of means to set down such a view, copy, exaggerate and vulgarize the insight of others.

Mere subject or symbolism, as we have said with reference to Giotto, has nothing to do with the attain-ment of mystical effects. A Cézanne still-life commun-icates more of the quality of life, seems a profounder revelation, than a Madonna by Andrea del Sarto or Murillo. A painter such as Turner, however, relies al-most solely upon the use of particular subjects. Flashy illustration of landscape seen through rain, mist or fog, is utilized to replace any genuine perception of the true inwardness of things. Meanwhile, the tech-nique, the actual use of plastic means, when it has any distinctive quality, is a superficial imitation of Claude's.

A similar counterfeit mysticism is that of Böcklin. His famous picture, *Die Toteninsel*, might be an illustration for one of Edgar Allan Poe's tales. Of a fresh and personal perception of color, of light or of line, it shows none. It is not plastic art at all, but literature, and literature which is decidedly trite, melodramatic and specious. If this is mystical art, then so are the Doré illustrations to Dante's *Inferno*. The whole force of such painting is due to suggestions of things and events which have nothing whatever to do with painting: it has all the unreality of an opium dream. To take it seriously as art is the same thing as to make the sign of the cross in order to ward off smallpox infection.

A final illustration of such mysticism is the work of the American painter, Arthur B. Davies. In his pictures we see dreamy-looking nymphs in strange landscapes, swirling movement and flying hair which suggest the wind sweeping over wide open spaces—all the paraphernalia of popular romantic mysticism. But, as with Turner and Böcklin, this striking subject is not embodied in a personal or distinctive plastic expression. His means are simply the clichés of painting, notably of Botticelli, employed to give pictorial setting to commonplace literary images. His vivid rhythmic movement is chiefly linear and is supported by no original use of color or light or space. Plastically, his painting is that of a skilled eclectic. His superficial adaptation of other men's contributions yields an appeal obvious but cheap, and his mysticism is only a dreamy dalliance with fancies.

ART AND DAYDREAMING[1]

LAURENCE BUERMEYER

DAYDREAMS, like works of art, are a refuge for unsatisfied desires. Of the many things we want, we actually get but few; but in our reveries we have all that the heart can desire. To the eye of the beholder, our circumstances may seem shabby, our abilities commonplace and our persons unlovely. To our own, when resolutely fixed upon them, they may appear somewhat the same, though probably never quite so much so. But it is not often that our eye is resolutely fixed upon them. At the first opportunity it looks away from them in their ordinary form and seeks and finds a golden counterfeit. Then it is that beggars ride, that the humble sit in the seats of the mighty and that unrequited love exists no more. We no longer find in the past anything to blush for, nor anything to fear in the future.

Unfortunately, the change is unmade soon after it is made. Castles in Spain are delightful but not permanent. Even while they last they are never quite convincing, at least while we retain our sanity. Unless they possess some footing on the solid earth, their flimsiness is apparent to those who inhabit them. This footing, in the sense of actual reality, they cannot of course be given, but—to drop figurative expression—a certain amount of actual sensation will vivify a great deal of imagery, and that degree of contact with actuality is what much that passes for art is designed to

[1] From Laurence Buermeyer, *The Aesthetic Experience*, The Barnes Foundation Press, Merion, Pa., 1929.

provide. The country estate, the retinue of servants, the motor cars and yachts and throngs of admirers which our fancy cannot quite make real, become much more real if we read of them or see them on the stage or in the moving picture. A very large proportion of all paintings, the enormously greater part of fiction and drama and almost the whole of the "art of the screen" have no other purpose than to supply this body, this solidity, to daydreams. We live ourselves into the personages who are presented to us there, share their possessions and celebrate their triumphs. Hence the endowment of the hero and the heroine with all that is enviable, impressive and praiseworthy, hence the ignobility of all who oppose them, and hence the happy ending.

To see the relation of daydreaming to art we must go back to psychological fundamentals. We have seen that instinct or emotion, at every stage of development, expresses itself in envisaging, in terms appropriate to its own specific bent, the object that stimulates it. Such envisagement, when the emotion is guided by intelligence, is tentative: the admirable or contemptible traits with which the subject is invested remain in the hypothetical realm, and effort is made to find out how far they represent the truth. But for undisciplined emotion they are absolute, and, as when love is infatuation, no reconsideration of them is admissible. When emotion, instead of proceeding to its proper goal, loses itself in sloth or is paralyzed by the difficulty of making itself effective, its natural tendency to dwell in fancy upon its object absorbs all the energy which ought to go into action, and it dreams endlessly of the accomplishments which are beyond its power. There is no stage of enlightenment and discipline in the instinctive life which is finally and completely adequate, able to meet all emergencies: the habitual expression of an emotion may always fail to do justice to a new situation. Therefore daydreaming may appear at every level of development. It may find expression in action no less than in thought, in refusing to see actual things as they are, as well as in flying for refuge to things wholly remote from reality. These alternatives correspond, respectively, to evasion of a problem in life, and evasion in imagination. We shall begin with consideration of the former.

Suppose, for example, that I wish to repair a break in a friendship. Someone to whom I am attached has given me what I take to be ground for complaint by accepting the offer of my services in a time of difficulty, and then disregarding my wishes in a matter in which his acceptance of my aid ought to have bound him to consider them. If he were going to act counter to them, he ought to have at least given some reason. In the absence of any explanation of his action, I feel that I have been used as a means to an end, and discarded when useful no longer. My former experience of him has made it difficult to believe that he is really mercenary and ungrateful, but until I can see the justification for his behavior, I cannot with self-respect continue on my former terms with him. One thing is sure: there has been an error somewhere.

It is needless, for the purposes of the illustration, to consider all possible alternatives: two will be sufficient. I may have estimated my supposed friend wrongly in the past, or the situation may not have seemed to him to involve on his part the obligations that I considered it to involve. Have I been unreasonable in my expectations, or was there something in my actions which exempted him from making the return which I regarded as my due? If I am at all acquainted with human nature, I know that men, myself included, act from very mixed motives, that they find the difficulties of others not displeasing, since these give them the opportunity to enjoy their own security and power, and that it is very easy to make an enemy in doing a favor, if the favor is enjoyed as a means of gratifying one's own self-esteem at the expense of another's. To make sure that I have a grievance, I must be certain that my own motives were entirely disinterested, and that nothing in my manner could have been taken to indicate condescension, pleasure in my relatively advantageous rôle, or the impersonal benevolence of the professional altruist. In other words, I must overhaul my estimate both of my erstwhile friend and of myself, and try to see anew the incident from both points of view. If I succeed in solving the problem, I discover wherein I have been at fault, and wherein he has been at fault, the point at which we were at cross-purposes, the readjusted attitude and reformed habits required of both of us if relations are to be resumed. What the whole incident means is that the transformation of practice and feeling through the work of intelligence has broken down or at least been halted, and that effort is required for its renewal. I have failed in the art of life and must retrace my steps and seek fresh enlightenment.

In the discovery of traits and purposes previously overlooked in the person I supposed myself to know and in myself, there is the same increasing grasp of the real world, with corresponding clarification of my will and the means to its attainment, that we found to be everywhere the fruit of intelligence. The fruits of daydreaming are very different. The daydreamer refuses to meet his problems. In the instance just given, the problem cannot be solved without effort and at least some degree of discomfort. No matter where the

blame lay, I am revealed as inadequate in my judgment
of others and of myself, and the painful necessity is
laid upon me to learn to see and do differently. This
necessity may be shirked in a variety of ways. I may
elect to feel that those I care for should be forgiven
even unto seventy times seven, and overlook the apparent inconsiderateness and ingratitude on my friend's
part, supposing the while that my indolence, which forgets that justice must be rendered before generosity
can be offered, is really magnanimity. Or I may feel
that my friendship has been outraged and my dignity
offered an affront, and in breaking off relations see in
myself one who is above associating with the unworthy.
In either case, whatever was amiss is unrectified, and
I remain the self-righteous Pharisee who is guilty of
the very disloyalty of which he complains. Whether
sentimentality or vindictiveness carries the day, I remain unadjusted to reality, shut up in the world of my
own preconceived ideas.

In the art which is really daydreaming, the same
shirking of issues appears, with the same results. The
painter who sees with a conventional eye, who makes
of the original discoveries of other painters a mere
set of devices for showing again what they have already shown, is evading the labor of looking upon
Nature for himself. Of course he must be taught by
his predecessors to see as much as they have seen, but
he has no reason for existence unless he can sharpen
the vision they have bequeathed him in order to see
something more for himself. Otherwise he makes
merchandise of stale sentiment and second-hand pret-
tiness.

So also with the novelist or dramatist. The daydreamer who seeks to produce literature is always he
who appeals to conventional sentiments, who puts before us the stock properties of the literary *mise-en-*

scène. His situations, the purposes, sorrows and delights of his personages, are worn shapeless by long
usage. The feelings to which they appeal are rigid as
iron: they amount to what in psychology are called "fix-
ations." Any wave of strong popular feeling pro-
vokes an outpouring of such printed daydreams, all
melodramatic in essence, all, that is to say, invitations
to the reader to take sides violently and be assured that
whatever he is, is right. A nation at war furiously
repudiates the idea that the enemy has anything good
in him, and its prejudice is at once fed by a flood of
novels and plays in which the angelic and diabolic rôles
are fittingly assigned. Indeed, every sentiment widely
diffused throughout society provides a market for
works of a corresponding type, so that sentimental,
patriotic and pornographic books need be written with
only passable skill to be assured of at least some success.

   A word which the years since 1914 have made increasingly familiar to all of us, is almost a perfect
equivalent for daydreaming. Propaganda, though its
motives may be different, has results wholly analogous
to those of daydreaming. It is the art of putting only
one side of a case, of concealing, slurring over, or be-
littling whatever contradicts what we want to believe
or opposes what we want to do. It is the voice of
crude instinct, howling down anything that could give
it pause. Of course, to arrive at a conclusion and to try
to persuade others that it is true, is not propaganda;
the distinction between the two is that honest argument
seeks to bring to light the objections to its thesis and
to give them all the weight that is their due, while
propaganda attempts to huddle objections out of sight.
Melodrama is to art what propaganda is to argument.

   Among the more gifted and intelligent of contemporary purveyors of melodrama is Mr. Upton Sin-

clair.[2] His books are not necessarily to be condemned
because they were written to illustrate a particular
view of the world and its shortcomings: so was the
Divine Comedy. The ground of complaint against
Mr. Sinclair is not that he has convictions, but that
they spring from an experience which passionate parti-
sanship has blinded to every aspect of the truth but
one. It is possible to write of the hardships and op-
pressions to which labor is subject without making, as
does Mr. Sinclair, the oppressed laborer a combination
of all but the most flagrantly inappropriate virtues,
and the victim, never of circumstances, but always of
the heartless selfishness or malice of his exploiters.
The question whether socialism is a desirable or prac-
ticable scheme of reform does not enter the question
as here considered.

A writer with his eye on the facts, either of the abstract economic situation or of the situation as it
appears to the laborer himself, would never write as
does Mr. Sinclair. The hardships of the exploited
may be as great as any propagandist would have us
believe, but it is an offense against intellectual integrity
to imply that they are those which, in the same position, a person of other nurture, habits and standards of
life would be called upon to endure. Mr. Sinclair, to
make the light of martyrdom in which he surrounds the
laborer as vivid as possible, suggests or implies that
absence of the daily bath, of opportunity to hear symphony concerts, of the sort of association with his fellows that would be craved by, let us say, a character
out of Henry James—that these things are a cruel
deprivation to him. Correspondingly, we find slurred
over the ignorance, lack of self-control, inability to
understand general issues and to take an impartial and

---

[2] These comments on Mr. Sinclair were in the main suggested to
me by an unsigned article in the *Freeman.* I have not the date.

inclusive view of public affairs, which, far more than the malice of oppressors, stand between the proletariat and the more satisfactory way of life.

Mr. Sinclair thus falls short both as an ally of labor and as an artist seeking to depict an experience. The intelligent friend of labor, or the artist interested in the life of those who gain their bread by physical toil, would attempt to see exactly where the shoe really pinches, to discover what the individual of the submerged classes does desire and what resources he really has for getting it. In doing so, such a writer would strive, instead of covering up the shortcomings of his protagonist, to bring them fully, though to be sure sympathetically, to light, since only so can they be understood and, from the practical point of view, corrected. The West Virginia miner who read *King Coal* would be encouraged by it, never to take pains to fit himself for the performance of the function which, well or ill, the capitalist and the promoter do perform, but to feel himself merely wronged and abused and unjustifiably kept down, to nurse a grievance and to indulge in self-pity. Mr. Sinclair has not achieved the portrayal of any human being, has conveyed no insight into any actual experience, but has provided a drug for those who wish without understanding to enjoy the pleasures of becoming indignant and lachrymose—either over themselves or over others.

Art and daydreaming are alike in that they both show us a world nearer to the heart's desire than the actual world. Otherwise they are antithetical. Art is conduct and feeling enlightened by "fundamental brain-work" and finding the heart of their desire, entering by sympathy and imagination into the wider world of Nature and man. Daydreaming is conduct and feeling so dull or so feeble that they can only shrink into a private cell with painted walls.

AFFECTIVE THOUGHT IN LOGIC AND PAINTING[1]

John Dewey

Traditional theories in philosophy and psychology have accustomed us to sharp separations between physiological and organic processes on the one hand and the higher manifestations of culture in science and art on the other. The separations are summed up in the common division made between mind and body. These theories have also accustomed us to draw rigid separations between the logical, strictly intellectual, operations which terminate in science, the emotional and imaginative processes which dominate poetry, music and to a lesser degree the plastic arts, and the practical doings which rule our daily life and which result in industry, business and political affairs. In other words, thought, sentiment or affectivity and volition have been marked off from one another. The result of these divisions has been the creation of a large number of problems which in their technical aspect are the special concern of philosophy, but which come home to everyone in his actual life in the segregation of the activities he carries on, the departmentalizing of life, the pigeonholing of interests. Between science's sake, art for art's sake, business as usual or business for money-making, the relegation of religion to Sundays and holydays, the turning over of politics to professional politicians, the professionalizing of sports, and so on, little room is left for living, for the sake of living, a full, rich and free life.

[1] From *Journal of The Barnes Foundation*, April, 1926.

Recent advances in some fundamental generalizations regarding biological functions in general and those of the nervous system in particular have made possible a definite conception of continuous development from the lower functions to the higher. Interestingly enough, this breaking-down of fixed barriers between physiological operations and the far reaches of culture in science and art has also removed the underpinning from beneath the separation of science, art and practical activity from one another. There has long been vague talk about the unity of experience and mental life, to the effect that knowledge, feeling and volition are all manifestations of the same energies, etc.; but there has now been put in our hands the means by which this talk may be made definite and significant.

Naturally, the variety of physiological details involved has not yet been adequately organized nor has there been time to digest them and get their net results. In any case, the writer is not an expert in this field, and even if he were this would hardly be the place to expound them. But some of their net results are easy of comprehension, and they have a definite bearing upon art and its connection with the normal processes of life.

We may begin with the field of reasoning, long supposed to be preëmpted by pure intellect, and to be completely severed, save by accident, from affectivity and desire and from the motor organs and habits by which we make our necessary practical adjustments to the world about us. But a recent writer, Rignano, working from a biological basis, has summed up his conclusions as follows: "The analysis of reasoning, the highest of our mental faculties, has led us to the view that it is constituted entirely by the reciprocal play of the two fundamental and primordial activities of our psyche, the intellectual and the affective. The first consist in simple mnemonic evocations of perceptions or images of the past; the second appear as tendencies or aspirations of our mind towards a certain end to be attained, towards which reasoning itself is directed."[2]

An isolated quotation fails, of course, to bring out the full force of the points made. But what is summed up here under the idea of "affectivity" is that an organism has certain basic needs which cannot be supplied without activity which modifies the surroundings; that when the organism is in any way disturbed in its "equilibration" with its environment, its needs show themselves as restless, craving, desiring activity which persists until the acts thus induced have brought about a new integration of the organism and its relation to the environment. Then it is shown that thinking falls within the scope of this principle; reasoning is a phase of the generic function of bringing about a new relationship between organisms and the conditions of life, and like other phases of the function is controlled by need, desire and progressive satisfactions.

Rignano calls the other phase "intellectual." But the context shows that the basic principle here is one of practical adjustments. Past experiences are retained so that they may be evoked and arranged when there is need to use them in attaining the new end set by the needs of our affective nature. But the retention is not intellectual. It is a matter of organic modifications, of change of disposition, attitude and habit. The "stuff" from which thinking draws its material in satisfying need by establishing a new relation to the surroundings is found in what, with some extension of the usual sense of the word, may be termed habits: namely,

[2] Rignano, *The Psychology of Reasoning*, page 388, Harcourt, Brace & Co., New York, N. Y., 1923.

the changes wrought in our ways of acting and undergoing by prior experiences. Thus the material of thought all comes from the past; but its purpose and direction is future, the development of a new environment as the condition of sustaining a new and more fully integrated self.

It thus turns out, though the argument is too technical to be developed on this occasion, that the great gap which is traditionally made between the lower physiological functions and the higher cultural ones, is due first to isolating the organism from the environment, failing to see the necessity of its integration with environment, and secondly, to neglect of the function of needs in creating ends, or consequences to be attained. So when "ends" are recognized at all, it has been thought necessary to call in some higher and independent power to account for them. But the connection of ends with affectivities, with cravings and desires, is deep-seated in the organism, and is constantly extended and refined through experience. Desire, interest, accomplishes what in the traditional theory a pure intellect was evoked to accomplish. More and more expansive desires and more varied and flexible habits build up more elaborate trains of thought and, finally, the harmonies, consistencies and comprehensive structures of logical systems result.

Reasoning and science are thus obviously brought nearer to art. The satisfaction of need requires that surroundings should be changed. In reasoning, this fact appears as the necessity for experimentation. In plastic art it is a commonplace. Art also explicitly recognizes what it has taken so long to discover in science: the control of re-shaping natural conditions exercised by emotion, and the place of the imagination, under the influence of desire, in re-creating the world into a more orderly place. When so-called non-rational factors are found to play a large part in the production of relations of consistency and order in logical systems, it is not surprising that they should operate in artistic structures. Indeed, it may be questioned whether any scientific systems extant, save perhaps those of mathematics, equal artistic structure in integrity, subtlety and scope, while the latter are evidently more readily and widely understood, and are the sources of a more widespread and direct satisfaction. These facts are explicable only when it is realized that scientific and artistic systems embody the same fundamental principles of the relationship of life to its surroundings, and that both satisfy the same fundamental needs. Probably a time will come when it will be universally recognized that the differences between coherent logical schemes and artistic structures in poetry, music and the plastic arts are technical and specialized, rather than deep-seated.

In the past we have had to depend mostly upon phrases to explain the production of artistic structures. They have been referred to genius or inspiration or the creative imagination. Contemporary appeal to the Unconscious and the Racial Unconscious are the same thing under a new name. Writing the word with a capital letter and putting "the" before it, as if it were a distinct force, gives us no more light than we had before. Yet unconscious activities are realities, and the newer biology is making it clear that such organic activities are just of the kind to re-shape natural objects in order to procure their adequate satisfaction, and that the re-shaped object will be marked by the features known to belong to works of art.

It is a commonplace that repetition in place and time, rhythm, symmetry, harmony, modulation, sus-

pense and resolution, plot, climax and contrasting let-
down, emphasis and intervals, action and retardation,
unity, being "all of a piece," and inexhaustible variety,
are marks, in varying ways, to meet the requirements
of different media, of all artistic productions. These
are just the traits which naturally characterize objects
when the environment is made over in consonance with
basic organic requirements. On the other hand, the
fact that the spectator and auditor "clicks" so intimately and intensely in the face of works of art is ac-
counted for. By their means there are released old,
deep-seated habits or engrained organic "memories,"
yet these old habits are deployed in new ways, ways in
which they are adapted to a more completely integrated
world so that they themselves achieve a new integration. Hence the liberating, expansive power of art.

The same considerations explain the fact that works
of art of a new style have to create their own audience.
At first there is experienced largely the jar of dis-
sonance with the superficial habits most readily called
into play. But changes in the surroundings involve
correlated changes in the organism, and so the eye and
ear gradually become acclimatized. The organism is
really made over, is reorganized in effecting an adequate perception of a work of art. Hence the proper
effect of the latter is gradually realized, and then what
was first condemned as *outré* falls into its serial place
in the history of artistic achievement.

In *The Art in Painting*, Mr. Barnes has shown that
plastic form is the *integration of all plastic means.*
In the case of paintings, these are color, line, light and
space. By means of their relations to one another, design is affected: design, namely, in line patterns, in
surface masses, in three-dimensional solids, and in
spatial intervals—the "room" about objects whether

up and down, side to side, front and back. And Mr.
Barnes has shown that it is the kind and degree of
integration of plastic means in achieving each of the
elements of design taken by itself, and also the integration of each with all the others, which constitutes the
objective standard for value in painting. From the
psychological standpoint, this integration in pictures
means that a correlative integration is effected in the
total set of organic responses; eye activities arouse
allied muscular activities which in turn not merely harmonize with and support eye activities, but which in
turn evoke further experiences of light and color, and
so on. Moreover, as in every adequate union of sensory and motor actions, the background of visceral,
circulatory, respiratory functions is also consonantly
called into action. In other words, integration in the
object permits and secures a corresponding integration
in organic activities. Hence, the peculiar well-being
and rest in excitation, vitality in peace, which is characteristic of esthetic enjoyment.

Defective value can, of course, be judged by the same
measure. Some one of the elements may be deficient;
thereby adequate support is not given to the function-
ing of the other elements and a corresponding lack of
vitality in response occurs or even a feeling of frustration and bafflement. Or, what is more likely to happen
in pictures that may conventionally attain celebrity
for a time, some factor is overaccentuated—so that
while vision is captured and impressed for the moment,
the final reaction is partial and one-sided, a fatiguing
demand being made upon some organic activities which
are not duly nourished and reinforced by the others.

Thus it is not too much to say that the statement of
an objective criterion of value in paintings set forth
for the first time by Mr. Barnes will make possible in

time an adequate psychological, even physiological, analysis of esthetic responses in spectators, so that the appreciation of paintings will no longer be a matter of private, absolute tastes and *ipse dixits*.

By the use of the same conception of integration of specified means, Mr. Barnes has also for the first time given us the clue to the historical development of modern painting in terms of paintings themselves. In the earlier period, integration is in considerable measure achieved by means extraneous to the painting itself, such as associated subject-matter in the religious or prior (academic) tradition, or by undue reliance upon familiar associations between light and shade and spatial positions. The history of art shows a tendency to secure variety and relationship in plastic form by means of the element most truly distinctive of painting, namely, color. Lines, for example, have ceased to be hard and fast clear-cut divisions (in which case they are more or less non-integrative), and are determined by subtle meetings of color-masses which upon close examination are found to melt into one another. Similarly, light and shade were long employed on the basis of everyday practical associations to give the impression of solidity. But artists capable of greater differentiation and integration of their experiences in terms of color itself experimented in conveying tri-dimensional relationships by means of variations and juxtapositions in color. Then color was employed to build up structural solidity and its variations in single objects. Painters have also learned to render action and movement, not by depending upon associations with extraneous experiences—which always lead to an overaccentuation of some one feature, light or line, as in depicting exaggerated muscular poses—but by use of the relations of forms to one another, in connection with spatial intervals, this end being attained by use of color as means. The fact that this more subtle and complete integration usually involves deformation or distortion of familiar forms—that is, conflicts with associations formed outside the realm of painting—accounts for the fact that they are greeted at first with disdainful criticism. But in time a new line of organic associations is built up, formed on the basis of unalloyed esthetic experiences, and deformations—what are such from the practical everyday standpoint—cease to give trouble and to be annoying. They become elements in a genuine and direct esthetic grasp.

From the standpoint of the analysis of pictures, there is nothing new in these remarks to anyone familiar with Mr. Barnes' book. I have recurred to them only because the objective analysis of Mr. Barnes is in the first place so thoroughly in accord with the present trend of fundamental biological conceptions, and, secondly, because it makes possible an application of these biological conceptions to the whole field of artistic structures and esthetic criticism. It then becomes possible to break down the traditional separation between scientific and intellectual systems and those of art, and also to further the application of the principle of integration to the relationship of those elements of culture which are so segregated in our present life—to science, art, in its variety of forms, industry and business, religion, sport and morals. And it is daily being more evident that unless some integration can be attained, the always increasing isolations and oppositions consequent upon the growth of specialization in all fields will in the end disrupt our civilization. That art and its intelligent appreciation as manifested especially in painting is itself an integrating experience is the constant implication of the work of The Barnes Foundation as that is reflected in *The Art in Painting.* For to make of paintings an educational means is to assert that the genuine intelligent realization of pictures is not only an integration of the specialized factors found in the paintings as such, but is such a deep and abiding experience of the nature of fully harmonized experience as sets a standard or forms a habit for all other experiences. In other words, paintings when taken out of their specialized niche are the basis of an educational experience which counteracts the disrupting tendencies of the hard-and-fast specializations, compartmental divisions and rigid segregations which so confuse and nullify our present life.

PLASTIC FORM[1]

Albert C. Barnes

A painting is a work of art in so far as it embodies the artist's perception of what he finds moving and significant in the objective world. As the expression of a coherent personality, it must have order or form; and as the outcome of an insight which penetrates to essentials and reorganizes surface-appearances, it must be plastic. The word "plastic" is applied to anything that can be bent or worked or changed into a form other than that which it originally had, and for the painter the merely factual appearances of things are plastic: they can be emphasized, distorted and rearranged as his personal vision and design require. The means by which this transformation is effected are color, line, light and space. A painting, as we have seen, is primarily concerned with things in their visible aspects, but it may include such illustrative values as are communicable without the intervention of any agency other than the specific plastic means. Plastic form is the synthesis or fusion of these specific elements. To be significant, the form must embody the essence, the reality, of the situation as it is capable of being rendered in purely plastic terms. A painter's worth is determined precisely by his ability to make the fusion of plastic means forceful, individual, characteristic of his own personality.

Plastic unity is form achieved by the harmonious merging of the plastic elements into an ensemble which

[1] From Albert C. Barnes, *The Art in Painting*, Harcourt, Brace & Co., New York, N. Y., 1937.

produces in us a genuinely satisfying esthetic experience. Plastic form is significant, in the ultimate and highest sense, only when it is a creation: an expression of an individual human experience in forceful plastic terms.

The most obvious plastic element is color. It has an esthetic value quite independent of its function of representing the actual color of real objects. Indeed, the esthetic significance of color is the most difficult of all to judge and is the source of much confusion on the part of novices and even of advanced critics. The novice is subject to many pitfalls in this respect—the mere sensuous appeal of varying degrees of brilliance, individual preference for particular colors, unconscious comparison with well-known objects of definite color-content—none of these standards has any esthetic significance. The intrinsic importance of color, and its relation to drawing and composition, will be discussed in the chapters which follow.[2]

Another of the basic plastic factors is drawing—and here again reigns a confusion similar to that noted in connection with color. The novice looks for the type of drawing which is a replica of the way colored surfaces of real objects intersect to form line and contour. He forgets that the artist's work is not to copy literally the lines and contours of objects, but so to select, draw out, accentuate and modify its essential aspects, by a fusion of all the plastic means, that there emerges a *creation*, constituting his individual version of the object. Success is a matter for esthetic judgment and not for simple comparison with the original object.

In the flat surface of a painting, color and line make up all the objects depicted. If there were no attempt to indicate the fulness of spatial depth, if objects were placed as flat representations on a single plane, color

[2] See chapters on Color; Drawing; Composition—Albert C. Barnes, *The Art in Painting*, Harcourt, Brace & Co., New York, N. Y., 1937.

and line would be the only plastic elements possible. But such a painting would have no esthetic significance unless there was an arrangement of the colored and drawn masses into some sort of relation with each other; and this arrangement is termed composition. Even in the pattern of a carpet or wallpaper, composition, in this sense of relations, is present. To have an esthetic appeal, the distribution of the elements in a pattern must have such a sequence of line and mass, a relation to each other, that their arrangement, order, balance are satisfactory to our sensibilities. Thus, mere pattern is the beginning of esthetic expression in so far as it shows that the creator has chosen one particular arrangement in preference to others physically possible, but without as much esthetic significance. In other words, color and line have been *composed* and the result is a design, a union of the two to give a single esthetic effect. Design is present when the color, the line, the composition, instead of being independently conceived, mutually affect one another and form a new unit. To alter any of these elements would disturb existing relationships and would destroy that particular unity. A design is completely satisfying esthetically when that particular arrangement of masses, that particular coloring, those particular shapes and sizes of objects, harmonize better with each other than would another set of relationships between the same elements. And this principle of unity may be said to be the ideal according to which all paintings may be judged. The design of a picture consists of the general plot or handling of the various details, and it is the factor which should be uppermost in the mind of the person who wishes to discriminate the plastically essential from the irrelevant. Design in plastic art is analogous to the thesis of an argument, the plot of a novel, the general structure of a symphony, the "point" of an anecdote: that is, the feature or detail which assigns to each of the other elements its rôle, its bearing, its significance.

A word of caution is necessitated by the present widespread confusion of pattern with design and with plastic form. Pattern, as defined in the preceding paragraph and in passages on cubism,[2] is always discernible in a good painting, but plastic form is present only in a relatively degraded stage in the "abstract" painting represented by cubism. Pattern is merely the skeleton upon which plastic units embodying the universal human values of experience are engrafted. Critics of the so-called advanced school prove by their writings that all that they see in paintings is mere pattern, although they endow it with the oracular mystification of such terms as "plastic design" or "significant form." The needed clarification of the meaning of form is furnished by Professor Dewey in the following statement: "Unless the meaning of the term (significant form) is so isolated as to be wholly occult, it denotes a selection, for sake of emphasis, purity, subtlety, of those forms which give consummatory significance to everyday subject-matters of experience. 'Forms' are not the peculiar property or creation of the esthetic and artistic; they are characters in virtue of which anything meets the requirements of an enjoyable perception. 'Art' does not create the forms; it is their selection and organization in such ways as to enhance, prolong and purify the perceptual experience. . . . Tendency to composition in terms of the formal characters marks much contemporary art, in poetry, painting, music, even sculpture and architecture. At their worst, these products are 'scientific' rather than artistic; technical

[2] See Albert C. Barnes, *The Art in Painting*, Harcourt, Brace & Co., New York, N. Y., 1937.

exercises, sterile and of a new kind of pedantry. At their best, they assist in ushering in new modes of art and by education of the organs of perception in new modes of consummatory objects, they enlarge and enrich the world of human vision. But they do this, not by discarding altogether connection with the real world, but by a highly funded and generalized representation of the formal sources of ordinary emotional experience."[3]

In any design, whether or not involving distortion, there are two important principles which deserve mention. These are rhythm and contrast. It is rhythm that first strikes our attention and produces the pleasure that holds us longest. No plastic element in a painting stands by itself, but is repeated, varied, counterbalanced by similar elements in other parts of the picture. It is this repetition, variation and counterbalance that constitutes rhythm. Each of the plastic elements may form rhythms with like elements — line with line, color with color, mass with mass — and each of these rhythms may enter into relation with the rhythms formed by other elements. The simplest form of rhythm is that in which the bending of a line is matched by similar modification in another line. This may be a simple repetition, or it may take the form of a meeting, intersection and balance of lines in which duplication plays a small part, as in Poussin's *Arcadian Shepherds* (Louvre). Color may be likewise repeated, varied, balanced, in such a way that the rich, pervasive, powerful rhythm gives to the painting its chief characteristic, as in Renoir's *Bathing Group* (The Barnes Foundation, No. 709) or in Giorgione's *Concert in the*

---

[3] John Dewey, *Experience and Nature*, pp. 391–393, Open Court Publishing Co., Chicago, Ill., 1925. Professor Dewey's text has been slightly condensed.

Open Air (Louvre). These rhythms, supplemented by rhythms of line, light and mass, permeate every part of the picture, contribute to the composition and form an ensemble which constitutes design in its highest estate. Such fusion of rhythms, at its best, has an effect upon our sensibilities comparable to the harmonious merging of chords and melodies in a rich symphony in music.

As with rhythm, contrast may be of various sorts. Matisse's work is an example of very successful color-contrast. Chiaroscuro, as Rembrandt used it, derives its powerful dramatic effect from the contrast of light and dark. In many Dutch landscape-paintings, a placid episode is contrasted with dramatic trees and sky. A vivid contrast between foreground and background is to be found in Fra Filippo Lippi's *Virgin Adoring the Child* (Uffizi): the Virgin and Child are disproportionately larger than the figures and masses behind them, and much lighter in color. In this case, the fact that the background has the effect of a screen greatly heightens the general contrast. The power of Giotto's Assisi compositions is largely due to his success in unifying the two sides of his pictures even when the contrast between them is so striking that they seem radically disparate.

Contrast also may be between different sorts of technique: broad areas of color may appear in one part of the picture, divided colors in another. This sometimes occurs in van Gogh, who also diversified his effects through contrasting direction and size of the brush strokes. The principle of all esthetic contrast is that of combining variety with unity, but it advances beyond the general principle in emphasizing the fact that variety is effective in proportion as the difference between the elements involved is unmistakable and dramatic.

To the experienced observer of paintings, it is the design that is revealed at first glance, and determines whether or not the painting is worthy of further attention. Judgment of a painting consists in nothing more than the determination of the artist's degree of success in integrating the plastic means to create a form which is powerful and expressive of his personality. Defects in plastic form are revealed by ineffective use of line, color poor in quality or inharmonious in relations, inadequate feeling for space, stereotyped, formulated, or perfunctory use of means, overemphasis of one or more of the plastic elements. In short, plastic form is lacking when the halting, inadequate, unskilled use of the means fails to effect the unity indispensable in a successful work of art. Either the artist has nothing to say or he lacks the command of means to convey an idea in plastic terms.

Painting which makes no attempt to portray spatial depth, that is, the third dimension, represents plastic form at its simplest. It may embody fluid graceful line, harmonious color, flat masses and surface-space, all so composed that the relations establish plastic form of a high order, even though quite simple. It is true that scarcely any painting is absolutely flat, even that of the Byzantines or Persians: there is usually some indication that the different parts of the painting are not literally on one plane, as are the figures in a rug. The objects almost invariably appear to be at varying distances from the spectator's eye, though this effect may be achieved in ways other than the utilization of perspective or deep space. In many Persian miniatures, for example, different scenes are depicted upon the same plane, but they are placed one above the other; thus a substitute for perspective is achieved. While the design in flat painting may be satisfying, such plastic forms remain comparatively meager and correspondingly deficient in reality.

In general, if there were no depth, there could be no solidity, no rendering of planes one behind the other, as they exist in the world as we know it. It is obvious that to render the depth and solidity of objects, the illusion of deep space must be created by plastic means. In flat painting, in which objects can have only two dimensions, they can have no depth, cast no shadows, cannot bulge or recede, and cannot be felt to be solid. Color remains superficial, sequence of line is chiefly mere pattern, light can play no rôle except to modify the quality of color, and composition is reduced to arrangement of objects above and below, to right and to left. But when deep space is conceived, color, line, composition and pattern are endowed with new possibilities of individual and interrelated treatment, which increase greatly the painter's power to create new and more complex plastic forms which possess a multitude of relations impossible in merely flat painting.

Plastic form and reality go hand in hand—that is, an attenuation of means results in a form which leaves out of account much of the actual quality of things which in art, as in the real world, moves us so deeply. When a painter uses any of the plastic means inadequately, the fulness, the richness of his work suffers to the extent of his lapse, for it is a characteristic of good art that it gives a reality more convincing, more penetrating, more satisfying than actual objects or situations themselves give.

While it is true that painting which portrays spatial depth is, in general, richer in plastic values than painting which approaches flatness, it is *not* true that mere depth or three-dimensionality of objects is the factor which determines the relative worth of such paintings.

It is possible to get an effect of depth by tricks of perspective or modeling, in which event the third dimension becomes mere virtuosity and the result is that instead of reality we get a specious unreality, more unreal than a frank two-dimensional pattern. Spatial depth and massiveness of objects have esthetic value only when they are achieved by plastic means harmoniously coördinated with the other plastic elements; that is, when they function as elements in a unified design. Therefore, it is obviously absurd to judge the relative merits of two painters by the success with which they render the illusion of a mass extending into deep space. A figure by Renoir, for example, has not as a rule the massiveness of a figure by Cézanne; such a figure would not enter harmoniously into his lighter, more delicate general design; Cézanne's design, in contrast, conveys the effect of austerity and power, and anything but a massive figure would be a disturbing factor. In short, spatial depth and three-dimensionality of objects are not to be judged by any absolute standard but only by their contribution to a unified, meaningful plastic form.

The merits of relatively flat painting and of three-dimensional painting which realizes solidity and spatial depth can be compared only when we observe how the artist has used color and light. One often sees paintings, in which color is merely laid on the surface like a cosmetic; it has the quality of tinsel, of something added after the object has been constructed. Instead of increased reality we get an effect of falsity, of unreality, and the painting lacks organic unity. Color is usually not a property merely of the surface of objects as we perceive them in the real world. The gray of a stone seems to spring from its depth, to go down into the body of the stone; the color is perceived

as part of the structure of the stone, so that the gray-
ness and the solidity are felt as a single individual
reality. In painting, the failure to include color in
form reduces the degree of conviction, and makes the
total effect relatively cheap, tawdry, unreal.

Not less important than color, in attaining a convincing three-dimensional character, is the use of light
and shadow. In painting that is two-dimensional, light
functions through modification of hue or tint so that
the shade of a color is partly determined by the light
that falls upon it. In three-dimensional representation, massiveness of an object is achieved by having
the brightest light fall upon the point nearest to the
source of illumination, from which point there is a continuous gradation to deepest shadow. In other words,
solidity is rendered by color and light correlated, and
that correlation constitutes the modeling of forms. It
is obvious that this correlation makes possible another
esthetic effect: such use of color and light that they
may each form independent and separate rhythmic
patterns, which in turn form rhythms with the other
plastic elements. For example, in Bellini's *Allegory
of Purgatory* (Uffizi), the pattern made up of the light
and shadow placed in various parts of the canvas, is
one of the principal components of the plastic form:
it is relatively independent of the function of the light
and shadow in giving indications of position and contour. Similarly, in Titian's *Man with Glove* (Louvre),
the striking pattern formed by the light, focused on
the face, shirt-front, hands and glove, renders the
solidity of these various units, and also does much to
organize the picture. In general terms, the artist has
used this particular plastic means to portray the essence,
the reality, of the subject and also to enrich and vivify
as well as unify the design.

The plastic element which determines the character of three-dimensional painting is deep space, and this is achieved by the use of perspective. It need not be literal perspective as we perceive it in the real world: it must be used plastically, that is, changed or adapted by the artist to particular needs. Perspective conjoined with the modeling makes possible what is termed "space-composition." This is something over and above the third dimension achieved by the utilization of line, color, light and perspective to make an object appear solid. Space-composition is such an arrangement of things in the depth of space that the intervals, back and front as well as up and down and to right and left, are felt to have a pleasing relation to each other and to the objects which they separate. Space-composition moves us esthetically when each object is so placed in its particular position that we perceive the space around the object in a definite relation to the space around each of the other objects, and that all these spaces are unified, that is, composed. If there were no objects, space could not be felt as an order of definite intervals; hence space-composition involves both the objects *and* the intervals of space. It is the sequence of objects and spaces so ordered that they form a pattern, which we perceive as a thing in itself. Space-composition is successful when it is unified with the plastic form as a whole; in other words, when the painter has been so successful in suggesting planes receding, advancing, and interacting with each other, that the whole series of spatial intervals between objects, as well as the objects themselves, interests or charms us. Space-composition contributes enormously to the reality of the total effect, since in our commerce with the real world we not only see objects but move among them. We live in a world of space and we see

9

objects in relation to remoter objects: a tree with a wall beyond it, a house against a background of hill or forest. Our mind is filled with these forms. When an artist enriches them with his deeper perceptions and feelings, and molds them into designs richer than our unaided powers could construct, we share his larger vision and deeper emotions.

We have seen that plastic form is satisfactory when all its elements and aspects are organically integrated. As one progresses in the study of plastic art, a great variety of falls from plastic unity reveal themselves. A painter, unable to enter fully into his subject, to see it in its concrete fulness and with an eye to all its relations, or one with an insufficient command over all the plastic means, is incapable of achieving a unified painting. He may single out for emphasis some one feature and slight the others, treating them sketchily, perfunctorily, or conventionally. When this happens, we have what is termed formula painting or academicism, and while the execution may be very skilful, the skill is mere virtuosity: the painter, no matter how adroit, is not genuinely an artist. Line, or light, or modeling, or perspective, or the relations with surrounding objects that enter into space-composition — any one of these may be accentuated to the point of submerging the other aspects of the object or situation. When this occurs there can be no proper integration of the plastic means, and the result is comparative unreality.

As we have already seen, the unreal is the uninteresting and we cannot accept as real what we feel does not represent an object or situation *in its concrete fulness*. This principle, so true in real life, is equally true in all the forms of art. For example, in poetry, Swinburne's spontaneity, variety, and subtlety of rhythm produce an exceedingly brilliant effect. But the flow and surge of his verse is soon seen to conceal an inner emptiness; mere rhythm is made to serve for the imaginative grasp of the subject that should vary both the ideas and their expression by all the poetic means. This constant repetition of rhythm without other poetic content becomes mere virtuosity. Verbal magic destitute of meaning constitutes unreality. In music, Berlioz and Liszt have a great command of orchestration, but their themes are almost invariably commonplace and conventional, their ideas are thin, and the orchestral dressing fails to conceal the essential triviality. Here again one factor is given an exaggerated rôle to cover up a lack of real substance, and the effect is one of showiness or melodrama, of unreality.

The conception of plastic form, as integration of all the plastic means, will be used in this book as the standard and criterion of value in painting, and hence all the analyses and judgments that follow will be an illustration of its meaning. To clarify what is meant by integration of plastic means we may anticipate the later discussion and consider Raphael as a striking example of inadequate plastic form. Raphael has often been looked upon as one of the greatest of all painters, and he was undoubtedly a master of his medium. He had a great command over line, his ability to use light to indicate contour and to make a pattern was of a high order, and in space-composition his gifts were unsurpassed. But these accomplishments were largely borrowed, his line and light from Leonardo, his space-composition from Perugino. His color is superficial and undistinguished in quality; it is thin, dull, sometimes garish, and it seems rather an afterthought in the design. His composition is almost invariably conventional; it has not the freshness and the inevitable fitness that we see, for example, in Giotto, so that for all the spaciousness and airiness of his pictures we never get the impression of a really original and powerful imagination at work. His borrowings are made in some measure his own; but they are not sufficiently changed to indicate that they are really a creation of a strong personality and a distinct mind. His subject-matter lacks originality and it has the sweetness and softness to be expected in a conventional and sentimental mind. In other words, he had no vigorous personality to serve as the crucible in which the qualities of things should be fused and welded into a new form. The result is that his particular means remained disjoined from his conceptions as a whole, and his light, line and space-composition stand out as isolated devices, as exploits of virtuosity. He did achieve a form of his own, and his great technical skill enabled him to attain results extraordinary in their own way, but the efforts are often specious and the effects tawdry.

For examples of the use of plastic means so disintegrated as to be mere tricks or mechanical stunts, we may examine the picture of Guido Reni entitled *Deianeira and Nessus* (Louvre). We find almost nothing expressive of the painter's individual grasp of the subject, and correspondingly there is no real synthesis of the plastic means employed. The pattern and composition are effective, but these are taken directly from Raphael and executed less competently. The impression of movement is rendered skilfully, but it is so much overdone that it suggests histrionics rather than art. The color is without charm or originality, and is simply laid upon the surface. It is so little integrated in the plastic form that another set of colors might be substituted with no damage to the total effect of the picture. What we have is a mere assemblage of devices without inner coherence and contributing to an effect that is conventional, strained and exceedingly tawdry.

Recognition of the balance or integration of plastic means which constitutes plastic form comes only from experience in looking at many kinds of painting. There can be no rules by which to fix the degree to which variety and brilliance of color, elaboration of grouping, rhythm of line, or any other plastic effect, must be realized. Colorists like Titian and Renoir cannot be accused of overaccentuation of color: they realized other aspects of the world in plastic terms equally strong, so that it is clear that they did not conceive *exclusively* in terms of color. In the work of both of these painters we see significant line, movement, composition, effective spacing, both on the surface and in the third dimension. Color serves not as the only source of effect, but as an organizing principle. Renoir's drawing, for example, is done in terms of color, and though the incisive line characteristic of Raphael or Leonardo is absent, the effects to which line contributes—movement, fluidity and rhythm— are rendered with great success. Although the kind and degree of three-dimensional solidity which we find in Michelangelo or Cézanne is absent from Renoir's figures, these figures do not seem vaporous or unreal. They have substance, mass, actuality, though not in the same manner and degree as do the figures in the work of painters whose primary purpose was different.

The way in which emphasis upon one of the plastic means may be united with subsidiary but sufficient realization of the others is further illustrated in Rembrandt. He employed chiaroscuro, that is, a bright area surrounded by darkness: light melting into heavy shadow serves as the technical method in most of his

pictures. He avoids overemphasis of his special means
by making chiaroscuro function as color more power-
fully than any colors of Leonardo or Raphael. In *Old
Man* (Uffizi) and *Hendrickje Stoffels* (Louvre), minute
variations in the golden-brown light give a richer, more
glowing and actually more varied effect than all the
colors of the spectrum used by a lesser artist. When,
as in *Unmerciful Servant* (Wallace Collection, London),
he introduces bright color, the effect is one of marvelous
depth, richness and fire. This same combination of
economy of means and great effectiveness is to be found
also in his line and distribution of masses. In space-
composition the use of chiaroscuro narrowly circum-
scribes the space at the painter's disposal, yet in
Unmerciful Servant the effect of roominess achieved is
comparable to that of Perugino or Poussin.

   In general terms we may say that in painting, as in
all other forms of art, whatever quality is selected as
setting the dominant note must be ballasted and made
real by being shown in a context of other qualities, and
when this is not done the effect becomes conventional,
cheap, tawdry, unconvincing and unreal.

   The "reality" which we consider to be the essence of
art-value in painting may be illustrated by reference
to the subject-matter portrayed by the French painters,
David and Delacroix. In David, there is constant
recourse to stage-settings, poses, themes, reminiscent
of classic antiquity. In Delacroix's exotic, Byronic
themes, there is a similar indication that the world in
which we actually live is beneath the artist's serious
attention. In both cases we are conscious of an artificial or theatrical quality, and this conviction that
the painters are playing a game or acting a part is not
affected by the fact that the histrionics were doubtless
free from deliberate insincerity. What they portray of

poignancy, pathos, tragedy, significance, existed in the world about them as well as in remote times and distant places. If they did not find them near at hand, we are justified in concluding that they did not know what they are, and that their portrayal of them is essentially a caricature, a set of figments out of daydreams.

This condemnation of "classicism" and "romanticism" is not based upon literary considerations, but upon plastic ones: antiquarianism or sentimentalism betrays itself in limited and unoriginal command of plastic means. The painter does not draw inspiration for his art solely out of his own personal experience but depends upon other painters for the methods by which his pictorial effects are produced. David's "classic" calm, or rather coldness, is due to a line which he took from Raphael and Mantegna and which they had taken from ancient sculpture. It is not something which he actually saw as a part of a personal and coherent view of reality, but a studio-device to which the qualities of color, mass and space were added as an afterthought. These qualities do not really fuse with the line to produce an impression of reality, but remain adventitious, just as the "noble" or "distinguished" figures and situations painted remain strangers and phantoms in the world in which we actually live.

The same is true of Delacroix. The stormy emotion, the exaggerated gesture and violent drama are almost as spectrally unreal as David's "nobility," and they point to the same inability to *see* the actual world about him. Delacroix does not seem so artificial either in subject-matter or in plastic quality as David, because romanticism was for him less a pose than classicism was for his predecessor, and because he did more to modify and reorganize what he took from others. His color represents an advance over Rubens' in that he showed a degree of originality in the methods he took from him. Consequently, he seems more real, and so more interesting and a greater artist, than David.

We realize how essentially fantastic David and Delacroix were when we compare them with later painters. The concern with actually existing scenes, persons and situations made of Courbet and his successors the legitimate successors of Velásquez and Goya, in making us see the objective qualities of things, divested of the subjectivism that constituted the romanticists' exhibited world of self. To sympathy with Courbet's insight we owe the important painters of 1870 — Manet, Monet, Degas, Sisley, Pissarro, Renoir, Cézanne — and their imaginative telling of the story of life in a real world. Of that group, Renoir and Cézanne deal most objectively with the whole range of experience as men find it verified in themselves, free from the trifling, the insignificant, the preoccupation with theory, technique, virtuosity, or personal vanity. If one looks beneath the dissimilarity of techniques, Renoir and Cézanne are seen as close kin in dealing with the fundamental, universal attributes of people and things. Both treated the familiar, everyday events that make up our lives. We see, feel, touch the particular quality that gives an object its individual identity. Each of the painters created a world richer, fuller, more meaningful than that revealed to our own unaided perceptions. Each mirrors, so vividly, a world we know by having lived in it, that we get a sense of going through an actual experience. Both are great artists because they make art and life one by convincing us of the truth and reality of what they see and feel and express.

PATTERN AND PLASTIC FORM[1]

Laurence Buermeyer

In Mr. Clive Bell's book, *Art*, published in 1914, is expressed a conviction and a standard widely influential in contemporary art-criticism. The burden of Mr. Bell's contention, that the distinguishing excellence of a work of art has nothing to do with its subject but that it depends on what he calls "significant form," an independent and specifically esthetic relation between the elements of the work of art, is not original with him. It is clearly foreshadowed in Pater's assertion that art at all times strives towards the condition of music, in which the appeal to emotion is made without any recourse to images of real things. For this view Pater himself never claimed any essential originality: he regarded it as a simple generalization from the work of the school of Giorgione. So far as the effect of Mr. Bell's book was limited to driving home to the popular consciousness the truth that a picture is not good because it resembles its original, points a moral or tells an entertaining story, he was to be commended for a real service to the cause of education. The same thing may be said of his work of undermining the saccharine tradition which goes back to Raphael. Since the views against which he contended were overwhelmingly dominant in the popular consciousness, his book undoubtedly exercised a beneficial influence in many quarters.

Unfortunately, however, he did not content himself with exposing the more flagrant errors of popular

[1] From *Journal of The Barnes Foundation*, January, 1926.

esthetics, but offered an esthetic theory of his own, as far removed from the truth as were the views which he attacked. Starting with the premise, unexceptionable in itself however little original, that a picture is not necessarily good because it mirrors accurately some real thing, he draws the conclusion, which does not in the least follow, that the goodness of a picture is totally and absolutely independent of its relation to any real thing. The only alternatives which he contemplates, in other words, are slavish imitation and wholly abstract or non-representative art. It is the contention of the present paper that this sharp distinction leads to a reduction of "significant form" to what may better be termed "pattern," that it makes decorative design as we find that in rugs or in wallpaper the ideal of all plastic art, and that "significant form," as Mr. Bell understands the word, would more accurately be described as "insignificant" or "meaningless" form.

A picture, Mr. Bell says, is good if it possesses "significant form." We should naturally expect such a statement to be followed by a definition of this all-important quality. No such definition is ever even attempted. Instead we are told that "significant form" is such an arrangement of the elements in any work of art as is productive of esthetic emotion. When we ask what esthetic emotion is (a necessary question, since according to Mr. Bell most of what passes for esthetic emotion is mere sentiment), the answer is that it is the emotion which is produced by significant form! Of course, nothing is ever fully definable in terms of anything else; definition in the end resolves itself into mere pointing, an indication of some immediate experience which must be had or felt if the definition is to be intelligible; but it is generally regarded as the mark of intelligence, and certainly of scientific analysis, to defer this recourse to the merely immediate as long as possible. However impossible it may be to find words for ultimate realities, we are entitled to expect that relations, the things with which what is defined has affinities, be pointed out. We find nothing of the sort in Mr. Bell, so that "significant form" remains wholly esoteric and recondite. The lady who by her reiteration of the only too familiar refrain, "I don't know anything about art, but I know what I like," earned Whistler's retort, "A quality, madam, which we share with the lower animals," seems to have differed in this respect from Mr. Bell only by her superior modesty. Mr. Bell, it appears, knows what he likes and calls that, and only that, art.

Admitting the value of Mr. Bell's castigation of popular errors, it is indeed a question whether the good his book has accomplished among the esthetically illiterate is not more than counterbalanced by the harm it has done among the discriminating. It is important that the specific which characterizes a work of art and distinguishes it from a mere report of objective fact should be recognized and valued. This form, as it appears in painting, is perhaps better termed "plastic form" than "significant form;" it does furnish the criterion of properly esthetic quality; but the manner of Mr. Bell's advocacy of it, the obscurity in which he has shrouded it and the Olympian assurance with which he dogmatizes about it, have seriously compromised its recognition. Oracular mystification where clear definition is the first requisite, and display of unbounded certitude in the early stages of analysis, where everything ought to be tentative and hypothetical, are perfectly adapted to compromise any cause.

The source of Mr. Bell's vagueness is not far to

seek. It is due to the absolute divorce between form and subject, to the repudiation not only of copying, but of every type or degree of interpretation. In opposition to Mr. Bell, we shall seek to show that plastic form is only relatively independent of subject, and that while subject does not in any degree prescribe the detail of an artist's work, it does furnish the point of departure and relatively, at least, fix the conditions of success. When the clue which it offers is entirely discarded, when truth, imaginative or interpretative as well as literal, is utterly banished from art, the artist is reduced to playing with sensations, to devising patterns which have, to be sure, many elements of esthetic appeal, but which are far from sufficient for great art.

We shall attempt to show this in detail by examples of the sort of criticism to which pure abstractionism leads. The general criticism, however, may be illustrated in music and literature as well as in painting. To condemn program-music, the bleating of the sheep and blowing of the wind in Strauss' *Don Quixote*, is one thing; to say that the best music is the most "pure," the most destitute of any expression of human emotion, is a very different thing: it is to exalt Haydn above Beethoven. Similarly with literature. It is often said that esthetically style counts and ideas do not count, and as evidence the case of Dante or of Milton is cited. The belief of these men in what Santayana calls the Christian epic now finds little echo in most cultivated readers, but the value of their style, the greatness of their literary stature, no one denies. To say, however, that their ideas, the content of their poetry, are dead, is to forget how much of their work goes beyond any mere scheme of supernatural salvation, how much of it expresses human feeling and aspiration as they appear in realms wholly non-theological. To say that, because any particular idea becomes obsolete eventually, the permanent value of poetry can be achieved by some one who has no ideas but is concerned to make a deft arrangement of words, is utterly false, and it is the precise analogue of the view that great painting springs not from any vision of the *world*, but from a fondness for making decorative upholstery.

The view of which Mr. Bell has been taken as the representative is thus the view, already combated in this book,[2] that art is an affair of the museum, a separate compartment in life into which we can enter only by turning our back upon the rest of life. It is not necessary to debate further this persuasion or prejudice in its general form; it may be useful, however, to point out the difference made by it in the practical procedure of education. If the view is true, then training in art, either in the appreciation or the execution of works of art, is a training in special tricks of the trade, devices or rules by which good patterns may be made and distinguished from bad. Specimens of such tricks, examples of such rules, are what we find in picture galleries, to which accordingly the potential artist or connoisseur is directed to go for the acquisition of something as essentially abstract and specialized as skill in playing chess.

The opposed view, here defended, is that what the picture gallery offers is of course valuable, but that it is valuable as the means of seeing, through the paint and canvas, the objective world. Not, of course, the world as a mere matter of physics or chemistry or impersonal sensation, but the world seen by the individual painter. The reply of Renoir to the questioner who

[2] See Laurence Buermeyer's essay, *Art and the Ivory Tower*, page 66 of present Volume.

asked him where one learned to paint, "*Au musée, parbleu!*" may be interpreted to mean what the pattern-makers mean, or—a very different matter—that it is through the vision of others that the painter sharpens his own. Which interpretation is to be chosen, Renoir's own practice makes abundantly clear. No modern painter, assuredly, combined a greater store of illumination derived from the traditions of the past with a fresher eye for the life about him, the unhackneyed, unstereotyped *things* of the contemporary scene. Our contention, in brief, is that the primary purpose of education in art is refinement and enrichment of the act of seeing, and that the plastic form which is not an expression of such seeing is trite, superficial or merely decorative.

Mr. Bell is to a large extent responsible for the prevalent confusion between pattern and plastic form, between merely decorative arrangement of line, color and mass, and the organization of those elements by which a convincing reality ("convincing," not "photographic") of an artist's experience with an objective world is achieved. Imitating Mr. Bell's objectionable mystification and dogmatism, and throwing to the winds nearly every principle of psychology and logic, a host of writers have added other absurdities, in efforts to prove that art is something essentially separate from everyday experience. They thus lose the clue afforded by imaginative interpretation of the reality of things and fill in the resulting vacuum with elaborate definitions of pattern that extend from deification of platitudes, such as "significant form," all the way to mechanical formulas which are alleged to have a mathematical foundation and are baptized by the meaningless catchword "dynamic symmetry." Each of these concoctions is guaranteed to contain the secret of all great

art. One of them offers a set or table of the elements
of design, comparable to the table of chemical elements,
and gives directions for combining them into satisfactory forms, thus reducing all "design" to an arrangement of lines and areas in two dimensions. Not a
suspicion, apparently, occurs that all such elements and
relations are wholly relative to the particular purpose
of the painter, to the aspect of reality of which he is
giving his personal version, or that in great art the
rules laid down are as often broken as they are obeyed.
Rules of this sort are useful to anyone who has nothing
of his own to say and who wishes to learn to repeat
what someone else has already said. They are useful
to the real artist or student in precisely the same way
that crutches are useful to the athlete.

What lends plausibility to the confusion of plastic
form with pattern is the fact that a pattern, a decorative arrangement of superficial qualities, is usually if
not always to be found in works of art. Decoration,
in other words, is a quality of painting, and a valuable
quality, if it is not made the be-all and end-all of art.
The mathematical formulation of pattern, with its
attendant rigidity, is not essential to the reduction of
plastic form to pattern, so that the case for pattern is
really stronger than many of its advocates make it out
to be. Decorative arrangement of line and mass, however, at its best falls far short of the esthetic richness of truly expressive plastic form, and some illustration of this fact must be given if the true relation
of the two is to be made apparent.

In every great painter the presence of pattern can
easily be demonstrated by an analysis of his pictures.
In Giotto, for example, the rhythm and sequence of
line, distribution of masses, and contrast and harmony
of color, have an immediate and obvious decorative

effect, but the expression proper (not of course merely
facial expression but imaginative insight) goes far beyond decoration. It resides in the restraint and dignity
with which the figures are conceived, in the mystical
quality conveyed largely by a pervasive, transfiguring
color-glow and by a convincing spaciousness, attained
by few and, in themselves, rather schematic indications
of perspective. These things enter also in the pattern,
but it is in their service in revealing a world which only
Giotto was capable of seeing that their most moving
esthetic effect resides. This is true also of El Greco,
whose mystical world is revealed no less convincingly
than is Giotto's, different as is its fervidness from the
serenity of Giotto.

For other examples we may take Rembrandt and
Manet. In both, of course, the pattern is present. In
Rembrandt it is formed largely by gradations of light,
contrasts of light and shadow, by which colors usually
dull in themselves are made to glow and display an
extraordinary richness, and by which masses scarcely
defined by linear contour are given body and reality,
and are organized in space. The pattern in Rembrandt, however, is much less clear-cut, rhythmic and
decorative than, for example, in Botticelli. Rembrandt's enormous superiority over Botticelli is due to
something quite apart from pattern; it is due to his
ability to make the play of light over flesh seem to
illuminate the depths of personality, set forth the living
human being who is portrayed. This is done by no
mere emphasis of the ordinary signs of emotion, the
facial gestures indicating pain, hope, sorrow or com-
passion, all of which depend upon more or less casual
associations of ideas. It is truly plastic, and yet much
more than decorative. It contains what plastic form
always, and decoration never, achieves: a grasp of the

essential nature of a thing, the unique quality which makes the thing what it is, which is shared with nothing else in the world. Rembrandt's painting of human hair, for example, is much slighter as decoration than Botticelli's; certainly it is equally far from photographic literalism; but it is infinitely more moving, because it gives us, as Botticelli's does not, an essential reality and not a superficial embellishment.

In Manet this reality is primarily achieved by the use of broad brush strokes which, omitting irrelevant detail, yet give the natural, essential quality of things in their familiar matter-of-fact aspects. Different as these aspects are from those which engaged the attention of Giotto, El Greco or Rembrandt, they are equally essential and distinctive. The critic whose eyes are closed to everything but pattern can see in these brush strokes merely the elements in a particular type of decoration. This decorative aspect is indubitably there, it is an important part of the total effect, but to attach exclusive importance to it is as grave an error as to consider only the illustrative aspect of Manet's work.[3]

Critics of the "advanced school" may be expected to reply to the foregoing contentions that they revert to the popular literary standard of plastic criticism. The difference between plastic form, as here conceived, and merely literary form must be pointed out. If in Giotto or El Greco the effect, as above expounded, depended upon identification of the persons portrayed as Jesus, the Virgin, or the other figures of the Christian hierarchy, the charge would be justified. There would then be reliance upon what we know *about* the things

[3] For more detailed analysis of the work of Giotto, El Greco, Rembrandt and Manet, see Albert C. Barnes, *The Art in Painting*, Harcourt, Brace & Co., New York, N. Y., 1937.

10

shown, and not upon what we actually see upon the canvas. The things would be labels, not realities. But in all the painters in question the illustration is given in good plastic terms. We see and feel the reality as the painter saw and felt it, and we need no extraneous associations to eke out what is actually presented. What is characteristic of merely literary painting is that the image set before us is trite and meaningless in itself, and that it derives its interest from the part played by the thing represented in practical life. In true plastic form, what is represented is significant not as an arbitrary symbol but as something of which the meaning is felt immediately, as an integral part of the actual image.

The interpretation of plastic form as pattern involves a denial to the painter of all effects that involve more than mere sensation. According to it, the funded results of past experience can never be more than adventitious associations, irrelevant to pictorial design. It is evident that the ejection of the meanings upon which human values depend, on the ground that they are inferred and not actually perceived, cannot stop short of such reduction to the bare immediate; it is equally evident that such rejection seriously compromises some of the purely plastic effects which are to be found in the work of the greatest artists. Space-composition and modeling, for example, depend upon revived experience of movement and touch; they are not directly given by paint on canvas; and if all meaning is to go, they must go too.[4] With them go all rhythm and movement in deep space, and landscape-

---

[4] Hambidge did exclude space-composition from the range of legitimate plastic effects. Clive Bell's careful avoidance of specific statement on any point makes it impossible to say whether he would exclude it or not; in any case, however, his logic leaves no place for anything so "representative."

painting and figure-painting join portraiture in the limbo of the "merely literary."

These consequences are ordinarily found so repellent that only a few pamphleteers, special advocates, and purveyors of new esthetic pills and powders are willing to accept them. But they may impose also upon critics of real discernment, such as Mr. Roger Fry. Mr. Fry's knowledge and experience are extensive, and his integrity does not permit him to pronounce upon matters of legitimate doubt with the unlimited certainty usually characteristic either of the extremely ignorant, or of the charlatan. He shares, however, the conception of form set forth by Clive Bell, at least to the extent of assuming that form is not only relatively but absolutely independent of the qualities of what art represents. This assumption is fully in harmony with his view of imagination as radically and essentially disjoined from practical life—the cardinal principle of what we have called the museum-theory of art.[5]

[5] See Laurence Buermeyer's essay, *The Esthetics of Roger Fry*, page 230 of present Volume.

AN EXPERIMENT
IN EDUCATIONAL METHOD AT
THE BARNES FOUNDATION[1]

Violette de Mazia

In guiding his pupils to a sound appreciation of art, Dr. Albert C. Barnes followed a pattern which he had developed in a lifetime of study. His authority in the fields of education and the arts stemmed not only from a lifelong devotion to the philosophies of James, Santayana and Dewey, but also from years of study on his own in the leading museums of the world. He believed that the approach to aesthetics should be as disciplined and methodical as the approach to physics or chemistry. Abhorring what Santayana called "an emotional drunk," he worked to create a standard by which art could be enjoyed intelligently and judged with as little subjective bias as possible. The Barnes Foundation was the result of Dr. Barnes' unceasing interest and research in the fields of science, philosophy, education and art. It was, thus, that both the art collection and the educational activities of the Foundation were conceived from the start as inseparable organic parts of a single, completely-integrated entity.

The success of the Foundation's program is a dream come true. More than sixty years ago the dream had come to John Dewey, at that time already acclaimed the world's foremost leader in educational philosophy. His studies had convinced him that the functions of philosophy and education, in their broadest sense, are

[1] Adapted from Violette de Mazia, *The Barnes Foundation*, House and Garden, December, 1942—Copyright, 1942, The Condé Nast Publications, Inc.

essentially the same. Indeed, so closely linked in his thinking were the purposes of each that, in the course of his activities in both fields, Dr. Dewey moved steadily toward his conception that education is, primarily, philosophy expressed in action. He believed that philosophy is of value as a guide to more intelligent living only when its findings pave the way to better methods for solving problems encountered in the everyday affairs of life. These were the views he put to work wherever his influence could be exerted—in the classroom and in social groups of varied interests, in which he was frequently a leading participant. No well-informed person can deny that the progress in educational methods during the last three decades is due more to Dewey's contributions and influence than to those of any other person.

The basic principle expounded in Dewey's books is that education is *not* something by itself, nor is its primary function the formal training of youth for future adulthood. On the contrary, education is a lifelong necessity because it is the chief means by which society perpetuates its habits, customs and ways of life, and in so doing keeps itself from dying. In this sense, adults, whether they be savage tribes or members of highly civilized society, are in need of a continuing process of education. Dewey points out that people learn most thoroughly through *shared* activity: that is, they learn by *using* things with others in their group. This conception of shared activity was one of Dewey's most fundamental principles—that the sharing of experience is the real goal of education; that it is the essence of true democracy, as well as one of the most potent factors in attaining it in society at large.

These fundamental concepts of education as a continually-developing process inspired Dr. Barnes to put them to a practical test, and, at the turn of the century, he initiated an experiment in a small chemical plant, with a group of twenty adult workers, whose schooling had been of the slightest.

The routine of work at the plant was so organized that two hours of each weekday could be devoted to class instruction by a member of the staff thoroughly grounded in Dewey's ideas. The tools necessary for any experiment were in this case the workers' practical duties at the plant. Their various activities, together with the class sessions themselves, developed into a genuinely coöperative effort. In an atmosphere that was completely democratic, the workers developed initiative and found greater incentive to expansion of their individual abilities, which led to growing efficiency in operation and management of the plant, to increased financial returns for the enterprise and its employees, and to more leisure time resulting from both. The additional leisure was employed for further cultivation of the workers' interests, and was directed, in part, to discussing some of their personal problems with the purpose of inculcating the essentials of sound thinking stripped of academic trappings. The fundamental concepts in Dewey's epoch-making books, *Democracy and Education* and *School and Society*, were simplified and brought within the comprehension of all the workers, no matter what their previous education.

The other set of educational tools consisted of a collection of paintings which covered the walls of the plant's half dozen office-rooms. The workers' curiosity about these pictures and their desire to understand them resulted in a program of lectures designed to acquaint them with those essentials of psychology and aesthetics that govern any intelligent approach to art. This novel systematic approach was widely discussed by outsiders who heard about the experiment; and when practicing artists and students of art began to visit the collection and asked to be permitted to join the classes, both the scope of the program and the facilities for working it out had to be increased. To provide for this need, The Barnes Foundation was formally organized, and in December, 1922, its charter as an educational institution was granted by the State of Pennsylvania.

The educational program formulated by The Barnes Foundation was a continuation on a larger scale of the experiment begun with the factory workers, but the experiment as it developed was more specifically directed to the understanding of art by application of the objective method which is a prerequisite for all scientific investigation. The knowledge acquired by Dr. Barnes in the fields of science, education and art served as the groundwork of a program of training for the Foundation's own teaching staff and for other teachers in colleges and universities throughout America.

The aim of the Foundation is not to defend any particular school or work of art. It is, instead, to provide a method for objective study and impartial appreciation of the art-expressions of all periods, and students enrolled for such studies have come from all parts of the world, and have included individuals of all strata of society, of all races, and of all shades of political and religious beliefs.

One of the fundamental principles in our teaching is that "art is a fragment of life presented to us enriched in feeling by means of the creative spirit of the artist."[2] In opposition to the common misconception that art is something apart from the workaday world, to which

[2] Mary Mullen, *Approach to Art*, page 5, The Barnes Foundation Press, Merion, Pa., 1923.

one turns in moments of leisure, or perhaps in the name of "culture," the Foundation's approach takes art out of its usually detached, esoteric world and links it up with life itself.

To provide instruction for learning the techniques of painting is not a part of the Foundation's educational program. All our efforts are in the direction of teaching students how to learn to see—that is, to perceive the aspects of everyday life that are significant from the standpoint of their broad human values, as these are expressed in paintings, sculpture, music, literature, etc. We point out the inadequacy of time-worn methods used in other art schools—that is, the practice of imparting *facts about* art, to be handed back in parrot-like fashion in recitations or in examinations given to determine students' final grades. That such practice is widely prevalent—even in schools of highest repute—is a fact vouchsafed us by students who are still attending them at the time that they are members of the Foundation's classes. We witness the harm done by the imposition of rules which stifle the creative impulse, and we are unsparingly critical of the mind-lulling effects produced by such educational procedure, as these are regularly revealed in questions, comments and attitudes of students from other schools, who frequently become the most outspoken critics of the type of instruction they are receiving elsewhere—or which they have received in the past. Facts about art and artists have their proper place in any courses given in art appreciation, but little or no progress can be made in developing sensitivity to the arts unless ample opportunities are provided for study and analyses in direct contact with as many authentic works of art as possible. These requirements are fully met in the Foundation's courses by means of the extensive art collection and the method of instruction employed. There is no substitute for this type of activity, which in the Foundation's classes is *shared* activity—that is, students are encouraged to discuss freely problems raised by art, and by life itself, of which art is but a part.

The goal of our first efforts is to eradicate the almost universal, confusing habit of looking at a painting for what it is not intended to be, *i.e.*, not a record of its subject or a likeness to familiar situations; not a mere display of craftsmanship or propaganda of a religious, moral, social or political nature.

Our next objective is to enable the students to develop new habits of perception by use of the scientific procedure of objective analysis. In observing the characteristics of a work of art and their interrelationships which determine its form, they become acquainted with the artist's individuality as he experiences the world around him and creatively adapts the contributions of his predecessors.

The Foundation's gallery is not a museum, in the usual sense of being an assemblage of relics which, for the most part, are valuable only as documents for study by historians or academicians. Any work of art brought into the gallery is given its place without the customary concern for either its medium of expression or the era in which it was created. The Foundation's collection was built up, organized and studied with the purpose of making evident the fact that, the inherent attributes of human nature having remained the same throughout the ages, there is no fundamental difference between the great art of the past and the great art of the present: both forms reveal to the competent observer a set of objective factors and relationships that endow all works of art with the power to call forth feelings of aesthetic satisfaction.

The gallery contains the world's foremost collection of modern paintings as well as a large number of important Old Masters which reveal the sources used by painters in subsequent periods. The value of the collection is further enhanced by the unique opportunity it provides to observe the unfolding personalities of several important artists represented in the collection, and to study their development from their earliest to their latest or most mature forms.

Exhibited with the paintings is a comprehensive selection of furniture, telling a continuous story of original ideas and good craftsmanship from the time of Queen Elizabeth to the end of the 18th Century. The collection also includes such diverse art objects as Greek, Egyptian and African Negro sculpture; early European and American iron-work and pottery; iron-bound tool boxes from colonial "covered wagons," etc. These, together with the paintings and selections from musical compositions and literature, are used in class demonstrations to illustrate both the continuity of the respective traditions and the methods that artists of each epoch have used to create entities expressive of their own eras, milieus and individualities, by selective adaptations of preceding forms to their own interests and purposes. The study of the important traditions in art is, therefore, an integral part of our program.

As was foreseen, the student's curiosity is usually aroused by the unorthodox grouping throughout the gallery of apparently disparate paintings and other works of art. He strives to understand our reasons for bringing old and modern masters into close proximity in the same room or on the same wall, or for placing a Persian vase on a Pennsylvania Dutch dower-chest, flanked by a pair of early American andirons and set at the base of a large triptych by Matisse. Discon-

certed by this break with the conventional ways of displaying art objects, and seeking a new orientation, the
student soon begins to discern in these diverse things
similarities in line, color or rhythm. He discovers their
common denominator of broad human values and their
common source in human nature. In so doing, he finds
the key to the distinctive harmony of these unconven-
tional but purposive compositions, and is likely in the
process to derive a stimulus to creative work of his own.

We are often called upon to explain the meaning of
"composition" and "good taste," terms that are too
frequently used vaguely, loosely and with little understanding. Composition, or the placing together of
various items—whether these be the constituents of a
single painting or of a group of art objects or household
articles—is the equivalent of a clear, orderly presentation of meaningful ideas in a logical argument. In
every instance, the identity of each constituent is preserved; it is reinforced by relationship to the characteristics of its fellow constituents, and contributes its
share to the meaning and harmony of the all-inclusive
entity.

To avoid the numbing effect of monotony, sufficient
elements of variety are required, yet adequate balance
must be maintained to achieve a satisfying oneness of
effect in the total organization. Chairs, for example,
on each side of a bookcase, sconces on a wall, or a grouping of cups and saucers inside a cupboard, need have
only a certain set of qualities in common (*e.g.*, amount
of space each fills, size of the intervals between them,
general color tonality or type of pattern) to yield a
sense of symmetry, all the more pleasing because of the
differences in color, shape, etc., of the individual
objects. These variations within the undisturbed
oneness of the over-all character supply anchoring

points of interest which enrich the content of the ensemble and stamp it with distinctiveness of character.

Ability to create composition of this organic sort entails knowledge of what has been done before and awareness of what needs to be done now because of the *purpose* to be fulfilled. Thus conceived, composition admits of no set of rules, standards or conventions. It is invariably determined by the "composer's," the artist's, intent, in the sense that it is what he wishes to express that governs his selection and disposition of the material used. The aesthetic merit of his composition and its degree of creativeness depend on the range of the artist's imaginative perception or insight—on his feeling for rhythm, drama, unity, and the intrinsic possibilities of his medium of expression. Composition, that is to say, can be as distinctively personal as one's expression of countenance, which never fails to reveal the person's background and the degree of his sensitivity—in a word, his personality.

When sensitivity to the harmonious relationship of parts is backed up by intelligence in the use of one's knowledge and experience, it may be defined as "good taste." Good taste can be developed and, as has been proved, can be taught. Aesthetic feeling is latent in every normal human being; the requisites for its development are the student's interest in the subject, an eagerness that impels him to do whatever may be required for fruitful results, and a course of study directed toward his *learning to see*, learning, *i.e.*, to perceive the meanings of things in their complex and subtle interrelationships. Indeed, the Foundation's main purpose in its use of the objective method is, precisely, to replace the free-floating "disembodied emotion" of the untrained with knowledge deriving from personal, direct trans-acting with the object of their interest.

We have gathered abundant proof that until aspiring artists grasp the meaning of these principles and develop a set of intelligent habits, they can never reach the gateway to genuine personality or individuality of expression, which is one of the *sine qua non* factors that make a man an artist.

The enthusiasm manifested by all interested in the Foundation's philosophy and principles has conclusively demonstrated that when education (teaching and learning) is animated by a deep-seated interest, it offers a fascinating challenge to discover more effective methods by which life can be continuously improved and transformed, through use of initiative and creative powers, into ways of living that yield more profound satisfaction.

The initial experiment with the factory workers and the subsequent development of the original ideas into the Foundation's program for systematic class-work, made it obvious that whenever the above-outlined plan for studying art is carried out with groups of students, their individual members are led not only to a sharing of the artist's experience, but to a singular heightening of aesthetic gratification whenever the experience is shared with their fellow-beings.

The Foundation's educational aims and practice, conceived, planned and organized by Dr. Barnes and carried out by its Faculty, are clearly set forth in the ten volumes of research in art and education written by members of the Foundation's staff. Most of these books are employed as texts in universities and colleges, in the public school system of large cities, and as standard works of reference in public libraries both here and abroad. We take pride in the fact that eminent authorities in the field of education have acknowledged the important contributions to American culture resulting from The Barnes Foundation's successful efforts to raise the prevailing level of art instruction by exploring a phase of education practically untouched before, and not as yet systematized into educational practice in any other institution offering courses in the study of the arts.

It may not be amiss to call attention at this point to Professor Dewey's remark (appearing elsewhere in this volume) that the most thoroughgoing embodiment of his educational views is found in an institution concerned with art; and referring to the successful application of those views as exemplified in practice at The Barnes Foundation, Professor Dewey describes that experiment in education as work of a "pioneer quality comparable to the best that has been done in any field during the present generation, that of science not excepted."

LEARNING TO SEE[1]

ALBERT C. BARNES and VIOLETTE DE MAZIA

THE fundamental error in all unenlightened intercourse with works of art is that no account is taken of the axiom that to see means to perceive what in any object or situation makes it significant for experience. Most of the looking at pictures, by those untrained to see, is a search for something to be recognized as already familiar from past experience: it is totally unrelated to the experience which prompted the artist to make of the painting a record of what he saw and felt in his intercourse with a particular objective situation. A beholder who does not see and feel the particular meaning of the painting as an expression of the artist's reaction to the world, is merely looking, not seeing; and such looking is productive of no more benefit than such other essentially similar diversions as looking at a photograph album or the colored illustrations in a magazine. To have a landscape stir up the pleasant memory of a familiar scene, or a portrait that of a friend, is merely to recognize, not to perceive; that is, to refresh one's memory, not to grow in experience by increasing the value of what one already knows through perception of new relationships and values. Recognition, in other words, is seeking a resting place in the past instead of being alive in the present. How widespread is this confusion of values on the part of the layman, and even in what passes for education in art, can be grasped only by a first-hand study of the situation.[2]

[1] From Albert C. Barnes and Violette de Mazia, *The Art of Renoir*, The Barnes Foundation Press, Merion, Pa., 1944.

[2] See Mary Mullen's essay, *Problems Encountered in Art Education*, page 251 of present Volume.

Seeing a picture, that is, perceiving its meaning as an embodiment of an artist's experience in his contact with the world, differs in no essentials from the perceiving of any other object in life, whether the object be a chair, a spark-plug, a map, or what not. In each case, perception, in the true sense of the word, must include two ever-present and determining factors: the qualities of the object itself as they appear to the senses, and the contribution of the individual's mind and body to what the senses communicate. It is only when these two elements interact, mutually affect each other in a single, continuously unfolding, uninterrupted process, that perception furnishes the material of experience. The impact upon the senses of each of the qualities of the object is a stimulus to a set of reactions in the percipient, and each successive impact and reaction modifies the significance of those preceding, and establishes new sets of relationships. Unless this uninterrupted flow of new and mutually-affecting relationships takes place the object is not grasped as a composite entity, an individual thing with its own identity, a form conveying a particular meaning for us as an experienced object. Perception, in short, is an organic blending of data furnished by the alert senses of a live animal with the accumulated store of the meanings of past experience, through which the data are digested and assimilated as a new and integral part of the total fund of experience. The process entails a continuous reorganization of the motor-energies of the perceiver and an ever-changing series of readjustments between the new material and the background of accumulated meanings which constitute mind.

It is obvious from the nature of the perceptive process that a defect in any of its aspects results in faulty perception, and, perforce, stunted experience: if the senses are not constantly alert, only isolated parts of the object are taken in; a break in the continuity of interaction between what the senses furnish as nutriment and the perceiver's store of knowledge, prevents new accretions to that store; a limited range of accumulated past experience means an inferior and impoverished store of fuel to be kindled by the sense stimuli into the warmth of new experience.

The foregoing account of the essentials of the psychology of perception makes clear how dependent the value of any artist's work, and indeed of any scientist's, is upon the *quality* of the creative person's perceptions. The work is never an inventory of facts but an embodiment of the interaction of these facts with the background of experience of the worker. Correspondingly, in any study of the work of artist or scientist the subjective element qualifies the objective, and this entails judgment, a judgment of values; in this again the conditions of success are alert senses, a rich background of experience, and a continuous interaction of what is furnished by these two factors. It follows, therefore, that the work of artist or scientist, as well as the study of that work by an outsider, may be gauged intelligently only by fixing the attention upon the control of the material of perception in both its subjective and objective aspects.

This attitude is expressed in all intelligent intercourse with our world: to be relieved of a throat affection, one consults an experienced laryngologist in preference to a general practitioner of medicine; if the specialist is not available, the family doctor, instead of a layman friend, is requisitioned. The reason is that first-hand observation of objective facts is meaningful in proportion to the quality of the background, of the stored values of experience, brought to bear

upon interpreting the significance of what is observed.
A painting, like the throat affection, has its own objective marks of identity determinable by perception; in
both cases, each attribute stands not alone but as an
element in a composite of other and mutually-affecting
elements. In the perception of paintings, as of other
things, the eyes are but as the sentinels at the out-
posts whose duty it is to report to headquarters —
the mind of the army — every sign that may indicate
a situation calling for the conjoined action of all the
organization's forces. If the sentinel fails to see the
sign of possible danger or advantage, or if headquarters fail to grasp its significance when it is reported,
there is no chain of interactions, and either loss of
opportunity or disaster may result. To scrutinize a
painting for the objective qualities which make it a
work of art, is a process of discrimination and this
practice finds its counterpart in all intelligent effort
to appraise values, in any realm of experience whatso-
ever. Even a dog practices it before he growls at a
stranger or shows the signs of pleasure in greeting his
master.

Discrimination in any situation in life entails a
picking to pieces of the situation in order to effect a
reunification of the pieces in a form representing an
appraisal of values. To stigmatize as mere dissection
this indispensable first step toward discrimination, is
to deny the basic rôle of analysis in the only kind of
appraisal of values entitled to respect: judgment based
upon objective facts. Only as each constituent part
is isolated and examined for what it is in itself, can
its fitness to the whole be determined. Thus analysis
itself is inseparably connected with the unification, the
resynthesis of the elements picked apart, which embodies the sought-for values. The creative artist exer-

cises such analysis not only in what he selects from Nature for his own interpretation but every time he transforms a significant trait characteristic of a preceding tradition—and no artist ever fails to make such selections from Nature or such drafts upon the past. The trait has to be abstracted, picked out, from its original setting before it can be utilized as working material in a new creation. The abstraction is a mark of the insight which enables the artist to grasp what is significant in a traditional form and recast it in his own expression. The failure either to make the abstraction or to use the abstracted material creatively is the abiding characteristic of academic art.

This looking back at the past by the artist, and his incorporation of selected meanings in the expression of new experiences, are paralleled by the dual process of perception and expression in every normal human being, and by every social movement as civilization progresses. What was most significant to human beings of past generations is retained by each subsequent advance in civilization, and the inherited values are enriched by other and equally basic human experiences born of the interaction of creative beings with an ever-changing environment. Such accretions constitute the most vital strand in the thread of life because they are the medium through which contemporary events are expanded in range and deepened in significance by what was most important in the preceding ages. The accretions also verify and deepen the significance of worthwhile experience of the past.

Each expression of significant experience is so deeply rooted in human nature that it survives the attacks of the contemporary critics who, insensitive to fresh experiences in a new and different world, stagnate in the dead past. The life histories of Galileo, Rembrandt,

El Greco, Renoir and Cézanne furnish examples of the imaginative insight surviving onslaughts of contemporaries who blindly accepted the unqalified sovereignty of the past. The work of these creators shows what their contemporary assailants never came to know at all; that a tradition survives because it embodies the spirit of highly-endowed individuals fully and freely alive to the forces that give individuality and distinction to their milieus and times.

Translate this blind clinging to the past and its opposite, the reacting of a creature alive with all his senses and mind to the world about him, into the terms of the perceptive process as it has been described, and we find stated one of the most fundamental problems of education and also the method of approach to its solution. Both the problem and its solution stem from the universal human tendency to confuse *recognition* with perception, a static condition with a dynamic process. Recognition is the servant of the dead past because it takes in only what is already familiar. If perception ends with recognition, instead of merely beginning with it, no connection is made between sense-stimuli and the background of accumulated experiences, and the process is halted before it can develop that uninterrupted reaction between the object, the senses and the mind, which constitutes real living. What happens is identification, reference of the object or situation to a stereotype preserved in the mind as a model.

The perception which leads to discrimination is no such abortive process and reaches no such dead ends. It begins only when some observed trait or attribute, impinging upon the senses, stimulates the individual's accumulated store of meanings to absorb the new material and to undergo itself a process of reconstruction. The vitality, the dynamic character, of the reaction is evidenced by the familiar warmth and glow pervasive of the whole self when a new experience is born—when one learns to swim, sees the dénouement of a skilfully presented drama, the form of a painter's individual expression of human character or of the contemporary scene. The warmth and glow are as positive and as real as they are when experienced in front of a fire on a cold day; in each case they result from, point to, an actual expenditure of energy. It is the expenditure of energy which makes perception difficult; the effortless, automatic process of recognition is easy, but it fails to generate the warmth of being alive.

Thus far our outline of the nature of perception has assumed that there is no difference between the process as it takes place in our contact with a painting, a part of the world of esthetic enjoyment, and with, for example, an automobile, an object which serves its purpose when it transports us from one place to another. The process in each case *is* identical; even though the *qualities* perceived are not the same, the two categories, esthetic and practical, are not mutually exclusive. A painting which is a work of art may also be a congruous object of furniture in a room; an automobile, by both the form of its structure and its efficient performance in travel, may be the source of esthetic pleasure. The prevalent tendency to confine esthetic enjoyment to what are termed works of art has no sound psychological foundation; it rests rather upon the erroneous assumptions that esthetic quality is something superimposed upon material, and that there is a fundamental difference between the perception of the artist as he creates and the beholder's perception of the esthetic form of the finished product.

To dispose of this misconception we need only reflect

upon two such widely separate experiences as that of an epicure taking his dinner and that of a sculptor modeling a statue. The epicure may supply sharp appetite, sound digestion, a knowledge of what constitutes good cooking; and the dinner may provide the best quality of food, irreproachable cooking, agreeable companionship, and a setting satisfactory to the most cultivated taste. The meaning of dinner, however, consists not merely of properly prepared food placed in front of a hungry person, but of a series of interrelated transactions between food and consumer.

If the series of these mutually-affecting elements unfolds harmoniously, their orderly progress and the gourmet's perception of them flow in a composite whole and become a definite esthetic experience, infinitely more exciting and more fully satisfying than the mere appeasement of hunger. The whole experience has a unity arising out of a pervasive excellence intrinsic not only to each of the subjective and objective components but also to the specific relationships between them: the epicure's background of culture appreciating the art and science of the cook, the personal qualities of the companions, the attributes of the setting, etc.

Let a break occur—a sudden indisposition of the diner, a dish badly seasoned or served, an impertinent remark of a companion—and the clash brings disorder in the sequence of events and interrelationships; the epicure's enjoyment of the meal is interrupted, and the esthetic quality of the experience aborted. The connected links which would have organized the parts of the dinner in a harmonious ensemble have been severed by episodes, the incongruity of which destroys the pervasive satisfying quality of the dinner as a whole. The quality of excellence flowing smoothly through the courses of the successful dinner was the decisive factor in the epicure's enjoyment. His background of culture and his acute senses, by their interaction with the environment, created that unity and quality which made the orderly dinner a satisfying experience, authentically esthetic, in contrast to the revolting experience of the disordered meal. The value of the dinner as a human experience depended, therefore, as much upon the creative process as it took place in the epicure's personality as upon conditions external to him.

The sculptor's modeling of a statue, though it creates a form more capable of objective verification, differs in no essential point from the experience of the epicure. The sculptor too makes use of an external material, clay or marble, that must have qualities capable of satisfying his need for expression; otherwise, his esthetic feelings would lie fallow and his frustration be as poignant as the cry of the body for food. He too has criteria of excellence which prescribe the qualities of the material and the manner of its organization which will make it answer his purpose; the organic connection between these subjective and objective factors is likewise vital for his esthetic experience.

As the sculptor works, his job is to perceive and, if necessary, alter and correct, the relationships between the feeling he wishes to embody in the clay and the effect obtained by the way he handles his material. At every movement of his hand, his eyes inform his mind just how far the external object has traveled toward the fulfilment of his conception. Every action upon the material is inevitably directed by what the sculptor saw, felt and did in all his preceding activity, and at the same time it is colored with the qualities the finished form is taking in his imagination. At each step it is the perception of relationships between what the hand has done and what the mind holds which guides and controls the continuous unfolding of the process in its subjective and objective aspects, in the reciprocal interaction and the concurrent development of both the original conception and the material object created. Only when the sculptor has achieved an orderly balance between what he has in mind and what the object reveals to have been done, does the creative process come to an end and the experience yield satisfaction.

Adventitious and irrelevant details apart, a common esthetic strand enters into the perceptions of both the epicure and the sculptor. As each progresses in his experience he perceives a set of *immediately felt relationships* between subject and object, and his series of perceptions proceeds to its conclusion in an orderly manner with no irreparable break in the continuity of the quality of the components. The epicure no less than the sculptor is a creator because he perceives the quality of the relationships that makes the experience a fully satisfying consummation and unity, and hence a dominantly esthetic experience.

The esthetic strand in all human activities consists precisely in this perception of immediately felt relationships of subject and object, and of parts to each other and to the whole. This type of perception is the *sine qua non* of the art of the painter, sculptor, writer and musician, as it is also of the art of the baseball player, the golfer, the epicure, or of any one enjoying intelligent social intercourse. The prerequisites in each case are alert senses trained to perceive significant objective attributes, and an unobstructed interpretation of these data by the background of stored meanings. The new values are incorporated in the accumulated experiences and serve as a guide to the individual's future activities.

Progress in learning to see pictures as records of enriched experience is of necessity slow, even when interest is genuine and application wholehearted. A set of habits essentially new and of a very special character must be gradually built up to supplant those ingrained in us by our adjustments to other phases of life. Progress has begun when the beholder, pausing for reflection, becomes conscious that his senses are feeding upon the objective traits of the painting, that the nutriment furnished is stirring his imagination, and that a *feeling* of warmth pervades his whole organism.

The word "feeling" is italicized in order to emphasize the fact that Nature herself furnishes experiential evidence that the perceptive process is not a cold intellectual affair, fundamentally different in character from the emotion that takes possession of a person when a work of art is appreciated. This warmth *is* the emotional factor productive of the consciousness of heightened vitality characteristic of every genuine experience. Heat is always the product of the expenditure of energy, whether in a stove, a dynamo, or a living body. A live animal attains to experience because of his alert interaction with the world, and the energy expended is always manifested. When feeling reaches the degree of warmth attendant upon esthetic experience, it is the organism's shout of victory proclaiming that something vital to it has attained fulfilment, that the forces of the individual have joined combat with and vanquished those in the external world. But a shout of victory is never the whole body of the experience: it is merely the outward sign of emotion born of the entire experience and, for the moment, preponderant over its other aspects. Consciousness, in other words, abstracts the esthetic strand from the composite whole and endows the total fabric of experience with a specific flavor.

The emphasis by many writers upon emotion as the chief, sometimes as the exclusive, characteristic of the enjoyment of art is largely responsible for the prevalent gush of sentiment so obstructive to genuine appreciation. It is easier and more natural for a large proportion of humanity to gush than it is to impose upon itself work in a field that holds no real interest for it. Gush is a mere explosion of disembodied feelings: the ghost of experience wandering aimlessly in an alien world of material objects. An *expression* of emotion is part of, inseparably connected with, the objective factors that gave it birth.[3] It acquires a very substantial body when it becomes an integral part of both the object or situation and the mind of the percipient, as it must if these factors have interacted sufficiently to produce perception in its true sense.

Excess of emotion is unabsorbed feeling; it spills over into a vacuum and inhibits the process of perception, thereby preventing any production of the material of experience.[4] Emotion of this sort is quite a different thing from the excitement about a subject that penetrates to the store of accumulated meanings of experiences and uses them as fuel for the fire which warms every vital experience. Emotion is

[3] "It takes the wine-press as well as the grapes to express juice, and it takes environing and resisting objects as well as internal emotion and impulsion to constitute an *expression* of emotion." John Dewey, *Art as Experience*, p. 64, Minton, Balch & Co., New York, N. Y., 1934.
[4] A sentimentalist is one "whose physiological complexion involves more poignant emotion than his ideas can absorb." George Santayana, *Reason in Art*, p. 64, Charles Scribner's Sons, New York, N. Y., 1917.

abiding only when it has an abode, a body; when it is feeling *about something*, to which it is so organically bound that the two are inseparable. Gush, sentimentalism, is free-floating emotion, unattached to anything; when emitted in the presence of a work of art, it lacks any specific relevance to its object. Its quality, in other words, is the very antithesis of that which makes feeling esthetic.

Another pitfall in the development of esthetic discrimination lies in confusing technical skill with the meaning of the picture as an expression of the artist's experience. A painter may possess a high degree of technical skill and still remain a mere craftsman, utterly incapable of creating a work of art. Mere recognition of such skill is as far removed from genuine understanding of painting, and is quite as irrelevant to it, as sentimentalism. Mere technical skill and the outpouring of excessive emotion are kindred vices in that each is a dis-located phase of a totality, usurping a sovereign rôle. Thus emphasized and isolated, technique loses its appropriate function as an instrument for expression, and becomes itself an expression of vanity and manual dexterity, and hence of dull perception and stupidity. Technique thus masquerading as art is mere virtuosity, an isolated set of muscular adjustments—in extreme cases a mechanistic avalanche which sweeps away all the essentials that make a picture significant. Sensory stimulation, if present, either falls dead upon mind or calls forth for reproduction a stereotyped formula. In this mechanical performance, perception is either aborted or still-born, degraded into mere recognition of already known facts which perforce leaves the trained observer cold.

In its proper instrumental function, technique rep-

resents a set of adjusted muscular activities controlled
by what the mind of the painter undergoes under the
stimulation of the senses. It is an integral part of a
process which links together the sensory stimulation,
the imagination, and the hand's movements in a single,
continuously unfolding operation, the activity of which
never ceases until the created object has absorbed the
feelings inherent in the experience. Creative production, in other words, is organically integrated with
esthetic perception. Attention to technique, therefore, in the study as well as in the painting of pictures,
is to be restricted to ascertaining the part which it
plays as a strictly subordinate instrument of artistic
expression.

From the foregoing account of the nature of perception, it is apparent that esthetic quality is not confined to our perception of works of art, but pervades a
large part of ordinary practical life. We have seen
that there is no essential difference between perception as it takes place in the producer of works of art
and in the non-producer who is able to grasp the experience which a work of art expresses. What the personality of the artist underwent in producing the object
is duplicated in the creative act of any person who
perceives the meaning of the object.

The significant difference between the artist and the
layman is that the former is infinitely more sensitive
to the esthetic possibilities of particular things, and
this sensitivity guides his perceptions as well as his
embodiment of them in objective forms. The work
of art is thus a coherent record of the sensitivity and
individuality of his perceptions; to read the record
one must learn the language, share the artist's per-

ceptions and experience. The basic problem of learning to see, therefore, centers inevitably around the
knowledge of what to look for, and how to interpret
it when found. What must be sought in works of art
is their form, and this is to be interpreted as the expression of a personality and an experience. The nature
of expression in its relation to form is the topic to
which we next turn.

EXPRESSION AND FORM[1]

ALBERT C. BARNES and VIOLETTE DE MAZIA

LIVING organisms, from the lowest to the highest, rarely find ready-made in the world the conditions indispensable to their continued existence and well-being; consequently, their greatest concern is to rectify the discrepancy, to establish the conditions which will provide them with what they require. This is the process of adjustment to environment in which all life fundamentally consists, and which finds expression in the attitudes or acts of the live creature. Man, indeed, is truly alive only in so far as he keeps aware of the possibilities and chances offered him by the environment to attain the equilibrium needed for his life progress; in this sense only, may he be justly called a live animal. The adjustment in question is a process in which the two factors, live animal and environment, are in a constant state of activity upon one another; and expression is a record of these activities, whether it be embodied in an artist's work or revealed in the behavior of a lost dog tracing his way back home from a great distance.

The adjustment between the animal and his environment is made possible by the fact that the world as a rule presents opportunities and resources as well as menaces; if it is wholly hostile, as it is to a man overtaken by an avalanche, no adjustment is possible. Adjustment, in other words, is not only to, but *by means of* the environment; the living being can do

[1] From Albert C. Barnes and Violette de Mazia, *The Art of Renoir*, The Barnes Foundation Press, Merion, Pa., 1944.

nothing except in so far as his energies engage with those which, actually or potentially, are already under way. He cannot even run away from danger unless the environment provides him with a sure footing and a place of refuge. The interaction between the live animal and his environment, through which a continuous and cumulative change is effected in both, constitutes, as we have seen, the actual process of experience. It begins with a felt discrepancy, proceeds with definite steps taken to establish harmony, and concludes, if the adjustment is successful, with an achieved equilibrium, a consummation in a sense of satisfaction or well-being. An experience, thus successfully consummated, expresses the nature both of the individual and of the situation itself.

Unless the impulse which begins and animates the process of adjustment is specifically directed to the conditions responsible for the breach of harmony, its expenditure of energy is futile, since the cause of the trouble remains unchanged. In a panic, we may run away from a fire which could easily be put out by pouring upon it the glass of water standing on a nearby table; in a fit of rage, we may stamp and shout, disregarding entirely the measures by which, if we composed our emotions and collected our energies, we could immediately dispose of the offending circumstances.

Only by an abuse of language can such outbursts be termed an expression of either emotion or personality; when they are over, the obstacles to adjustment remain unaffected, and the force which might have been used to rectify them has not been employed, but dissipated. Impulse, in a word, can be effective only in so far as it is from the start directed and controlled by an intelligent *purpose;* that is, in so far as it takes account, not of the fearsomeness or obstruction of the situation in general, but of the particular features which come between the individual and whatever end he may be striving for. Active effort, thus brought to bear upon the actual obstructions, institutes a new order of things propitious to the well-being previously threatened; a significant change is introduced into both the material situation and the active individual who has acquired a new adjustment, a harmonious relation to his environment. The relevance and adequacy of the reaction to the stimulus constitute it a genuine ex-pression, a pressing out or extraction of essential quality both in the living being and in the environment.

Expression, in the proper sense of the word, thus begins only when the purpose directing the expenditure of energies is to convert the obstacles into agencies contributing to the attainment of the needed adjustment. Purpose means an end forecast in consciousness through the help of meaningful images garnered from previous experiences and stored up as a background of funded knowledge. It remains at the stage of sheer imagination—therefore futile as expression—unless the individual uses it to direct his activities toward control of the situation by removal of the obstructions to adjustment.

When purpose is thus in command, the obstacles themselves become active stimuli to that coördinated interplay of thought and action which constitutes intelligence, and the original impulse toward adjustment imparts to the specific measure taken an intense driving force. The process of adjustment, in the course of its forward movement, absorbs into itself the qualities of the external conditions acted upon, as well as those of the acting individual, and unifies them in the consummatory act expressive of the total situation or experience. In the practical world intelligent purpose thus finds its expression, achieves its end, by discovering the relevant qualities of an actual situation and in devising the measures which must be taken if the possibilities of the situation are to be realized. Neither the sensitivity of perception which discovers what the objective situation is, nor the sagacity which discloses how it can be changed into what is desired, is possible except through the use of meanings stored up from past experience: it is the discriminating use of these meanings which imparts effectiveness and reality to the expression.

Expression in art entails the same acuteness of perception and employment of relevant meanings as every other intelligent execution of purpose in the practical affairs of life. Like the "practical" man, the artist is moved by some object or situation to feel and to do. What he does is not an attempt to arrest or alter the course of natural events, but to depict them, to paint a picture, carve out a statue, write a poem or symphony. The art in his picture, statue, poem or music is a record of an experience, an expression of his sensitiveness, intelligence, feeling and personal individuality.

The artist, stirred by some specific aspect of the world, reacting with his whole personality—his senses, habits of perception and interpretation, imagination, emotional attitudes and muscular adjustments—is impelled to extricate, to draw out from the object of his emotion the particular set of qualities and relationships that called forth his response, and to reincorporate them in a form of their own, in the process of which the work of art comes into being. The form of the work of art is thus literally ex-pressed from the original external stimulus as well as from the artist's personality and the clay, paint, musical tones or words used as a medium. As the process goes on, the artist's

stir of excitement, at first directed upon the situation as a whole, is gradually differentiated as the
separate aspects of the situation emerge one by one
into attention, and as each of them assumes its individual place in the total form and its distinctive
feeling-tone within the harmony of the whole.

These successive steps are never independent: each
proceeds out of what has gone before and paves the
way for what is to come, while all are suffused with
the general feeling characteristic of the impression as
a whole. In the process, both the artist himself and
the material on which he is working undergo a change.
As the material is refined, clarified, purged of what is
irrelevant, reshaped and more meaningfully unified, the
artist's own feelings are transformed; the excitement
which at first incited his activity expends itself in the
work of perception and organization; mere intensity
becomes enduring vitality; and eventually the sense of
composure and peace, characteristic of all successful
adjustments to life, supervenes. The end and fruition
come when equilibrium is established between what the
situation had im-pressed upon the artist and what he
succeeded in ex-pressing from it through the use of his
medium. Nature has thus been transformed through
the interplay of forces between the artist and the
external world; raw material has been given meaning
by an intelligently directed purpose; the emotional
content of the artist's experience is concretely embodied
in the objective attributes of the created form.

The exploration and organization of subject-matter
through which the artist executes his purpose of con-
ferring upon it a definite form, always proceeds more or
less tentatively. Until the end is reached, both the
form to be achieved and the detailed handling of its
components, remain indeterminate, and creative expres-

sion manifests itself, in imagination or in fact, as the qualities revealed to sense are taken account of, weighed, emphasized, slurred over, or distorted, as they are judged suitable or unsuitable to the office intended.

At the same time the design itself, the purpose, assumes more definite character; it is not something fixed from the start and imposed by force upon matter to which it is unadapted, but a way of ordering which ex-presses, draws out, the nature of the material itself, the subject-matter as well as the medium of expression. Both the projected form and its components thus undergo a process of investigation and canvassing, checked at every move; the process is not unlike the movements of a person entering a dark and unfamiliar room, littered with he knows not what, conscious only of a need to find a resting place. The inquiring, groping and testing continue until what is found answers the specific purpose in view, enters into the required relationship with what has gone before. In the whole ordered set of relationships each part both determines and is determined by every other; *this thoroughgoing interdetermination of parts constitutes form in a work of art, as it does in a machine, an organism, or the intelligent execution of any purpose.*

The fact that every detail of a work of art is shaped with reference to a specific purpose establishes unity of an artistic form, and the realization of the purpose by such objective means makes its form perceptible to a qualified observer. The individuality of the form arises from the fact that it is the expression of a unique personality; conversely, the artist's personality, his distinctive individuality, is revealed by the objective qualities of the form itself and by nothing else. Form is thus a book of record of the artist's mind and soul, and the medium through which he publishes his experience and communicates it to the world.

Form in a painting is a harmonious merging of the plastic means—color, line, light and space—through which the artist gives expression to his experience, and it is so permeated with his own personality that its meaning is all its own. A successfully painted landscape, compared with the scene depicted, reveals what the artist has done to and with the original components of the subject—trees, houses, earth and sky—to make them and the nexus of their relationships expressive of the distinctive way in which he sees them, the very specific meaning with which his senses, his feelings, his background and active impulses, endow them.

This meaning is objective; it is a version of the natural scene itself, but the extraction of it, the revelation of what the natural scene essentially is, is an act of creation, possible only to one who has the artist's specific endowment, his trained perceptions, and the funded meanings which his past experience has stored up. In his painting, therefore, nothing remains as it was in its original condition: color, line, surface-texture, the shape, degree of voluminousness and distribution of masses, are all altered, sometimes even to the point of gross distortion, in the process of their incorporation in the new form created by the artist. This penetration to essentials, and the reorganization of mere fact to make it expressive of an experience, is what distinguishes art from every form of imitation and photography. The artist does not meaninglessly repeat what already exists: in one and the same act he shows what *it* really is, and what *he* is.

This creative transformation of natural appearance by artistic insight may be termed *drawing*, if the word be understood not in the arbitrarily limited sense usually given it, but as the whole intricate process of drawing out what is essential in any given situation.[2] Every exciting object contains a mass of detail a large part of which has no relevancy to what the artist feels in perceiving the object; on the other hand, what is significant in it for artistic expression may be far from obvious. Expression, that is to say, involves selection, emphasis, and the addition of material which only the artist can discover and supply. The drawing out of what is fundamental and significant is therefore the essence of the expressive act, and it involves all the aspects of the thing depicted, the color, illumination and spatial arrangement, as well as the line. A landscape, a figure or a still-life drawn in this manner not only represents the essentials of the subject as it occurred in nature, which any spectator is free to interpret differently, but it conveys to the trained beholder a record of life and nature, enriched by what the artist's mind and spirit have drawn out, and by what his funded experience has fed to his imagination. Drawing in the full sense, in other words, *is* expression.

The abiding appeal of art to human beings springs from the presence in it of the characteristics which lend interest and poignancy to life itself: movement, contrast, rhythm, symmetry, coherence of parts, unity of form and meaning, and individuality of purpose, are common to nature and art. The regular recurrence of night and day, of the seasons of the year, the systole and diastole of the heart, are natural rhythms to which we are all subject and which profoundly affect our lives. The alternation of these rhythms in nature lends

---

[2] For a fuller account of drawing, see Albert C. Barnes and Violette de Mazia, *The Art of Henri-Matisse*, page 80, Charles Scribner's Sons, New York, N. Y., 1933.

contrast and movement to life, as their repetition and interdependence, their interweaving and dovetailing, lend unity; they thus provide both variety and unity, the indispensable conditions of satisfactory living.

In the world of actuality, however, the harmonious adjustment of natural rhythms to human purposes is only occasional, and it constantly tends to give way to monotonous repetition or to chaotic disorder, either of which is destructive to the individual's well-being. The artist, therefore, deliberately modifies his subject to make rhythm ubiquitous, and at the same time he discards, in the interest of variety and contrast, the mechanical uniformity characteristic of many natural rhythms. The pervasiveness of rhythm is one of the most important agencies of unification; understood in the widest sense, as embracing color, lighting, shape and mass as well as line, and also such general qualities as grace, charm or power, rhythm establishes unity, the reciprocal determination of every part by every other and by the form as a whole.

In making rhythm more definite and pervasive than it is in the natural world, art brings to a conclusion a tendency which, as Professor Dewey points out, is manifested in all perception. The eye reports things and events to the mind, and the mind interprets them in a series of pulse-beat waves, through which what is seen is gradually unfolded. The details, that is to say, do not enter consciousness simultaneously but as a progressive series, in which contrast between the parts is emphasized along with the common relationship to the whole which maintains unity. When perception has the fulness characteristic of genuine experience, it has a definite form with distinctive movement, rhythm, variety and balance, and is already well advanced on the road to art; art, indeed, may be regarded as simply the consummation of the striving toward fulness and order in perception, and as its objective record. Art thus contains the values of experience in a purified and heightened form. The keenness of the artist's perception, the intensity of his feelings, the vitality and reality of his experience, in a word, blend every part of the authentic work of art in a continuous rhythmic flow, which springs out of and coördinates the rhythms and contrasts of every detail.

The inherence of rhythm, contrast, symmetry and balance in the organic unity of all the parts of a form, as distinguished from their factitious superposition, is the criterion by which genuine artistic expression may be differentiated from its simulacrum. The importance of this differentiation in any intelligent study of art may be appreciated by a brief glance at this aspect of Renoir's work, prior to our detailed survey of his paintings. Rhythm in Renoir is an element pervasively ingrained in the structural form of the picture, a continuous ebb and flow of all its constituents. The outstanding rhythmic feature is in itself a composite of numerous factors which, in turn, are organized in a great variety of subsidiary rhythms and, by an ever-expanding set of relationships, reënforce and increase the significance of the total form.

Often in Renoir these infinitely varied and intricately intertwined series of rhythms bear striking similarity of quality, extending at times to a close correspondence in structure, to the rhythmic sequence of themes and variations in Beethoven's symphonies. This kinship can be readily perceived by a trained observer tracing with his finger the rhythms in Renoir's *Noirmoutier* (The Barnes Foundation, No. 163), for example, as he listens to the second movement of Beethoven's *Fifth Symphony*. In both the painting and the music, the main rhythmic movement, a swinging lilt, is extremely fluid, powerful, colorful; if picked up at any point in its course, it develops constantly in variety of content and in mode of expression; each addition to the prevailing rhythm punctuates the basic underlying movement with refreshing throbs of new meaningful units. It is a powerful, all-pervasive rhythmic surge that stirs the percipient's whole personality to sympathetic vibration.

Renoir's rhythm is never a mere repetition, it is a varied recurrence of elements with modifications usually in more than one of their components. The variations not only create rhythms of their own, but enter into the rhythmic corporate body of all the main plastic elements; that is, through their immediately felt influences upon their context, they become dynamically related to the other rhythms and also to the pervasive feeling of life and force distinctive of the composition as a whole. So thoroughgoing is the unity resulting from the rhythmic interpenetration of all the constituents, and so continuous is the transformation of each by every other, that only upon analysis can the rhythms be separated from the other aspects of the formal structure. In the whole painting there is no break in the compositional continuity of the rhythmic movement: each interval between punctuations or accents is in itself a unit of subtle rhythms and contrasts. Composition, in other words, is an uninterrupted progressive sequence of rhythmic contrasts in color, line, light, space, mass and pattern. Renoir's own glow of vitality is communicated to the spectator as the latter's own energies are reorganized by the constantly varied and ever-widening pulsating rhythm which feeds his mind and stirs it to activity. In short, the part played by rhythm in Renoir's form is organic, growing out of the basic design and inseparable from it.

The fact that rhythm, contrast, variety, symmetry and balance are so vitally important in esthetic expression makes them also the principal means through which the surface-effects of art are speciously manufactured. The stock-in-trade characteristic of all such specious effects consists mainly of rhythms mechanically imposed upon subject-matter, and distributed throughout the composition in accordance with shopworn formulas, to obtain balance.[3]

A simulation of rhythm by units which monotonously repeat one another in the way they are constructed and placed, is far from the rhythmic contrast that effectively recalls and organizes the spectator's store of accumulated meanings. The artificially manufactured rhythms, in any field of art expression, in their failure to renew or even sustain the original sense-stimulus, differ in no essentials from the ticktack of a clock, or the monotonous rows of horizontal and vertical bars in a rail fence. Reaction to them is barren of significant meanings: at best the senses are titillated, as by the repetitive patterns of sound in jazz music, instead of being made to convey to the entire personality the compelling and profound human values expressed in genuinely creative esthetic forms.

The difference between the rhythms in Renoir's work or Beethoven's and those in manufactured concoctions can be detected at once by the trained observer; in the former the interplay of rhythms and contrasts constitutes the very substance of the construction and is the very means by which the depth and significance of the artist's experience is conveyed to the spectator. The contrast between the manufactured rhythms and those

[3] *E. g.*, the paintings of Thomas Benton; the poetry of Edgar Guest; the sculpture of George Barnard; the music of Vincent Lopez.

of Renoir is that between a pattern of lines, colors and masses factitiously arranged and barren of meaningful content, and a rhythmic expression loaded with significant meaning.

What is true in general of the rhythms in manufactured art is true also of their arbitrary distribution throughout the composition in order to obtain a symmetrical appearance; the symmetry thus speciously secured is merely a physical equilibration of quantities and expanses: it is on the same esthetic level as that which the grocer obtains when he weighs a pound of sugar. The only sort of balance that counts esthetically is the symmetry arising from the intrinsic *qualities* of the balanced units themselves. Professor Dewey calls attention to the fact that symmetry is itself a phase of rhythm and can be separated from it only on reflection.[4] Symmetry, in short, is bound up with, is a product of, the organization of rhythms; it is one of the media through which expression of experience attains to esthetic status; and in all genuine art, symmetry, no less than its constituent rhythms and the dynamic movement they engender, is a quality emerging spontaneously from the form, not imposed upon it from without. Thus in all fully-expressive works of art, contrast, which forms the basis of drama, and rhythm, which conduces to unity, are the two variable qualities,

[4] "Symmetry and rhythm are the same thing felt with the difference of emphasis that is due to attentive interest. When intervals that define rest and relative fulfilment are the traits that especially characterize perception, we are aware of symmetry. When we are concerned with movement, the comings and goings rather than arrivals, rhythm stands out. But in every case, symmetry, since it is the equilibrium of counteracting energies, involves rhythm, while rhythm occurs only when movement is spaced by places of rest, and hence involves measure." John Dewey, *Art as Experience*, pp. 178–179, Minton, Balch & Co., New York, N. Y., 1934.

by the interplay of which symmetry and balance are established and form is unified.

Because art embodies these universal qualities of life and nature, great works of art call forth in the sensitive percipient a wide range of human values over and above those which attach to the treatment of particular subjects. Indeed, works of art are great in proportion as they possess the power not only to impart the enhanced vitality characteristic of all genuine immediate experience, but to revive the feelings stored up from scattered experiences of the distant past. Thus art has the unique quality of containing within itself an epitome, a condensation, of the values of innumerable phases of life that cannot find expression through any other medium. Painting and music call up visible and audible images loaded with the "hushed reverberations" of past vital experiences in the everyday world, gone beyond recall except for the magic of pictorial and musical forms. The recalled emotion is all the richer, fuller, more moving, for having all the discordant concomitant factors of the original experience refined away and only a purified residue retained. The condensation and clarification of the meanings of the earlier experiences make the emotional content all the more poignant.

This capacity of art-forms to express the universal qualities of things, limited in range only by that of the perceiver's background of experience, rests upon the same psychological basis as the normal human tendency to transfer the values of one form of experience to that of another and different field. The determining part played by these transferred values in all forms of art-expression warrants restating here a detailed account of the matter as it appeared in another of our books.[5]

[5] Albert C. Barnes and Violette de Mazia, *The Art of Henri-Matisse*, pp. 30–31, Charles Scribner's Sons, New York, N. Y., 1933.

Human beings always and necessarily interpret the present, the given, in terms of the past. The fact is a truism as regards intellectual apprehensions: we understand anything only in so far as we identify it, place it in a context of familiar meanings; but what is not so generally realized is that this intellectual apprehension is accompanied by an imaginative or metaphorical extension of meaning which imports into the experience of the here and now at least a part of the emotional aura, the heat and glow, of our past sensations and feelings. Sometimes, especially when the importunity of practical necessities is relaxed and the situation is propitious to flights of fancy, as on a steamer passing within sight of land off the coast of the Riviera, material objects may attract to themselves swarms of images, and serve as figures in fantastic dramas. Fleecy clouds sailing over the sky often remind us of animals, persons, buildings; as they move and change, we may interpret their movement and change according to our fancy, and weave narratives about them. A portion of the cloud may detach itself and remind us of the spire or façade of a cathedral; or starting from faint or vague resemblances, we may see in it an elephant's trunk, a shining silver river, or the broad surface of a cliff. Or it may be a living figure moving in stately grace to the melody of a minuet which our memory has cherished for years.

Reveries of this sort are only the extreme development of a tendency to figurative perception which is present in all persons at all times. We say of a man that he is adamant, or soft, or a fox, and the emotional quality conveyed by the figure of speech, no less than our purely intellectual estimate, pervades and determines our attitude toward him. We feel in a Cézanne the qualities of a solidly constructed building; a Renoir picture of a girl recalls a rose in a garden on a morning in June. In short, there is scarcely an object or situation in life, or in art—the mirror of life—not fraught with emotional associations for which its objective qualities give no demonstrable ground.

Often the recall is not of memories and feelings as separate and distinguishable psychological facts, but of what Santayana calls the "hushed reverberations" of the original experience: vague thrills, obscure likings and dislikings, a sense of importance or triviality, of which we can no more bring to mind the basis than we can explicitly state the evidence which underlies many of our most fundamental beliefs. As with intellectual beliefs, there are in our minds in solution a vast number of emotional attitudes, feelings ready to be reëxcited when the proper stimulus arrives, and more than anything else it is these forms, this residue of experience, which, deeper, fuller and richer than in the mind of the ordinary man, constitute the artist's capital. What is called the magic of the artist resides in his ability to transfer these values from one field of experience to another, to attach them to the objects of our common life, and by his imaginative insight make these objects poignant and momentous. Far from being the exotic flower which "practical" people look at askance, art is an essential and vital part of life in that it reveals, expresses, the meaning, the universal significance and emotional import of innumerable facts and experiences which without it would be flat and commonplace.

This chapter may be briefly summarized as follows: every living being is constantly expressing itself by adjustment to its environment, an adjustment in the course of which both the organism and the environment are changed. The expression which constitutes art consists of both a more penetrating perception and a more thoroughgoing rhythmic organization of the material of the objective world. The qualities of real things are drawn out and resynthesized in a form which adds, to the values actually present in the reality, a whole range of others which the artist transfers from remote realms of experience. Art is thus a clearer, more luminous, and imaginatively richer version of the world of nature.

Every worthwhile artist, like any other normally developing human being, passes through stages of infancy, adolescence and maturity of personality and of expression. Consequently, the full significance of his life's work, his contribution to the traditions of art and to human experience, can be revealed and judged only by approaching the study of his form with the knowledge of the principles of the developing process through which personality and insight continuously grow. The next essay will examine the significant factors in development and growth.

EXPERIENCE AND GROWTH[1]

ALBERT C. BARNES and VIOLETTE DE MAZIA

THERE is a widespread impression that experience is something which, with the passage of time, happens to every one, that exposure to objective conditions automatically generates the ability to perceive and understand them. Thus a man who has spent twenty years in a profession is usually said to be "experienced" in it, irrespective of the qualities of mind, the habits of observation and reflection, that have directed his practice of it. Modern psychology and logic have made it abundantly clear that no such inevitable generation of experience takes place; not only objective conditions but active interest, alert senses, an open mind, a store of knowledge already in hand, and systematic reflection on the part of the individual, are the indispensable conditions of any discriminating sensitiveness to the world about him. What is inevitable in their absence is a counterfeit of attention, a mechanical set of habits, and the prematurely fossilized mind which, as William James says, makes the majority of human beings incapable of growth after the age of twenty-five.

The organic connection between growth and experience is obvious in every aspect of experience itself: all the activities which enter into it have their function and meaning only as instruments of growth, and the reality of the experience as a whole is destroyed when the continuity of growth is broken. Except in so far as the organism utilizes the situations in which it is

[1] From Albert C. Barnes and Violette de Mazia, *The Art of Renoir*, The Barnes Foundation Press, Merion, Pa., 1944.

177

placed as food out of which to build up a constantly
more robust and individualized personality, its perceptions, purposes and achievements, either intellectual
or esthetic, are without substance or significance. A
survey of the various levels and types of experience will
show the continuous interaction with environment and
resulting growth to be essential to them all.

We have seen in the essay, *Learning to See*,[2] that
perception furnishes the material of experience through
a process of active intercourse of the individual with
his environment. Every living being is constantly
undergoing stimulation from some external object, responding, and again undergoing, in its entire organism,
the effects of the response. That such constant interaction with the surroundings is the first condition of
growth is revealed by the most striking feature in the
behavior of the lower animals. An animal is constantly
observing, investigating, and actively doing something
about the things going on in his vicinity. His activities
may be limited in scope, but they are never half-hearted
or perfunctory; he is, in a word, *interested* in his environment, and his interest shows itself both in a constant
attentiveness to it and in an equally constant expenditure of energy to adjust himself to it. A dog which
greets the arrival of a stranger by growling, that of an
acquaintance by wagging his tail, is testifying both to
his interest and to his discrimination, and the obvious
limitations of his world and his reactions do not in the
least affect the genuineness of his interest, the definite-
ness of his response, or the reality of his experience.

The behavior of even very young children exhibits
the same unjaded interest, manifesting itself in spontaneous curiosity, appropriate responsiveness, and freedom from affectation. It shows also, and even more

[2] Page 145 of present Volume.

clearly, the *ability to learn* which is always present when experience is real, and becomes more and more important as the test of such reality as life reaches higher levels. This will be apparent if we consider the familiar instance of a baby's touching a flaming object and thereby burning himself. The baby may repeat the act again and again without having a genuine experience: not until he connects what he did with what happened to him as a result of his act, does he grasp the meaning, *i.e.*, have the experience, that fire burns. Experience, in other words, involves not only doing and undergoing but perception of the relation between the two—and this, in a word, defines thinking. Such perception endows situations and the acts which they prompt with meaning: a flame (touched) means a burn; and the perception of meaning constitutes experience.

The simplest reflex action thus makes apparent the fact that two conditions are essential to experience—interest, manifesting itself by active attention and specific response, and grasp of meaning. In so far as a situation does not incite some one to do something positive and appropriate, he has no experience of it because he is not really alive to it at all. The action, even though nothing more than an unconscious adjustment of the organism to the situation, is always positive and appropriate. With the perception of the consequence of action, the meaning of the situation is revealed: the organism has fed on its environment and enriched its own substance. Mind is merely the store of accumulated meanings remaining from past experience, and it grows by adding to that store new meanings, likewise born of the uninterrupted interaction of individual and environment.

In mature life, intelligence consists in the explicit

13

use of one's store of accumulated meanings, and this is likewise a dual process of doing and undergoing, with reciprocal and continued interaction between the two phases. The problem for reflection is always set by a situation which as a whole is unfamiliar, so that no habitual course of action can serve as a response, but not too unfamiliar to be recognized as having a bearing upon our interests. The fact that it is not altogether strange means that our past experience can furnish us with suggestions about it, and the test of intelligence is found in the way in which such suggestions are used. If they amount to no more than guesses, means for bringing the inquiry to an immediate end, not only is any action premature and exposed to the risk of practical disaster, but the opportunity for growth is lost.

If, in contrast, the suggestion is treated as a hypothesis, which as its implications are developed points to additional observations which will justify its acceptance or rejection, we avoid as much as possible the danger of practical loss, and at the same time turn the situation to our intellectual advantage. Often a number of hypotheses may call for consideration before we can reach a conclusion, and the final decision may be a compromise between conflicting hypotheses, but when it is attained the action supervening has acquired a new status: it is no longer mere trial and error, but experience. Whether the action itself succeeds or fails, it brings illumination, and its results are thus available for the interpretation of similar situations in the future. The reality of experience is thus attested in reflective as in spontaneous behavior by the fact that the continuity of development is maintained: the organism has been nourished by the objective situation, in and through the process of amplifying its own store of meanings, its mind.

Another factor of the utmost importance in the process by which the matter of experience is assimilated to yield fresh insight, is the ability to perceive analogies between things superficially different. No problem is solvable by any one who lacks a fund of knowledge out of which suggestions or hypotheses may arise, but even when this is present individuals differ enormously in the degree to which they can avail themselves of it for the interpretation of unfamiliar situations. The extremely literal-minded or habit-bound can take in a situation only if it repeats practically point for point one already encountered. Their past experiences can be revived only as wholes; such are the persons who are unable to give an accurate and succinct statement of anything, or to tell the simplest story without adding a multitude of irrelevant details. Lacking the capacity to select, reject and eliminate, they are helpless in the presence of complexity, and their development is arrested by problems which to the intellectually resourceful would be a challenge and stimulus to growth.

At the other extreme are those who can detect very slight resemblances and in so doing discover the indispensable clue to the solution of a problem. All interpretation of really formidable novelty requires this ability to discriminate between the essential and the adventitious, and to carry away from experience a grasp of generalized connections applicable to innumerable things which need have no obvious common quality. Experience thus requires, in addition to living interest and a reflective habit of mind, an ability to look beneath the surface and distinguish what is fundamental from what is trivial.

Interest, perception of meaning, the use of suggested meanings as hypotheses, and a penetrating discrimination of essentials, together with a background of meanings retained from the past, are thus necessary for that continuous active interplay of forces between the individual and environment which alone constitutes experience. These activities, operating in every aspect of the individual's behavior, so expand and relate it to its context of absent, past and future conditions that action is no longer a response to a single fact, but to the totality of the situation. These factors in experience are distinguishable, but not isolable: in the absence of any one of them the continuity is broken between the individual and his environment, he fails to function as a complete organism, and the supply of nourishment required for his continued growth is suspended. If, for example, interest is not wedded to reflection and action, it speedily becomes emotional indulgence, and this, as our account of perception has shown, has no fruit in experience; and reflection itself, if not checked by experiment, is nothing more than idle speculation, a form of day-dreaming. Experience, in a word, is an organic whole, and is arrested or perverted the moment the reciprocal interaction of its elements is interrupted, and its supply of food from the objective world thereby cut off.

This statement of the nature of experience, in its application to practical affairs and science, would probably not be disputed by any well-informed person. It is almost universally supposed, however, that in esthetic creation intellectual processes have little or no part to play: that the effort in practical affairs to determine, by painstaking observation, elaboration of hypotheses, and recognition of objective connections, exactly what the facts of the situation *are*, is in esthetic creation replaced by something more emotional and "intuitive," often called "inspiration." As we shall see further on in this essay, the idea of inspiration corresponds to an important phase or aspect of growth, but the aspect is as characteristic of intellectual growth as of esthetic, and the belief that artistic creation and reflective thought are in any sense opposed is a radical error, fatal to adequate understanding of either.[3] Far from being opposed, they are in psychological essence the same: the fundamental fact in both is interpretation of an objective situation in the light of the individual's whole personality and background; in both, this interpretation is made under the spur of specific interests, controlled by the purposes of the organism as a whole, and directed to action. In other words, genuine experience in reasoning and in artistic creation is a continuous process, each using the problems which arise and the material furnished by the past as food for an ever-renewed growth, and resulting in a constant reorganization both in the individual and in the world.

As already noted in the essay, *Expression and Form*,[4] all the elements or phases characteristic of practical and intellectual experience are also present in the esthetic:

[3] ". . . the idea that the artist does not think as intently and penetratingly as a scientific inquirer is absurd. A painter must consciously undergo the effect of his every brush stroke or he will not be aware of what he is doing and where his work is going. Moreover, he has to see each particular connection of doing and undergoing in relation to the whole that he desires to produce. To apprehend such relations is to think, and is one of the most exacting modes of thought. The difference between the pictures of different painters is due quite as much to differences of capacity to carry on this thought as it is to differences of sensitivity to bare color and to differences in dexterity of execution." ". . . To think effectively in terms of relations of qualities is as severe a demand upon thought as to think in terms of symbols, verbal and mathematical. Indeed, since words are easily manipulated in mechanical ways, the production of a work of genuine art probably demands more intelligence than does most of the so-called thinking that goes on among those who pride themselves on being 'intellectuals.'" John Dewey, *Art as Experience*, pp. 45–46, Minton, Balch & Co., New York, N. Y., 1934.

[4] Page 160 of present Volume.

without interest and a store of accumulated meanings, both of them involving all the activities of the organism as a whole, no such thing as esthetic expression could exist. Just as the physician detects symptoms to which the layman is blind, the artist too sees more than the man whose eyes have not been opened by specific training and active experiment. What the artist sees is, for example, more numerous shades of color, interrelations of volume and space, sequences and rhythms of line, but these things are as far from being divined intuitively or spontaneously composed into a single whole, as are the indications of health or disease.

Like the scientist, the artist is able to see only because he has learned to see: the traditions of art play exactly the same part in stimulating and directing his activities of mind and body, and in nourishing his growth, that the facts and principles of science do for the physicist's or chemist's. Indeed, each of the traditions of art may be described as a systemized way of seeing, in which particular aspects or qualities of the visible world are selected and arranged in a characteristic type of organization. To have mastered the traditions means, therefore, to have seen the objective things about us from many points of view, to have acquired a rich store of material for the esthetic interpretation of reality; and this is precisely the same thing as to have an ample supply of possible meanings for the interpretation of a practical difficulty or scientific problem.

The use in science of suggested meanings as hypotheses to guide observation is paralleled in artistic creation by the artist's use of traditions tentatively or experimentally, following them not as rules or laws to bind his own seeing, but as suggestions, means of illumination, to be adhered to in so far as they reveal what he as an individual wishes to express, but discarded or modified whenever they are irrelevant to his purpose. So used, in balanced coördination with the particular object or scene which provides the problem of seeing and the opportunity of growth, the traditions feed his esthetic activity and give it direction and meaning; otherwise, they are mere blinders, limiting his vision and stunting his growth. The distinction is that between authentic art and academicism, and illustrates once more the difference between true experience, in which interest, knowledge and all the powers of mind and body coöperate to produce a personal achievement, and the meaningless repetition of undigested formulas which constitutes the entire stock in trade of academic painters.

The ability to discover analogies between things superficially very different, to utilize the essence of an experience in a new context, appears in art in the ability to extract from a tradition the elements responsible for its basic significance and to make of them instruments for the creation of a new form which need have little or no obvious resemblance to its prototype. This is what characterizes all profoundly creative art, such as Cézanne's, or, as we shall see in detail, Renoir's.[5] A painter who is able to distinguish in the traditions what is essential from what is adventitious has at his command an immensely extended range of values: he can observe his world with an incomparably more penetrating insight than one who has no choice but to see things, in the main, as they have always been seen. He can, in other words, nourish his experience from all the resources of the past, incorporating its richness into the very fiber of his personality without compromising his own integrity; if he retains unimpaired his capacity for

[5] See Albert C. Barnes and Violette de Mazia, *The Art of Renoir*, The Barnes Foundation Press, Merion, Pa., 1944.

growth throughout a long career, his work may then come to be an epitome of all the most significant values of tradition, made fresh, distinctive and personal by the completeness with which everything irrelevant to his own vision is eliminated.

The vital importance in art of a constantly increasing capital of esthetic meanings may be illustrated by a comparison of Monet's work with Renoir's. Because Monet's sensitivity and interest were practically restricted to the field of out-of-door light-and-color effects, each new impact upon his senses called forth a type of reaction similar to previous reactions; selection and interpretation took place each time according to the monotonous dictates of his fixed set of habits and limited background, and correspondingly failed to enrich the latter by expanding the boundaries of his vision.

Renoir too was interested in the impressionistic interpretation of nature and in Monet's technical method of expressing it; but the impact upon his senses, and his interpretation of what was being done by his contemporaries, instead of limiting his field of vision, quickened his sense of perception and broadened his insight. Thus the impressionistic form itself, in Renoir's hands, acquired a richer meaning because his keener perception and greater freedom of receptivity had discovered in it fuller possibilities than were ever suspected by its originators.

A set of landscapes by Monet offers great variety in subject-matter, especially in the character of illumination at different times of the day; but the essential quality expressive of the interaction of the scene with the man's personality is monotonously alike in all. Monet, in other words, was awake to only certain phases of life beyond which his specialized vision seldom reached; Renoir, on the other hand, was continuously unfolding in his perception of Nature; he consistently inquired for, discovered, selected, established, organized and expressed new pictorial effects, connections, relationships, values and meanings, all reflecting a wide field of life activities, and a profound assimilation of the great traditions of painting. In contrast to Monet, Renoir could paint the very same spot of landscape a number of times and each version would reveal an essentially different ramification of his spirit and feelings.

An understanding of the fact that the process of creation is essentially the same in art, in science, in philosophy and in all intelligent living, makes it possible to see, in each, the type of development or growth which occurs in cases of "inspiration." All art, as Santayana observes, is automatic, but this in no way implies that it occurs as a spontaneous sudden birth, without a long period of gestation. What automatic means here is that the experience which a work of art records cannot be consciously planned for in advance: that often, after a long series of fruitless efforts, the artist is visited by a flash of insight, a burst of inspiration, and that because of the absence of deliberate design on his own part, he may think of his vision as something which has come to him, rather than as something which he has produced.

This absence of conscious contrivance, however, which is characteristic of all art of the first rank, becomes intelligible as soon as we understand that mind and conscious reflection are not at all the same thing. The mind is a system of meanings, each of them the indelible record of an experience, and its growth consists in a more precise definition and a more fully organic interconnection of these meanings as a result of interaction with the environment. This growth may and in fact largely does go on without explicit awareness of it on our part, and sometimes when we finally do become aware of it we find that our personality has been changed to its depths, that our changed attitude makes us see a vast number of things in a totally new light.

A familiar form of this is religious conversion, but it occurs also throughout the whole range of experience, intellectual as well as esthetic. Its explanation is what William James calls "subconscious incubation," a germination so gradual that we do not realize that it has taken place until it is almost or quite complete. The suddenness of our realization, however, does not in the least indicate that the change itself was sudden. There has been no breach of continuity, no interruption of the steady assimilation of appropriate nutriment from the environment which can alone make growth possible, and when the new insight bursts upon us, analysis can always discover its relation to all that we have done and undergone. Interest, the system of habits and meanings which constitute the individual's real though often unconscious personality, have all left their mark upon it; they are bred into its substance, and in their absence it would never have been forthcoming.

Religious conversion, indeed, is only an exaggerated form of an experience which every one has constantly. We often find that the solution of our problems does not come as a result of a single uninterrupted process of thought, beginning with a difficulty or perplexity and proceeding forth to a conclusion; instead, after a long course of observation and reflection, we may remain completely at sea. The process may be repeated over and over without yielding a satisfactory conclusion; suddenly, however, perhaps when we are not thinking about it at all, what we have been looking for flashes upon us. Clearly, in the interval something has gone on, but it has been below the threshold of consciousness, and we know it only by its results.

On a more extended scale, the changes in our attitudes toward people largely take place in the same fashion. Often no question is definitely raised, but after a lengthy association we wake up some day to find that an infatuation has been outgrown, or an aversion changed into respect. The final result represents a long continued summation of stimuli upon a mass of piled-up observations the significance of which was not felt at the moment, but which when assimilated grew into a final and dramatic alteration of our whole attitude and disposition of mind.

Growth or development, however continuous in essence, thus shows an alternation of rapid and obvious advances with pauses; the pauses are periods not of stagnation but of gestation, in which the activity of the organism continues unabated but takes the form of preparation for a new variety of expression. Indeed, the absence of such pauses is likely to point, not to uninterrupted development, but to the fact that the individual has reached the limit of his growth early, and is therefore unable to attain any more profound ordering of his experience. Haydn and Matisse are artists who, for all their ability, remain at approximately the same level once their maturity is reached: Beethoven and Renoir, in contrast, develop not only in technical mastery but also by advancing constantly to more exalted realms of experience and to higher levels of personality.

Since advances of this kind cannot possibly be planned beforehand, and yet represent the most important order of development, deliberation or conscious reflection is only one, and not the most vital, phase of that growth of mind and body which takes place when a living organism, by the operation of all its powers, draws nutriment from its world. It follows that in the profound thinker, as well as in the creative artist, the most significant part of growth takes place during the periods of gestation, when his subconscious is in control; that his experience too is basically a matter of active commerce with environment, and that his explicit reflection is instrumental to making an adjustment of his whole personality to the objective world. His emotions are deeper than his reasoning, and they determine the purposes which his conscious intelligence devises means to carry out.

This conclusion is of the utmost importance for the understanding of both art and intellectual activity.[6] Modern psychology, in showing the essential identity of experience in all its forms and phases, has revealed the possibility of analysis of art by the same means which have proved so fruitful in science. Such analysis, in fact, is indispensable to any real understanding of art or participation in the artist's experience. However little the artist is capable of formulating abstractly the purposes which animate his activity or the principles which guide it, their operation is demonstrable in the inherent rationality of his work, which is an orderly, coherent creation out of the material of experience, the culmination of a continuous growth which has drawn substance from all that he has done and that has happened to him. Conversely, a profound and living philosophy is first and foremost the reaction of a living being, fully alive to his environment and participating with his whole mind and body in all its activities.

As little as the artist, can the philosopher always

* See also John Dewey's essay, *Affective Thought in Logic and Painting*, page 95 of present Volume.

identify the true basis in experience of much that enters into his world: the sources of his nutriment are too varied, subtle and elusive to be brought completely into consciousness. Largely because of this elusiveness, it is vital that they be perceived and made intelligible; it is only in the light of them that we can hope to share his experience and judge of the validity of its result. The artist, like the philosopher, invites us to enter into his mind and view his world. If we are to accept his invitation to share what is offered, we must feed our mind and grow through the active and unremitting enlistment of all our powers in the attainment of discriminating insight into what he has to show.

THE EVOLUTION OF PLASTIC DESIGN[1]

Albert C. Barnes

The line of demarcation between painting which is and which is not modern is difficult to draw with exactness, but it is clear that impressionism made a sharp break with the traditions that preceded it. For practical purposes, contemporary painting may be said to date from the age of Courbet, Manet, Monet and Pissarro. In the work of these men, the motives of the later men are present, although not disengaged from the traditions which went before. The chief point of difference between the old and the new may be said to be that the moderns exhibit greater interest in a design which depends more upon its plastic content than upon subject for its esthetic value.

In order to show the development of this interest, it will be necessary to trace the evolution of plastic design as something in itself, apart from the subject of the painting. Criticism of any work of plastic art is valid in so far as it concerns itself with the form the artist has created out of the means at his disposal, namely, line, color, light and space. That is as true of the work of the Renaissance painters as it is of Cézanne or Matisse, and there can be no reasonable doubt that what makes the art of Giotto great is not the religious subject, but the plastic form, the design, by which deep human values are conveyed. A variety of circumstances prevented the early Italian painters from making a sharp distinction between their

[1] From Albert C. Barnes, *The Transition to Modern Painting*, The Art in Paintng, Harcourt, Brace & Co., New York, N. Y., 1937.

interest in design and their interest in illustrating a religious or historical narrative. The spirit and state of culture of the early Renaissance required that painting fulfil definite public functions. It was necessary that church frescoes should illustrate religious motifs, that portraits should reproduce their originals, that pictures ordered by states or guilds should portray specific occurrences of interest to their purchasers. The general conditions were such that books were accessible only to the few, and their function was largely taken over by painting. All these circumstances made it impossible that properly plastic or pictorial motives should operate without constraint. The history of the transition to modern painting consists of an account of the removal of all such irrelevant compulsions, and of how the employment of the various plastic means came to be more and more directed to the realization of plastic design. Such an account will make clear the essential continuity between painters apparently as diverse as Piero della Francesca and Picasso, Tintoretto and Cézanne.

Design, as it is found in modern and contemporary painting, appears in the work of the early Italians whenever literal reproduction is so modified that the arrangement and handling of objects make a more esthetically moving plastic form. Giotto is, in his way, as far from literalism as Renoir. If we compare Giotto with his inferior contemporaries, we see at once that a large number of his simplicfiations must have been conscious departures from photographic representation. These departures are of the very essence of the appeal of his themes, and are clearly expressive of an interest in plastic form for itself. Even though his designs are always accompanied by a narrative, they embody more the spirit than the details of the narrative;

in other words, they express a human interest of essential value in terms truly plastic, and such expressiveness is inevitably an enhancement and not a distraction. In this sense Giotto seems far more modern than such painters as van Dyck, Reynolds, or David, in whom the rôle of painting is instrumental to such cheap human activities as personal flattery or surface imitation.

In the early Florentines, Uccello and Fra Filippo Lippi, interest in design was so paramount that academic critics propagate the obvious misconception that Uccello was principally an experimenter in perspective. But considered from the plastic standpoint, his work is a striking illustration of the value of a design which discards an imitative presentation of the spatial relationships of objects in favor of one which has greater intrinsic worth. Fra Filippo Lippi distorted perspective in still another manner, and achieved a design which is akin plastically to that used by many important painters since Courbet.

Design is the animating motive in drawing whenever there is simplification or deliberate distortion directed to heightening of esthetic effect; this is clearly discernible in Andrea del Castagno, in Michelangelo, in El Greco and other great painters. In all of them drawing is only partly representative and more esthetic or expressive in intent. In the fifteenth century Florentine, Masaccio, the deliberate distortions of line, light and color produce an appearance that is both naturalistic and infinitely more moving esthetically than any literal or photographic representation could be. The paintings of these great artists prove the absurdity of those ultra-modern writers who contend that plastic form is an absolute creation of the artist, in which no attempt is made to render the quality of anything in nature. We maintain that such form can be no more than decoration, that plastic form at its best does seek to give an equivalent of something real—of fundamental aspects, of essences, though not of insignificant detail. In fact, at all stages in the history of painting, from Masaccio to Manet and Matisse, the departures from literalism by which a more satisfactory design is secured, accomplish *also* a convincing effect of reality: we have not receded from the human significance of scenes and events but approached nearer to it.

Another form of modernism is anticipated in Botticelli, in whom design concerns itself chiefly with decoration. This inferior order of design has its modern counterpart in those cubistic paintings in which design is reduced to the level of mere pattern; this is in the same category, esthetically, as the pattern in a rug.

When a painter uses color which departs from the observable color of an object, that also constitutes distortion. Such distortion has been constantly practiced to enhance the value of design, notably by all the great Venetians. The Venetian glow, a circumambient atmosphere of color, is obviously a color-distortion introduced to modify, harmonize, emphasize and set off the colorful aspect of things, so that the effects are richer than those found in nature. The most original element in the work of Matisse, that is, his interest in color-combinations for their own sake, is thus clearly foreshadowed in the Venetians. But this similarity is overlooked because of the great differences in perspective, solidity, and the quality of the colors used by the Venetians and those used by Matisse.

Light is also distorted from its naturalistic effects in the interest of design. When used naturalistically, light accomplishes some degree of modeling and sets off color; but these are only a few of its functions in contributing to great effects in art. In Leonardo, for

14

example, it does much more than this. Its modeling
function is strongly accentuated and the way it falls
upon surfaces is not always in accordance with physical
laws, but is so modified that it makes a pattern cognate
with the general design. It would be manifestly absurd
to accuse Leonardo, one of the most advanced scientists
of his day, of ignorance of the physical laws that govern
the incidence and reflection of light; it is more reasonable to suppose that his distortions of light were used
deliberately, with the esthetic motive of forming a
specific pattern. Both Leonardo and Raphael used
light in the same manner, even to the extent of an
accentuation that disturbs the balance of plastic means.
A better use of light as an independent pattern that
unifies in the total plastic form is found in Piero della
Francesca, in most of the painters of the Venetian
school, in Poussin, and in most of the important
moderns and contemporaries.

Line, light and color are all highly distorted in
El Greco, partly to heighten the effect of religious
mysticism, but mainly to achieve a form of intrinsic
interest which adds to the direct moving power of the
picture without going through the circuit of appeal to
the emotions aroused by religious imagery. Rembrandt's chiaroscuro is distorted light employed for two
distinct and obvious purposes; first, to show an objective
fact, such as the three-dimensional solidity of a head;
second, as a means of giving to a particular arrangement of color and line a specific quality more moving
than that yielded by ordinary illumination. Even in
Velásquez, where the effect of the picture as a whole is
apparently realistic, the realism, like that of Masaccio,
is attained by many departures from exact reproduction, all of which contribute directly to the creation of
a form far more effective than any distribution of

objects literally depicted. In all these painters there is interest in illustration, but the purely plastic interest is also present, though it has not yet appeared in isolation.

The actual process of transition is to be seen in the impressionists, in whose work literal representation is scarcely attempted; the drawing is very broad, and much greater liberties are taken with the actual coloring of objects than in the earlier painters. With the Impressionists it is the mode of presentation and not the object presented that counts. For example, in Manet's *Olympia* (Louvre) it is apparent that the interest lies in the composition and that the story is unimportant. The strangely modeled and proportioned woman placed in just that position and in just those relations with surrounding objects, creates a picture speaking its own language and esthetically more moving than any literally depicted story. This picture represents an advance toward abstract plastic form when compared with, say, Rubens' *Judgment of Paris* (National Gallery, London), in which it would be much easier for the spectator to lose his way in the narrative.

One of the most important practices of the Impressionists, the distortion of perspective, is clearly apparent in the fifteenth century Florentine, Uccello. The Impressionists varied the effect by rendering foreground, middle distance and background as a homogeneous area of light-and-color which serves to unify the composition.

This relative freedom from literary or photographic interest, that is, from the interests which are not plastic, recurs in all the Impressionists. Their very technique, the use of divided color, is itself a departure from literalism, since it replaces a merely imitative rendering of colored surfaces by one in which the colorfulness of objects is more imaginatively realized. In

Monet, the sense of design is less vigorous than in
Manet or in Pissarro, and he sometimes falls victim to
an interest in the effect of sunlight on color, which
interest is more photographic than plastic. But the
greater artists, Renoir and Cézanne, used sunlight
and divided tones only as means to the achievement of a design which is purely plastic. Their forms
are richer, more powerful, more convincing than those
of any of their predecessors in the nineteenth century.
They not only sum up the painters who preceded them
in much the same way as Poussin and Rubens summed
up the painting of the Renaissance, but they created
new forms that stimulated their followers to the creation
of still other and different plastic forms. From impressionism has been developed most of what is best in
contemporary painting. It may be said that in Renoir
and Cézanne, design is more completely realized in
terms of color than in any of the early great painters,
and that this would not have been possible without the
researches of Monet and those who followed him. To
these pioneers is due the credit for forging the instrument by means of which the effects characteristic of
modern art at its best were achieved.

THE TRANSITION TO CONTEMPORARY PAINTING[1]

Albert C. Barnes

In the essay *The Evolution of Plastic Design*[2] is mentioned the fact that the distinctive note in the painting of our own day is the development of interest in design as something comparatively independent of the ostensible subject of the painting. Almost all modern painting of any importance shows the influence of impressionism, especially as that movement was shaped and brought to its consummation by Renoir and Cézanne. In the work of both of these artists, the interest in achieving design primarily through the medium of color is paramount, but the interest in color takes a different form in the two men. Renoir's color is brighter, more sensuously charming, more decorative, and its effects are more varied, in spite of the fact that his palette consisted of nine colors, Cézanne's of seventeen. In Cézanne, color is used more directly in the interest of solidity or mass. But in both artists, color assumes a functional power to effect composition in a degree unexcelled in the history of painting. The emphasis upon color as the most potent of all the instruments of design is thus due chiefly to the researches of these two men.

In the evolution of their techniques, Renoir and Cézanne adopted methods that came, through Manet, from the Venetians, and from Velásquez, Hals, Rubens, Goya and Courbet. Their simplifications and general-

[1] From Albert C. Barnes, *The Art in Painting*, Harcourt, Brace & Co., New York, N. Y., 1937.
[2] See page 192 of present Volume.

izations were achieved principally by the broad brush
strokes that enabled Manet to give the essential quality
of things, stripped of adventitious matter, in a form
that added a new note to the tradition of painting.
The concentration on the essential visible reality, which
was the distinctive contribution of Velásquez, was revived and made a part of the living tradition of the
time, but with the addition of an independent non-
naturalistic design, which also reveals penetratingly the
nature of things. Manet's method of using his brush
had much influence upon Renoir and Cézanne; his
contribution as a whole was in solution in most of the
painting of the time, and it constantly reappears in
the work of subsequent painters. Unfortunately, his
brushwork survives also as an academic cliché, while
his form as a whole is caricatured and commercialized
by numerous portrait-manufacturers.

We have already summed up the details of the advance made by Renoir and Cézanne upon the impressionistic painting which constituted their point of
departure. In their forms, impressionism was further
fertilized by their use of the great traditions of the
past, and, together, Renoir and Cézanne represent the
highest development of plastic expression. Simplification and distortion are more obvious in Cézanne's work
than in Renoir's, and this fact has led to the view, at
present much in vogue among superficial critics, that
Cézanne represents a stage further in advance than
Renoir in the progress toward the goal of a pure art.
Such a view is due partly to an assumption which is
false, and partly to insensitive observation. The assumption is that which has been given currency by the
advocates of cubism and other ultra-modern art-forms,
namely, that pure art involves a complete breach with
reality, that plastic values are totally detached from

human values. We have already seen the falsity of this assumption, and it will be further indicated in the discussion of cubism.[3] The critics' fault in observation is that of failing to see in Renoir a more complex and profound originality than in Cézanne.[4] The obvious surface-characteristics of Cézanne's work lend themselves to detection by academic critics, and imitation by academic painters, more readily than do the complex fundamental characteristics of Renoir. Cézanne's distortions, the simplicity of his compositions, and the comparatively limited effects of his palette—all these are easily seen and mimicked, but are far from explaining his power. Cézanne's greatness depends upon the use of color to achieve his peculiar effects of convincing massiveness, spaciousness and compositional relations. To appreciate these, it is necessary to be able to abstract color and discern its function, its structural and organizing power; alleged appreciation not based upon such discernment is plain illusion and self-deception. But where the ability to grasp such color-values exists, there will also be ability to see in Renoir's paintings greater wealth of color-relationships, based upon the use of an infinite variety of shades and modulations with light. Color-chords in Renoir's canvases are far richer and more numerous than in those of any painter before or since his time. The difference between Renoir and Cézanne is this: Cézanne concentrated his efforts upon a much narrower range of problems; he attained a quite individual strength, but he became something much nearer a specialist than Renoir. The specialist is, of course, more advanced in his particular province than

[3] See Albert C. Barnes, *The Art in Painting*, Harcourt, Brace & Co,. New York, N. Y., 1937.
[4] See Albert C. Barnes and Violette de Mazia, *The Art of Renoir*, pp. 216–221, The Barnes Foundation Press, Merion, Pa., 1944, and also Barnes and de Mazia's essay, *Cézanne and Renoir*, page 301 of present Volume.

a man of broader activities, but he is not therefore more
original. It is true that Cézanne was extraordinarily
original in his own sphere, but Renoir's originality was
the more universal, subtle and inimitable. Critics
desirous of showing Renoir as at a disadvantage compared with Cézanne, point to Cézanne's more numerous
imitators among the painters of the last decade or two,
and assert that he has had more influence upon subsequent artists than Renoir. To any one with the slightest knowledge of history, the fallacy of judging the
fertility of a man's work by its influence on the members of the generation just following his own will be
apparent. The truth is that any profound or far-
reaching originality requires for its understanding and
use more than the very few years that have elapsed
since Renoir's and Cézanne's activities.

The art of painting as it emerges from the hands of
Renoir and Cézanne demonstrates as never before two
all-important principles: first, that of relatively abstract design, embodying the values of human experience but not tied down to a literal reproduction of the
situations in which these values are found in ordinary
life; second, the principle of color as the most essential
of all the plastic elements, the means most entirely
intrinsic to the medium of paint. This latter principle
means, pragmatically, that effects of mass, composition,
space, drawing, are most moving esthetically when
rendered in terms of color. Upon this foundation rests
all that is truly significant and important in contemporary art.

Factors contributing to the development of modern
design are found also in the work of Gauguin and van
Gogh. Other very important sources of inspiration are
Negro sculpture, in the case of Picasso, Modigliani and
Soutine; and the art of Persia, Byzantium, Egypt,

India, China and Japan, in the case of Matisse and his disciples.

In Gauguin, there reappear, with a different effect, the broad areas of color which are to be found in Manet. The areas are broader, more purely decorative, and do not show Manet's characteristic brushwork. In Manet the design is intended much more to render the essential natural quality of what is depicted, while in Gauguin the forms are less expressive and they function more obviously as means to a design which is much more nearly mere pattern. This undoubtedly makes Gauguin a less important artist, but it also made his pictures fertile in suggestions for the painters who followed him. In Gauguin's general exotic quality and in his unusual color-contrasts, there is an anticipation of the color-scheme which is used by Matisse with more subtlety, variety and power. Van Gogh's exaggeration of the Impressionists' spots of color into ribbonlike streaks gives a general animation to the canvas and a brightness to the color itself, in addition to making a specific design in which line reënforces color. In this respect, van Gogh's painting is more literally expressive, less merely decorative, than Gauguin's; but a similar step is taken toward the emphasis upon design, and the decorative motive is also strongly felt. The strikingly unnatural shades of color and the distortions of line and mass are steps in the same direction, and these, together with the other characteristics of van Gogh's work, have been utilized freely by contemporary painters.

Negro sculpture has enriched contemporary painting to a great extent. In the early periods of Greek sculpture, figures were conceived as combinations of back, front and side bas-reliefs. Design was too often encumbered by representation, so that the arrangement of masses—head, trunk and limbs—which would have made the most effective esthetic ensemble, is rarely found. Literature, in other words, stood in the way of plastic form. With Negro sculpture, the literary motive is submerged in the artist's distribution of masses in accord with the requirements of a truly sculptural design. There is no suggestion of bas-relief: the figures are three-dimensional through and through. Freedom from the adventitious or meaningless gives Negro art a sculptural quality purer than that of the majority of the best Greek work or of Renaissance sculpture, which is Greek in another guise. In this respect, Negro sculpture is quite the equal of Egyptian sculpture of the best periods.

Greek and Græco-Roman statues have had an enormous influence on the whole course of painting since the Renaissance, and the pictures in which this influence is most apparent, for example, those of Leonardo and Michelangelo, represent in a double sense a mongrel art. They are imitations, in painting, of another art and this other art is in itself hybrid, a cross between pure sculpture and flat representation. Hence the confusion of values in Leonardo and Michelangelo, and in all who showed the influence of their examples. This confusion was not incompatible with considerable achievement, since Giorgione, Renoir and Cézanne are clearly within the classic Renaissance tradition, but it has unduly limited the range of possible pictorial effects.

Negro art, in exhibiting a form which is in the fullest sense sculptural, has enforced a sharper distinction between the possibilities inherent in painting and sculpture, respectively, and it has also put at the disposal of painting a new source of inspiration. It is not a confusion of values when a painter finds inspiration in another art: the confusion arises when he directly imitates the methods of that art. Michelangelo's stone-like masses and Leonardo's rounded forms are such an imitation, but the use of Negro motifs in the work of Matisse, Modigliani or Soutine is not. The latter do not attempt to re-produce the three-dimensional qualities of Negro statues: what is taken over is rendered in terms proper to painting, and so has nothing of the mongrel quality which is found in the present-day revivals of Renaissance art. Matisse, Modigliani and Soutine avail themselves of the essential feeling, the spirit of Negro art, and give it force in a new setting.

The attempt in painting to use sculptural motifs or suggestions may either be quite unsuccessful, or produce an effect entirely other than that intended, as in cubism. Cubistic pictures, far from possessing the characteristics which the word "cubistic" would properly imply, often tend to go toward the opposite extreme of utter flatness. The great success of Lipchitz in applying the cubistic principles to sculpture suggests that the peculiar type of emphasis upon selected planes, advocated by Picasso, Braque and their followers, is a valid procedure in its proper sphere, however much of a fiasco it has been in painting. When suggestions supplied by sculpture are employed with due consideration for real and fundamental problems of painting, especially with an eye to the possibilities of color, as in the work of Soutine, the result is a very strong plastic form of which nothing in the previous history of painting is an anticipation. The achievement is of epochal importance.

Section II

CONSTRUCTION AND CONTROVERSY

FOREWORD[1]

Albert C. Barnes

There is a view generally prevalent according to which construction and controversy are alternatives, between which on any occasion we are compelled to choose. It is true that what is called "constructive" criticism is usually admitted as allowable, but by this is meant comment on matters of detail, a recommendation of patching and tinkering that leaves essentials untouched. Anything that goes beyond this to advocate drastic alteration, and of course extirpation, of the thing criticized, is condemned as "destructive" and explained as a love of ruin or chaos for its own sake. This seems to us a profoundly mistaken view, and one especially calling for examination. Indeed, we believe that The Barnes Foundation's policy of branding as radically false and pernicious what seems to it such, offers the most hopeful method of eliminating the irrational and antiquated practices so strongly entrenched in influential art and educational circles.

An attempt to bring into existence something essentially new invariably finds the ground on which it must build already occupied. Neither ideas nor material things can grow in a vacuum; from the start they must compete for their right to existence with the ideas or things already in control of the field. Sometimes, but not always, they can be grafted on the old, and when they can a policy of intransigeance is undesirable; when they cannot the only course is a simple struggle for existence. And since everything fights for its life, such a struggle cannot always be kept within the rules of decorum which regulates friendly association between

[1] From *Journal of The Barnes Foundation*, October, 1925.

individuals; but to consider decorum as the first necessity of debate is often to surrender a cause.

This is especially true when existing institutions are firmly established and surrounded by prestige which prevents any impartial examination of their right to exist. The attempt to call in question their validity is then treated as a piece of presumption, or else simply ignored. We all know that deeply-rooted habits do not yield to any merely abstract reasoning. Such reasoning is simply listened to at one moment and forgotten the next; nothing short of a severe shock can secure genuine attention to the matter at issue. An individual, for example, addicted to the excessive use of alcohol, will rarely or never give any real thought to what he is doing until the consequences of it are forcibly impressed upon him by such unmistakable danger-signals as loss of health or employment. Social institutions which owe their fixity largely to habit are in no different case. So long as the success of their workings is not challenged in a manner striking enough to arrest attention, the voice of mere reason beats upon deaf ears.

To attack in terms wholly free from ambiguity may thus be the necessary prelude to any fruitful discussion. Such attacks are frequently said to be "in bad taste." They are in bad taste if they spring from malice, desire for personal aggrandizement or any other motive than desire for the general good. If, however, all discussion that seeks to go to the roots of the matter, which does not assume the essential rightness of what is questioned, is in bad taste, then "good taste" is nothing but a weapon by which vested interests may fight any penetrating analysis of their prestige and privileges.

It is sometimes said that while criticism of institutions is permissible, criticism of persons is objectionable and offensive. Defenders of established institutions, when they invoke this principle, clearly intend its benefits to be confined to themselves: the "subversive" critic must expect "personalities," and usually, indeed, vilification.[2] The principle, however, is in general as paralyzing as anything could be to all serious attempt at betterment of existing conditions. All institutions are directed and utilized by persons, and if they are noxious the fact is apparent in the effect they have on individuals, including the individuals who profit by their operation. This is the ground for the legal maxim, that all guilt is personal. Its practical justification is shown by the ineffectiveness of all lawenforcement, so long as no individual can be made responsible for anti-social acts. It is true that individuals are very largely what institutions make them, and that consequently it is unjust to single out an individual for peculiar condemnation when anyone else, faithfully serving the same system, would have done the same thing in his place. This, however, does not alter the principle that he who holds a position must accept responsibility for whatever the position involves. Criticism is thus illegitimate only if it charges the individual with personal offenses over and above those entailed by his place in the system.

Criticism, however "destructive" in appearance, is

[2] Nothing is more illuminating, to the student of herd-psychology, than the controversial manners of the professional conservative. Bernard Shaw lists, in his *Quintessence of Ibsenism*, some of the expressions applied to Ibsen, his work and his admirers by London dramatic critics in 1891. Among them are: "A gloomy sort of ghoul, bent on groping for horrors in the night," "Morbid, unhealthy, unwholesome and disgusting," "Absolutely loathsome and fetid," "Garbage and offal," "Muck-ferreting dogs." The list might be prolonged indefinitely; it might be paralleled by the epithets applied to Manet and Monet by the French academicians of their day, or, in a different field, by those to which the Abolitionists fell heir in our own country.

15

always legitimate if it offers an alternative to what is criticized, and if it is free from animus. Whoever considers something wholly bad cannot without compromise of his convictions urge less than its total abolition. If that involves saying also that the activities of some individual have, in this respect, no justification for existence, the fact may be unpleasant, but the obligation is no less binding. In the long run, it is not even kindness to the individual to do anything else. The piercing of hollow pretensions is a humanitarian as well as an intellectual duty.

What prevents recognition of the fact is the current belief that no one should be subjected to searching criticism if his intentions are good. No more deplorable superstition could be found. The harm done by ill-intentioned persons is utterly trivial when compared with that done by those whose consciences approve their every act. No one doubts that crime and malice are deplorable and that they ought to be wiped out, but who cares to read a denunciation of criminals? The only anti-social acts which are significant enough to be worth discussing are those of men who are "doing their best," but whose best springs from demonstrably untenable convictions. The militarist, the religious persecutor, the defender of unintelligent subservience to mere custom and authority—these, who are not considered criminals at all, are the real enemies of humanity. Their guilt is shared by all who in the presence of unmistakable evils, take refuge in inertia or invoke prestige to stifle discussion. To refrain from bringing to light the harm done by well-intentioned persons is to resign one's self to futility.

It is in accordance with these principles that the polemics of The Barnes Foundation will be carried on. We shall have no hesitation in calling in question the grounds for anyone's prestige, his exercise of functions for which he is unqualified, or, in general, the value of activities which there is good reason for believing to be pernicious. Such criticism is not necessarily intended to convey any charge of personal corruption or wrong-doing, as these terms are generally understood. We have no interest in individuals except as their influence is a force in education, especially in education in art. When it is such a force, those who exert it should not and cannot expect immunity from a candid appraisement of their activities.

ART TEACHING THAT OBSTRUCTS EDUCATION

WE have been requested by many teachers of art in public and private schools, colleges and art academies throughout America, to make and publish analyses of some of the existing theories and practices with which teachers have been saddled by school authorities. The teachers themselves know how far many of the courses are from conceptions of art or education that could possibly be considered as intelligent; but they are helpless to rid themselves of the incubus so long as custom, unanalyzed prestige and lack of organization among teachers continue to prevail. What most of these courses do is effectually to stifle both self-expression and appreciation of art. The best they can do is to furnish mere formulas for people who paint bad pictures, perpetuate ugliness in the industrial arts, promulgate outworn principles of pedagogy, and thus erect almost insuperable barriers to that development of individual intelligence and the rational enjoyment of life, which are the chief purposes of education. The application of scientific method will be made to various systems which have considerable vogue in the teaching of art in public and private schools.

THE ESTHETICS OF BERNHARD BERENSON[1]

ALBERT C. BARNES

THE most influential contemporary writer on art is probably Mr. Bernhard Berenson; his views embody

[1] Adapted from Albert C. Barnes, *The Art in Painting*, second edition, pp. 414–425, Harcourt, Brace & Co., New York, N. Y., 1928.

most of the characteristics of academicism and irrelevant sentimentalism. His four volumes on the schools of Italian art set forth a theory of painting ostensibly based upon psychological considerations made sufficiently concrete to serve as a guide for judgment. As a specimen of the best kind of psychology and of criticism of plastic art that the academic tradition has produced, his theory will repay attention.

According to Mr. Berenson, the essentially important qualities of paintings are four—tactile values, movement, space-composition, and color, though the last is much the least important. He says that the purpose of art is life-enhancement, that tactile values, that is, modeling which gives the effect of solidity, stimulate our conviction of reality by vividly suggesting the actual feeling of an object, and thus enhance our sense of life. He maintains that the representation of movement causes us to rehearse in ourselves the muscular sensations which would be involved in performing the act or assuming the posture which the picture presents to us. Hence by the successful rendering of movement, or of a posture which invites us to a reposeful muscular state, our vital energies are stimulated. Space-composition, in giving us a vivid sense of the extensity of the world about us, enlarges our personality and makes us feel that we are living more abundantly. In his earlier work, Mr. Berenson dismisses color almost entirely, but in the final summary of his esthetic theory, at the end of his volume on the North Italian painters, he admits having underestimated the value of color, but still allows it only secondary importance. He writes: "Color is less essential (than tactile values, movement and space-composition) in all that distinguishes a master painting from a Persian rug." From all this it follows that painting is at its best when

it renders the human figure, and the additional reason
by which this conclusion is confirmed is interesting.
He says that all appreciation of art, all perception of
natural objects, involves a projection of our feelings
into the things we see, but in figure-painting alone is
this not illusion, since feelings akin to our own do
animate other human beings, but they do not animate
trees, rocks and mountains.   In short, his conceptions
are based upon the always untenable, and now obsolete, theory of *Einfühlung*.   No sound psychology has
ever maintained that in perceiving an object we
necessarily go through a process of internal mimicry
of it, and find it agreeable or disagreeable according
as the movements involved are or are not congenial
to our muscles.   Concerning the theory of *Einfühlung*,
Bosanquet writes: "It has been supposed that when we
take pleasure in a graceful curve, our eye is executing
this same curve, 'that we feel pleasure in this movement, or in the ease of it, and turn this pleasure into a
quality of the object whose outlines we follow.'   Well,
it simply is not so. The eye in following a curve moves
with jerks and in straight lines. 'The muscles of the
eye are mere scene-shifters.'"[2]

If the theory offered by Mr. Berenson were true,
any distortion of the human figure would invite us to
attempt to make movements or to put ourselves in pos-
tures which our bodies could not possibly accomplish,
and the effect would be objectionable to us.   We would
scarcely find pleasant our attempts to mimic the uncomfortable position of the nude in Manet's *Olympia*
(Louvre) or the contortions depicted in the best work of
El Greco.   His theory rests on the misconception that
art is essentially photography, and in this case, a kind
of muscular photography.   Incidentally, it may be

[2] *Three Lectures on Aesthetics*, page 24, Macmillan and Co., Ltd.,
London, 1915.

remarked that the whole theory of Berenson is adopted by Professor H. S. Langfeld, in a book which shows on nearly every page a total lack of real esthetic experience. It makes of art something completely comprehensible to a person who has had no personal or immediate contact with actual works of art.

In his explanation of "tactile values" Mr. Berenson exceeds the ordinary limits of sophistry. His emphasis of the fact that suggestions of touch give a note of conviction to our visual perception of an object, is only an elaboration of the platitude that the word "tangible" is a synonym for "real." It is undeniable that effects of solidity in a painting may add to the reality of an object, and so represent one of the innumerable ways in which our natural powers may be called into play by a work of art. But they have no such primary or unique importance as Mr. Berenson ascribes to them. To give them that importance is to fall back on the imitative theory of art and throw to the winds all considerations of design. For example, in the work of Claude, tactile values are very imperfectly rendered, though with no damage to esthetic value, since it is not by touch that we grasp the essential quality of landscape. Mr. Berenson's theory logically binds him to accept as great masterpieces the countless academic paintings in which tactile values are violently over-accentuated by painters who are merely skillful imitators. He shows that he fails to grasp the importance of the specific medium of an art and would make of painting something that could be at best inferior imitation of sculpture.[3]

[3] "The illustrator who communicates ideated sensations which compel us to identify ourselves with such virility, with such proud insensibility, with such energy and endurance, is an artist indeed." *The North Italian Painters of the Renaissance*, p. 60. He is speaking of Cosimo Tura. Our intention is not to contest his estimate of that particular painter, but his reasons for it.

In the light of theories so patently absurd, it is easy
to understand his overestimation of Florentine painting as compared with Venetian, as evidenced by the
very singular statement about Rubens: "In every other
respect (than technique), he was an Italian: and, *after
Michelangelo, to say Italian was practically to say
Florentine*."[4] Rubens was assuredly much more Venetian than Florentine. Mr. Berenson's confusion of the
values of painting with those of sculpture leads him to
overlook altogether the plastic values that make up the
real greatness of the painters of the Italian Renaissance.

By his emphasis upon space-composition, Mr. Berenson reduces relatively flat painting to mere pattern,
since his conception implies that composition in the
ordinary sense of the word, is relegated to a status
outside the formal character of a picture. Light, except as an aid to modeling, is never mentioned, yet
light as a pattern in itself and as a means of organizing a painting, was constantly used by the great Italians.

One of the gravest faults in Mr. Berenson's writings is his neglect of color. He regards it essentially
as only a means of embellishing surface. Its structural and organic values are never hinted at, either explicitly or by implication, yet color is the plastic element on which the most important achievements of the
artist depend. How important color is, has been indicated in our chapters[5] on Color, on Giotto, Piero della
Francesca, the Venetians, Rubens, Rembrandt, El
Greco, Velásquez, Renoir and Cézanne. It can hardly
be questioned that a sense of color is the one thing

---

[4] Italics ours.
[5] See Albert C. Barnes, *The Art in Painting*, Harcourt, Brace &
Co., New York, N. Y., 1937.

which no painter of the first rank has ever lacked. It is not without significance that Mr. Berenson's volume on Venetian painting is almost entirely an account of the social and political conditions of the time, and of the literary qualities of the painters discussed. In the conclusion to his volume on North Italian painting he recognizes the need of amplifying his account of color, but he has made no move to do so in the nearly eighteen years since the book was written. It is evident that he has said substantially nothing about color, because his essentially academic theory has blinded him to what, more than any other element, characterizes painting as an art. Such are the consequences of thinking of painting in terms of sculpture.

Mr. Berenson's mechanical standards, and his reliance upon irrelevant sentimentalities in the judgment of paintings, are due primarily to his fundamental classification of the qualities in plastic art under two heads, illustration and decoration. Decoration he defines as "all those elements in a work of art which appeal directly to the senses, such as color and tone; or directly stimulate ideated sensations, such as, for instance, Form and Movement." By illustration he means "everything which in a work of art appeals to us, not for any intrinsic quality, as of color or form or composition, contained in the work of art itself, but for the value the thing represented has elsewhere." He claims that in any given work of art these qualities vary quite independently of one another and he cites Raphael as great in illustration and, except as regards space-composition, comparatively inferior in decorative power; in Masaccio, he implies, the contrary is the case.

Such a classification represents the very essence of academicism, in that it assigns the values of a single organic whole to two separate and unrelated compartments. It omits the fundamental principle of art, the adjustment of form to expression, that is, of integration of the values of what is represented in properly plastic terms. He praises Raphael for the range and power of his imagination in reproducing classic and religious themes; but if we apply strictly Mr. Berenson's definition of illustration, that "it appeals to us for the value the thing has elsewhere (than in the painting)," then this representation of the themes of antiquity has *no* value, for painting. His definition of decoration, as the "intrinsic" appeal of a work of art, apart from all interpretations of its subject, implies that a picture is a combination of what is meaningless with what is irrelevant.

Mr. Berenson's reasoning ignores the facts that the form of a picture is always an embodiment of what the artist finds essential in some part of the real world, and that it is the distinction of the greatest artists that they give us what is essential and not what is adventitious; but there is no means of making a distinction between what is essential and what is adventitious unless we have in mind the object or situation represented. The artist gives us what is essential in plastic terms. Hence to judge his form we must have a clear grasp of the medium of painting, so that we can say whether or not it has been fully utilized—whether or not there has been overaccentuation or undue reliance upon any one plastic element. Art is expression, and the expression is always *of* something, and *by* means appropriate to the particular art in question. Mr. Berenson's isolation of these two aspects into separate compartments represents not an art judgment but the common human weakness that seeks to avoid a personal reaction in which we are ourselves obliged to go through the process of creative interpretation which resulted in the original experience of the artist. Psychologically, it is akin to that form of academicism in ethics that tries to judge a moral act in abstraction from the two essentials, the individual and the consequences.

In contrast to Mr. Berenson's implied view, we are contending that to appreciate a work of art, or any other manifestation of human instinct acting intelligently, we are obliged to put ourselves into the situation out of which the work of art sprang, and reproduce the artist's vision of it. This is a difficulty from which the academician shrinks; hence he resorts to the easy mechanical classifications. The shrinking takes the form of judging the factors or aspects in isolation, not as elements in an organic whole. It divides form from expression, just as it divides composition from color, and color from modeling, and in consequence it cannot judge any of them esthetically. It is only when we have seen what grasp of the world the artist is undertaking to set forth that we can say whether his work is important as an embodiment of human values, or whether he has succeeded in integrating the plastic means to make an intrinsically moving plastic form.

This criterion exposes the falsity of Mr. Berenson's estimate of Raphael's greatness even from the point of view of illustration. He writes: "The central Italian painters were not only among the profoundest and grandest, but among the most pleasing and winning illustrators that we Europeans have ever had." On the contrary, the cheapness of Raphael's means is reflected in the melodramatic character of his scenes, the softness and sweetness of his personages, the exaggeration of his spatial effects. His classic themes become mere suaveness, his religious themes, sugariness, when contrasted with similar themes rendered with the power of Michelangelo, the dignity of Giotto, the other-worldliness of El Greco. Any deficiency in the ability to achieve plastic embodiment results in a loss of human values in subject-matter; examples of this are found in Delacroix, Böcklin and Millet. In Giorgione, Titian, Rembrandt or Renoir, great plastic genius is expressed in forms which are deeply impregnated with human values, and these human values determine the proportion in which the plastic means are used, so that the forms cannot be appreciated or judged unless we retain our contact with what is expressed.

Mr. Berenson's classification entirely overlooks the important factor of decoration as it really exists in paintings. There is a general decorative texture in Paolo Veronese, in Rubens, in the Eighteenth Century French painters and in Renoir, which constitutes an important ingredient of the esthetic effect, but which is not particularly expressive of the essential character of the individual thing portrayed. When we say that Cézanne is stronger than Renoir, but that in Renoir there is a greater wealth of charm, we mean that in Renoir there is present much of this decorative element that is relatively absent in Cézanne. That distinction is unintelligible according to Berenson's principles, since both painters have the intrinsic values which he lumps together under the head of "decoration." Nor indeed do his principles permit of any appreciation of either Renoir or Cézanne, because both of those artists can be understood only by realizing that they, like Giorgione and Titian, and indeed like Giotto, achieve their effects chiefly through the organizing power of color. To that fundamental principle he never even refers, and the long series of his judgments shows that he has never in any degree understood or felt the force of it.

Mr. Berenson's work deals not with the objective facts that enter into an appreciation of art-values, but with a form of antiquarianism made up of historical, social and sentimental interests entirely adventitious to plastic art. It would be unworthy of serious attention except for the regrettable influence his writings have had in filling our universities with bad teaching on art and our public galleries with bad Italian paintings. The courses in art at practically all the universities and colleges in America are based upon the obsolete psychology, the unscientific method of approach, that make it impossible for students to obtain either a grasp of esthetic essentials or a real and personal experience with works of art. The instruction offered at such institutions is a mixture of spurious sentiment and historical data, elaborated into a system that has no relevancy to either the plastic values in painting or the principles of scientific education. Even worse is the fact that this deplorable tradition is given currency among the general public by books such as Professor Langfeld's and Professor Mather's, which offer in the name of public education in art something which has nothing to do with art or with education. This academic instruction, given both in the classroom and in popular books, is largely responsible for the confusion of values which has made the public the victim of sentimentalists and antiquarians who breathe with religious awe the names of great painters whose work they never understood.

Mr. Berenson has aided materially in the identification of the works of some of the early Italian painters by means of investigations that are primarily and fundamentally akin to those of handwriting-experts. In-

teresting as that work has been in itself, it has yielded
no data relevant to an appreciation of the values that
make paintings works of art. Indeed, the principal
effects of the activities of handwriting-experts in the
field of art have been bad ones. They have resur-
rected the names of a number of early, and very bad,
Italian painters whose work the picture-dealers sell
accompanied by an expert's certificate of authenticity;
in other words, antiquity, not esthetic merit, has become the guide in a traffic in the kind of pictures which
George Moore calls "cock-eyed saints painted on gold
backgrounds." The host of bad paintings in the public
galleries of Boston, Cleveland, Philadelphia, Detroit
and other cities, and especially in the Johnson Collection in Philadelphia, show the sad results of the expert-
dealer-author-university method of propagating counterfeit thinking and counterfeit art.

The especially lamentable feature of the whole system is that the fetish-worship is so entrenched and
buttressed by prestige that it is a waste of time to
suggest that a more rational method of studying art
be employed. Recently, we made a first-hand study of
the facilities, the personnel, the equipment, and the
practical results upon the students, in the department
of art in one of the largest and best-known American
colleges, whose courses are founded upon the kind of
psychology and educational practices above analyzed.
The revelations of the study were so representative of
intellectual and educational disorder, of such widespread social and economic significance, that my col-
league, Mr. Laurence Buermeyer, described the incident in his book, *The Aesthetic Experience.*[6] On
page 169 of that book Mr. Buermeyer writes: "Recently one of the American colleges applied for an

[6] The Barnes Foundation Press, Merion, Pa., 1929.

opportunity to provide its students with first-hand acquaintance with a very large and representative collection of works of plastic art. The collection, in range and quality, was without parallel in America; its owner, however, considered that it could be fruitfully studied only by those possessing an intelligent conception of human nature and of aesthetic principles. Compliance with the request was therefore accompanied by the condition that the college should coöperate to provide such a background; the coöperation involved, on the college's part, no more than a statement of the instruction already given, a statement sufficiently detailed to make possible a plan for such supplementation as might seem necessary. The college itself was not asked to provide the additional instruction, which would have been furnished as a part of the collection's resources, nor was it asked to modify in any way its existing courses in art. Nevertheless, the information sought was refused, apparently on the ground that to give it would have involved an admission that the instruction already offered might not be all-sufficient. Thus are daydreams sheltered from the destructive action of facts.

"The incident is striking because of the extraordinary contrast it presents between profession and actual practice, between the intelligent open-mindedness which may reasonably be expected of an institution devoted to the advancement of learning and education, and the somnambulistic adherence to precedent actually displayed. But it is not unique. It is a symptom of the intrenchment of vested interest and unchangeable habits which are as destructive to art as they are to life in general."

THE ESTHETICS OF FRANK JEWETT MATHER[1]

ALBERT C. BARNES

MR MATHER's reputation in the art-world depends essentially upon his activities in tracing the attribution of obscure Italian paintings. How far that criterion fell short of adequacy for the position he held as Professor of Fine Arts at Princeton University is revealed in his *History of Italian Painting*. A review of that book in the light of modern thinking and experience shows that it represents but another example of the obsolete psychology and unscientific method of approach operative in the courses in art in most of the American universities and colleges.

His book is composed almost entirely of biography, literary criticism, irrelevant rhapsodical effusions and sentimentalizings. There is a slender thread of reference to plastic qualities running through it, but the conceptions and standards revealed are banal in the highest degree. There is no attempt to set forth a coherent esthetic theory, either in general or as applied to painting. Such judgments as do appear reflect an utterly stereotyped academic theory of design which assumes that every painter is trying, or should try, to do the same things. In color, in composition, in drawing, in modeling, Mr. Mather assumes that there is one right way, and only one. In the whole book there is no indication that he recognizes the esthetic significance of any of these plastic means; indeed, his statements about drawing, color, composition, space, convey no meaning that would enable a student to grasp a conception either of plastic form in

[1] Adapted from Albert C. Barnes, *The Art in Painting*, second edition, pp. 412–413, Harcourt, Brace & Co., New York, N. Y., 1928.

general or the particular form that makes an individual
an artist as distinguished from a mere practitioner of
technical tricks. This initial blunder, by making design a fixed formula, eliminates personal expressiveness, and with it all true art.

No better example of the fact could be found than
in the treatment of Piero della Francesca, who is castigated for the undramatic quality of his work. Of
him, Mr. Mather writes: "His figures are finely constructed and beautifully placed, but emotionally unrelated. They merely exist rather splendidly, as do
some of Manet's figures. Indeed, the warning of
George Moore as regards Manet applies equally to
Piero. It is futile to seek from him anything but fine
painting." In saying that Piero's figures are "emotionally unrelated," he can only mean that they do not
convincingly suggest any narrative that would stimulate the sentimental rhapsodies with which the book is
surcharged in lieu of criticism of plastic qualities. In
the same discussion, we find it said that Piero sacri-
ficed color to atmosphere — a statement which shows
that Mr. Mather utterly lacks eyes to see that Piero's
silvery blue is differentiated into a wealth of tints
which form a rich series of subtle harmonies that
organize the paintings by means of color. The slightest grasp of the principles of design would have showed
Mr. Mather that Piero's coolness, the static quality
of his line, his subdued color, are parts of an essentially
detached, impersonal, yet individual design in which
drama would be as out of place as would the strongly
accentuated rhythms of Beethoven's *Fifth Symphony*
in Debussy's *Prelude to the Afternoon of a Faun*.

It is apparent that Mr. Mather has no conception
of plastic design as anything apart from narrative or
sentimental coherence. In commenting on a picture by
Masaccio, he condemns as an after-thought two fig-

ures absolutely essential to the composition, the rhythmic unity of the picture; what is true of these two
figures is that they have no part in the story. In
Giotto, he uniformly prefers the triter, less significant
compositional arrangement of masses to the more original and powerful; although he sees the sensuous charm
of Giotto's color, he is utterly oblivious to its really
multitudinous plastic functions, including that of tying
together the composition. In illustrating Giotto's development with age (really a retrogression in originality and the forceful use of plastic means) Mr. Mather
contrasts the ignobility of expression depicted in the
faces of some Mohammedans in an early painting, with
the nobility with which they are characterized in a later
treatment of the same subject. This greater magnanimity to an enemy is taken as an indication of
Giotto's growth in artistry.

In many instances, not even perfunctory attention
is paid to plastic considerations. For example, an important element in Fra Filippo Lippi's design, in which
he anticipated many of the latest developments in
painting, is the non-naturalistic portrayal of perspective. In this the background, rendered with abundance of clear-cut detail, is made to appear as a screen,
rising to the top of the canvas. The striking contrast,
combined with perfect harmony, between the figures
in the foreground and this background, is probably
Fra Filippo Lippi's most characteristic plastic achievement: it is due to his use of color, light and rhythmic
line. Mr. Mather, ignoring this pictorially significant
aspect of Fra Filippo Lippi's work, tells us that he was
"the first Italian painter to care greatly for the look
of everyday people," that he caused the art of Florence
for two generations to be "boyish and girlish." Of a
particular painting he says: "The picture gets its pe-

culiar sweetness from the gentle, girlish figure of the Maiden Mother, its quality of romance from the ledgy background watered by springs and spangled with modest flowers, its tang of reality from the chubby and stolid Christ-child and the boyish St. John the Baptist. You could almost see such a thing today along the shaded upper Mensola when a young Florentine mother has taken the children for a Sunday picnic." This is what passes for a scholarly analysis of plastic art.

But it is only when we reach a subject that lends itself to more rhapsodic treatment that Mr. Mather's discussion attains its most characteristic form. No single picture in all painting, perhaps, yields a richer harvest to the critic of plastic art than Giorgione's *Concert in the Open Air* (Louvre). In it we see color of the utmost sensuous richness used to build up volumes, create space and atmosphere, and hold the picture together; masses arranged in deep space in a complex composition which is completely unstereotyped and yet perfectly unified; line which is rhythmic, sensitive, expressive but never melodramatic; light and shadow employed to vivify color, lend conviction to perspective and glow to atmosphere, and to enrich the general form with a wealth of secondary but harmonious designs. Of all this utilization of plastic means to achieve a powerful design Mr. Mather says nothing; what he does say is: "My own reading is merely based on the contrast between the rustic and urban lovers, and an intuition that the courtier in peering so wistfully at the shepherd is merely seeing himself in a former guise. In lassitude, perhaps in satiety, beside a courtly mistress who is absent from him in spirit, there rises a vision of earlier simpler love and of a devoted shepherdess who once piped for him in the shade. The vision rises as his listless hand sweeps the lute strings in a chord unmarked by the far lovelier mistress at the fountain. The golden age of love, like Arcady itself, is ever in the past."

It is evident that literature, tempered with archaeology, absorbs the interest of Mr. Mather and prompts him to emulate, if not imitate, the rhetorical irrelevancies usually associated with Walter Pater's style in writing about paintings. As a compendium of biographical and historical facts his book is informative, and as a set of exercises in rhetoric it is entertaining for those who like sentimentality. But as an introduction to the study of plastic art it is worse than useless. It distracts attention from what is significant, and encourages the student of painting in the most pernicious of errors—that of confusing an emotional orgy with intelligent esthetic insight. It is merely another means of perpetuating the confusion of values; it has nothing to do with art and is fatal to education.

THE ESTHETICS OF ROGER FRY[1]

Laurence Buermeyer

In the greater part of even the best contemporary writing on art and on esthetics, there is an obvious defect. Either the writer's grasp of fundamental principles of psychology and logical method is unaccompanied by any first-hand experience of art itself; or his esthetic perceptions, vivid enough so far as they go, are not illuminated by any profound understanding of the source of all perceptions—human nature. The union of general understanding and specific

[1] Adapted from Laurence Buermeyer, *Some Popular Fallacies in Aesthetics*, The Dial, February, 1924.

sensitiveness, which alone can yield pregnant insight, is impossible in anyone who is not at the same time a psychologist and a connoisseur.

No better illustration of this fact can be found than the critical writings of Mr. Roger Fry. It is impossible to deny that Mr. Fry is one of the most acute of present-day observers of painting; he possesses also a certain fund of psychological information; but the psychology is largely popular psychology, a set of half-truths superficially understood. They constantly come between him and the direct experience of plastic art to which his natural sensitiveness would entitle him, and which a juster understanding of general principles would make accessible to him.

To see the influence of Mr. Fry's psychology upon his esthetics, it is necessary to consider at some length his exposition of both. They are set forth most systematically in his book, *Vision and Design*, in the chapters, *An Essay in Aesthetics* and *Retrospect*.

Art is not an imitation of nature. Its true nature can only be understood if we draw a distinction between the active and the imaginative life. We are conscious in both of a world of objects, but it is only in the active life that we are obliged to, or in fact *can*, do anything about them. In this realm the things of which we are aware contain a promise or a threat, they are the signals of events to come, events which we may wish to promote or to prevent. To this function as signal or guide, however, many of the qualities of things are irrelevant. If the letters on a sign-board directing us to our destination are clear, we need not inquire about the board's shape, size, age or material. Such features are ordinarily overlooked; and so in general the world of practice is an abridged and abstracted world. In the life of imagination, however, there are no practical exigencies, and we are at liberty to contemplate objects in their concrete fullness. To embody in permanent form the world thus contemplated for its own sake is the purpose of art.

Similarly, actual objects occasion emotions, but the intensity and urgency of these emotions prevent us from giving them detailed attention. We speak of being "overwhelmed with astonishment," "stunned with grief," "convulsed with anger." In imaginative life emotions are called forth in a weaker form and because of our relatively greater composure and self-possession we are able deliberately to exploit them. Such clearly observed and enjoyed emotion, together with the object that arouses it, forms the content of a work of art and represents the consummation of the imaginative life. That the determining factor in the release of imagination is the absence of practical activity is shown by the fact that children, in whom the practical motive has not yet developed, tend to draw objects, not from nature, but in harmony with their own story-telling proclivities.

To perform its function properly, an object must have unity and variety. Unity, to give the maximum of clarity in presentation; variety, to secure the maximum of stimulation, to lend all the interest possible. But since objects in nature may have these qualities, a work of art must also display the evidences of purpose, must indicate the feelings, the intentions of a conscious contriver. The sense of mutual understanding between the artist and the observer of his work is an essential part of the esthetic experience.

An object is beautiful, in other words, when it is a purposeful synthesis of varied parts. But beauty has a wider and a narrower sense. An object is beautiful in the narrower sense when it satisfies the conditions of unity and variety. To be beautiful in the wider sense it must arouse the emotions, and do so in purposeful and orderly fashion. If the accomplishment of this involves the sacrifice of conventional beauty in the object represented (as in Rembrandt and Degas) the sacrifice does not impair the esthetic value of the picture.

"Order" (unity), in so far as it promotes clarity of perception, consists merely of the balancing of the parts of a picture about a center line, which causes the eye to remain within the frame of the canvas. It effects such a presentation of the parts as to secure that each shall have a fundamentally harmonious relation with every other. This form of unity, with its correlative variety, is termed "sensuous," and with it must be combined emotional order and variety. These are secured by what may be called the emotional elements of design. They are, first, linear rhythm of contour; second, mass or inertia; third, spatial magnitude; fourth, light and shadow; fifth, color; and, a possible sixth, inclination of planes towards or away from the spectator.

All these qualities, with the possible exception of color, are characteristics of importance in real things, whence their emotional excitingness. They are, however, not particularly moving in isolation: it is their combination that lends force to them. This fact may provoke the objection that since the combination of them is formed in nature, art is imitation of nature after all, to which the answer is that in nature the union of qualities is not such as to realize the maximum of effectiveness. This is to be had only in the artist's combination of them.

To sum up the relation of art to nature: there are to

be found in nature at least occasional examples of fitness for the disinterested contemplation character- istic of art, but there is not the added consciousness of purpose that is involved in the esthetic experience at its fullest. The elements and some of the com- binations found in nature are legitimate raw material for the artist, but his reorganization of them may depart from natural patterns in any degree that his purpose may dictate.

So far this outline has followed the first of the two essays above alluded to. Mr. Fry's later views are embodied in the chapter *Retrospect* in which he makes some modifications of his theory. In the earlier view, it is assumed that the emotional response elicited by a picture depends upon the elements reproduced, whether literally or not, from the real world. Con- siderations urged by Clive Bell lead to the conclusion that what is called "significant form" is something over and above all represented material, something which may, none the less, arouse a genuine emotion. This, according to Bell, is the only truly esthetic experience. From the point of view of art, all else is adventitious. The view leads, logically, to the justification of paint- ing completely non-representative. Mr. Fry shrinks from this conclusion, since he is not prepared to dis- pense with representation of the third dimension; he is willing to admit, however, a pleasure in form, in arrangement of line, color and mass, quite apart from any pleasure in the thing represented. The question thereupon naturally arises: Does pleasure in the thing represented heighten the purely esthetic pleasure, or is it irrelevant? The latter view seems the more prob- able, but the issue remains in doubt, and the definition of significant form which avoids passing definite judgment is that significant form "implies the effort on the part of the artist to bend to our understanding some intractable material which is alien to our spirit."

The foregoing is, in brief, Mr. Fry's argument. Its dependence at every point upon Mr. Fry's psychological assumptions is obvious. Since art is *not* imitation, Mr. Fry assumes that it cannot be defined with reference to the object represented; hence a psychological definition is necessary. This is found, first, in "imagination," regarded as release from practice; second, in exploitation of a rather subdued and detached emotion; finally, in conscious intent to transmit imaginative vision and emotion to others. In its later development, the theory is complicated by the conception of "significant form," which Mr. Fry cannot make up his mind wholly to accept or wholly to reject. The conception, however, sharpens the distinction drawn between "sensuous unity and variety" and "the emotional elements of design," and leads Mr. Fry to lean to the former as the chief constituent in esthetic value.

It is not difficult to show that Mr. Fry's psychological principles are superficial, and that their net result is to lead him into the confusion between pattern and plastic form of which we have seen Clive Bell to be so conspicuous a victim.[2] In each of the cardinal points of his theory, in his view of imagination, of emotion, and of the nature of form, Mr. Fry goes astray in essential particulars.

Imagination, according to Mr. Fry, comes into being when practical response to a situation is absent. Such absence may be a necessary condition, but certainly it

---

[2] See Laurence Buermeyer's essay, *Pattern and Plastic Form*, page 123 of present Volume.

is not a sufficient condition. Recent investigation in psychology has made clear the immense part played in life by what is called "daydreaming," *i. e.*, the gratification of real wishes by imagined satisfactions. Daydreaming may go on in entire isolation from realities, or it may attach itself to them: we may picture ourselves as wealthy, powerful and famous in a purely imaginary world, or we may imagine the material things about us to be our property, turned to our purpose, made an instrument in our self-display. Such fancies involve a different sort of observation from that required in practical purposes: they arouse emotions which do not compromise us by their effects and which may be enjoyed for their own sake; they are, however, not an excursion into the realm of art, but a degraded form of practical self-indulgence. They constitute the resources of those too feeble to dominate the world, practically, intellectually or esthetically. They can be had without effort and the end of them comes not with any real consummation but with boredom. Esthetic imagination involves effort both in the artist and the spectator. It is active, not passive. Unfortunately, Mr. Fry's illustration of the child drawing things, not as they are, but as his fancy moulds them, actually suggests that what he has in mind is not esthetic imagination, but daydreaming. A child's fancies, as is well known to all who have made accurate observations upon children, are usually most practical in type, even when they serve no practical end. They relate almost wholly to the uses to which things can be put. A chair is something to sit in, a knife is something to cut with, and so on. Ability to conceive an object in terms of its structure or appearance comes much later: it is an accomplishment, not a spontaneous disposition.

Confusion such as this is particularly regrettable in an introduction to esthetic theory, since so much of what passes for art, pictorial as well as literary, is a commodity manufactured for the consumption of day-dreamers. The melodrama—and most novels and plays, not to speak of moving pictures, answer to this description—is flagrantly constructed to this end: its sharp moral classifications, its invariable assurance of triumph to the characters embodying the conventional virtues, invite identification with the "hero" of the piece and enjoyment of the hero's glories. It is no less obvious that the paintings of pretty girls and agreeable domestic scenes, which the public overwhelmingly prefers, are equally invitations to daydreaming. To say this is not, of course, to suggest that Mr. Fry confuses magazine-illustrations with works of art, but certainly his definition of imagination gives him no grounds for making a distinction.

The looseness of definition which facilitates the confusion has an important and disadvantageous effect upon the rest of Mr. Fry's theory. Since all preoccupation with objects not dominated by practice is regarded by him as imagination, and yet not all of it, clearly, falls within the sphere of art, something more is required. This something is the intention to communicate the emotions which imagined objects arouse. Nature, we are told, though it may be pleasing to our sensibilities, falls short of art because it expresses no purpose to please us. What is not intended to be beautiful is not really beautiful, since we cannot feel it to be the vehicle of a message from a spirit akin to our own. That art is always the bearer of a message, the *intentional* stimulus to an emotion, is the truth which Mr. Fry says Tolstoy taught him. The consequences of this view are surprising. If it is true, a landscape is beautiful if one believes in a God, the creator and architect of nature, but less so, or not at all, if one does not. A face is made more definitely the object of esthetic appreciation by the application of cosmetics.

To discover the error involved, we must examine more closely the statement that art seeks to communicate emotion by expressing it. Mr. Fry gives an illustration, taken from Tolstoy:

"Let us suppose a boy to have been pursued in the forest by a bear. If he returns to the village and merely states that he was pursued by a bear and escaped, that is ordinary language, the means of communicating facts or ideas; but if he describes his state first of heedlessness, then of sudden alarm and terror as the bear appears, and finally of relief when he gets away, and describes this so that his hearers share his emotions, then his description is a work of art. Now so far as the boy does this in order to persuade the villagers to go out and kill the bear, though he may be using artistic methods, his speech is not a pure work of art; but if of a winter evening the boy relates his experiences for the sake of enjoyment of his adventure in retrospect, or, better still, if he makes up the whole story for the sake of the imagined emotions, then his speech becomes a pure work of art."

A few general remarks about the nature of emotion will serve as preface to the criticism to be made of this passage. The expression of emotion is always, originally, a motor reaction. When angry, we may turn red and strike a blow; when afraid, turn pale and take to flight. Others, not directly affected by the original stimulus, may be contagiously affected by our emotion. Bystanders at a quarrel grow tense and irritable, and a cry of fear only too often starts a panic. The expression of an emotion thus does communicate the emotion; but it does so because the movements made by the angry or frightened person directly induce anger or fright in the spectator. Art is an expression of emotion, however, with a difference so considerable as to constitute a difference in kind. It seeks to do what no simple and ingenuous emotion ever does, *viz.*, reproduce the object which excited it. A man who has been insulted and is angry does not seek further affronts, nor does one in fear intentionally run additional risks. The purpose of the acts to which these emotions give rise is to rectify, change, put away or destroy the objects to which they refer. Only when an emotion is transformed under the influence of the esthetic interest does it attempt to re-create the situation that brought it into being. It may then perform the function of communication, but in a way diametrically opposed to the direct transmission of ordinary emotion. It directs the spectator's attention to its exciting cause instead of moving him by its outward expression, by exclamations and gestures. The example of the boy and the bear precisely inverts the true order of things. To make such a story effective a true artist would describe, not his feelings, his sensations of goose-flesh, dryness in the mouth, quick and shallow breathing, and so on, but the suddenness of the pursuer's approach, his menacing aspect, the swiftness of his advance, obstacles to flight, visions of teeth and claws and flowing blood. Even if a described emotion conjures up appropriate images and thus provides the listener with a concrete image, it is not *the* picture in the narrator's mind: communication has failed; the story-teller has not objectified his emotion or created an individual object. The emotion may be transferred, but it is not communicated.

The point has been discussed in detail because the

separation of emotion from the object that excites it, and the transmission of the emotion to others, are so essential to Mr. Fry's conception of the purpose and content of art. At the bottom of his conception lies the assumption, already criticized, that the imaginative life, defined as consciousness of objects without practical responsibility, provides the material of art. Over and above this material, there must then be a purpose which, because the imaginative life is not in itself enough, is always to communicate an emotion. As against this view, with the difficulties we have seen it to involve, an alternative may be suggested. Not all play of fancy, not all non-practical observation of things, is "imagination," in the sense in which imagination is the basis of art. Only when we single out and observe things for the sake of their appeal to a specific interest, an interest which is directed to insight into the things represented, in terms of the medium of the art in question, do the things observed really form the subject-matter of art. This esthetic aspect of things is ordinarily overlaid by qualities which have practical importance, but such qualities do not recede in our attention merely because they are at a particular instant unimportant. Our habit of conceiving things in terms of the uses to which they may be put dominates us as a rule even when we enjoy a respite from the need to be up and doing. To conceive, to see, the world from a detached and spectatorial point of view is itself a definite habit, involving a continuous readjustment of other habits, a fact which explains the expenditure of energy required for genuinely esthetic contemplation. This is true when we are contemplating either nature or works of art.

What is needed, in addition to this persistent and active interest in the esthetically appealing aspects of experience, to make the artist? Not, as Mr. Fry suggests, primarily a purpose to communicate with our fellows, to share an emotion. It is only by a figure of speech that we can talk of the emotion as anything in a work of art additional to the work's content. The emotion is present only in what is portrayed, in the selection of detail and form of organization; thus, and only thus, can a picture be said to embody emotion or purpose. And communication seems rather a collateral result than the primary purpose of the artist. Art, if this is true, is less a message than a revelation: a revelation primarily *to* the artist, and only secondarily *by* the artist, of the beauty actually or potentially in things. What essentially distinguishes the artist is not ability to make himself intelligible to others—this is the definition of craftsmanship—but the ability to see more clearly and profoundly than the average man the esthetic possibilities of the world about him. These possibilities may not be realized in actually existing particular things, and their revelation may consequently compel modification or distortion of the actual; but the purpose of the modification is not, as Mr. Fry asserts, to leave the stamp of humanity, of a spirit kindred to the observer's, upon the work; it is to make a more adequate revelation. It is true, doubtless, that we enjoy finding a kindred spirit in the artist, but the enjoyment in appreciation of art at its best may be less that of recognizing likeness than of recognizing unlikeness, less a discovery of ourselves in another than expansion of our own mind through the profounder vision of another's. "The light that never was on sea or land" is not an infra-red or ultra-violet ray, hitherto inaccessible to human vision. It is the light of our familiar world which we had seen only through a glass darkly, but which the artist has made us see face to face. It is this transformation of nature which supplies what justification there is for Mr. Fry's sharp distinction between the beauty of art and the beauty of nature.

The case seems precisely similar to that of the scientist. He also has a purpose, he creates something, and he communicates something. But his purpose is revealed in the content of science, his creation is at the same time a discovery, and his communication is secondary and incidental.

In his treatment of form, Mr. Fry falls into errors no less serious. In his separation of the "sensuous" and the "emotional" elements of design, he appears to be on the track of the legitimate distinction between decorative pattern and the structural or expressive form in which an artist expresses his personal and penetrating vision of the essences of things. But there is no reason for limiting pattern to composition, to the exclusion of line, light and color, and Mr. Fry's uncertain hold on the distinction in question is evident from the fact that he so readily succumbs to Clive Bell's reduction of all form to pattern. Although Mr. Fry does not explicitly take sides with Clive Bell on this point, his essential agreement appears in his treatment of Seurat in *The Dial* of September, 1926, and of Cézanne in *The New Republic* of August 5, 1925.

His comments on Cézanne refer almost exclusively to the pattern to be found in Cézanne's paintings. He notes the dignity, the reserve, the austerity, to be found in Cézanne's style, but these observations are the commonplaces of contemporary art-criticism, and have little to do with specifically plastic criticism. He notes also the rectangular simplicity, the recession, at right angles, of planes parallel to the plane of the picture,

in contrast with the diagonal organization of El
Greco's paintings; this, except for the reference to the
third dimension, is almost entirely a matter of pattern. Over and above this, he devotes himself almost
exclusively to comment upon the multiplicity of strokes
of pigment, the vast variety of subtle gradations of
color out of which Cézanne built up all his more extended color-areas. The infinitude of this variety, plus
its coördination, are what, he says, constitute Cézanne's
"immense richness of esthetic content."

Two things are notable in this analysis. First, it
reduces the characteristic quality in Cézanne to an
elaborate color-pattern, and this is not, in his account,
related to Cézanne's characteristic manner of organizing space. Nothing at all is said of the use made by
Cézanne of the delicately modulated color-scheme to
give, with a minimum of modeling by light and shadow,
the solid massiveness of objects, and their rhythmic
organization in deep space. Of the correlation, to this
end, of distortion with the use of color, nothing at all
is said. The rendering of space and solidity, with a
power comparable to Michelangelo's, in terms of
subtly-used color, and in addition to this the realization of convincing individuality in particular things in
a degree worthy of Rembrandt or Velásquez, is
Cézanne's distinctive plastic achievement, but it is an
accomplishment to which anyone concerned primarily
or exclusively with pattern must necessarily be blind.

Second, what Mr. Fry says of Cézanne's use of
color, its derivation from the impressionists and its
advance beyond them in variety, power and freedom
from literalism, is equally true of Renoir, and especially
of Renoir's later works. Merely from the point of
view of richness of color-chords, and their combination into a satisfying decorative unity, Mr. Fry's

17

eulogy is *less* applicable to Cézanne than it is to Renoir: the distinction between the two painters, the fact that Renoir's employment of color is the more distinctively decorative, is invisible to Mr. Fry because of his neglect of the distinction between pattern and truly expressive form. This is not to say that Renoir failed to catch the spirit or essential quality of things, but the essential quality, as he saw it, was more obviously natural, more joyous, more spontaneously appealing, than it was in Cézanne, therefore more fittingly set in a context of rich and brilliant decoration. No considerations relating merely to decorative pattern, in brief, are sufficient to account for either the distinctive quality of Renoir and Cézanne, or the characteristic difference between them.

From the foregoing examples it is apparent how grave are the consequences of error in fundamental esthetic and psychological principles, and how immediately such error is reflected in blindness to the specific qualities in individual works of art.

DYNAMIC SYMMETRY[1]

Albert C. Barnes

The theory of "dynamic symmetry" as the fundamental principle of plastic design, and the method of painting based upon it, do not merit serious consideration except for the light they throw upon current opinion and practice in the realm of art and esthetics. The method was originated by the late Jay Hambidge and is in use in many schools and art academies throughout the country. It has also influenced the work of a variety of painters popularly regarded as artists, and a considerable number of persons in authority in educa-

---

[1] From *Journal of The Barnes Foundation*, October, 1925.

tion are disposed to take it seriously. These facts confer upon the method considerable sociological importance.

Mr. Hambidge regarded himself as the rediscoverer of the secret of Greek esthetic design and believed that he thus anticipated another Renaissance. He intimates that in "dynamic symmetry" science and art are auspiciously wedded at last, and the means of transmuting base metal into gold is delivered to men. What his theory lacks in originality is compensated for in simplicity and naïveté. He writes: "Lines, angles and curves are regarded merely as defining areas which compose the units of a map-like arrangement within the boundaries of the picture-frame or the canvas stretcher." In other words, his plan consists in reducing the composition to a flat pattern in which the chief masses are outlined and placed with reference to each other by means of a series of rectangles. For the construction of these rectangles an extensive set of mathematical formulas is provided. That is the method — that, and nothing more. In short, Phidias, Praxiteles, Giorgione, Rembrandt, Cézanne and Matisse had a box of tricks which any person familiar with the use of cube roots can apply and produce great works of art.

The arguments offered in its behalf are, first, that much of the art of the Greeks lends itself to analysis in terms of the ratios given; second, that the method facilitates the enlargement of sketches, which is required when they are transferred to the final canvas; third, that it has proved useful to painters who have won prizes at exhibitions. The reduction of all pictorial design to flat pattern is defended on the ground that the use of deep space is a descent of art into photography!

To state arguments such as these is to make debate

superfluous. Yet his claim to "logic," to liberation of
creative energy, to avoidance of anything like a "studio-
trick to cover up poverty of thought," is made so
consistently and so confidently that the unwary may
be taken in, and it is therefore worth while to indicate
how grotesque the claim is. The initial reduction of
what in a painting makes it esthetically significant —
that is, pictorial design — to flat pattern, to mere placing of line and area, disqualifies at the start everything
that follows. The isolation of the elements in plastic
form from one another and from the form as a whole
is the esthetic sin from which spring nearly all the
esthetic vices. There is no integrity in art unless all
the means at the painter's disposal are conceived as
subsidiary to the effect intended. If the flat pattern
of a picture is treated as something which can be fixed
independently of, *e. g.*, the color, the result is as dis-
astrous as that of separating plot and characters
in literature or harmony and melody in music. Unless
composition, drawing, color and light are felt from the
start as aspects of a single plastic form, they are inevitably and necessarily just such "studio-tricks" as
Mr. Hambidge professed to repudiate.

The preliminary assumption that the design of a picture is to be regarded as a flat pattern[2] is made by Mr.
Hambidge dogmatically, although there is a show of
argument in its behalf. Giotto and the painters of
Greek vases are adduced as examples of the artists who
avoided perspective because of its "photographic
quality," in total disregard of the fact that the painting of vases is really a form of illustrative decoration
and is not representative of plastic art at its best, and

---

[2] Of course a flat pattern may have its own esthetic value; but to
make this value fundamental in plastic art is to reduce all painting to
the status of wallpaper or rugs.

that Giotto's use of perspective in an original manner was one of the principal means of obtaining striking and individual esthetic effects. Although Giotto did not portray realistic perspective as we know it, the effect of three-dimensional space is subtly indicated by such means as color. However, since this and other plastic functions of color escape Mr. Hambidge's formula, he forcibly excludes whatever makes the method inapplicable, and his argument here is obviously perfunctory.

If it is logical to make a dogmatic assumption violently in conflict with the first principles of the subject under discussion, then Mr. Hambidge's claim to be logical is justified. His claim is frankly based on the impressive array of mathematical formulas by which the rectangular patterns making up the groundwork of a picture are to be constructed. But to confuse logic with the simple and, in this connection, irrelevant use of mathematics is, at the present day, simply naïve, however awe-inspiring it may be to the uninitiate. When it is said of an artist that he "prefers to think out the arrangement of his pictures," what is meant, of course, is that such a person prefers calculation to sensibility or imagination. And, since calculation is easy and imagination hard, any such proposal to make the production of art possible to people who can learn formulas, but who lack great endowment, is sure to meet with general acclaim.

It is amusing to observe how the clichés of modern esthetics may be appropriated, in perfect unconsciousness, by those who have not the faintest conception of their meaning. Mr. Hambidge, forgetting that he had just joined in the familiar reprobation of the ideal of copying, justifies his mathematical method by its success in analyzing and reproducing the forms found in nature! Just so, after deploring the subject picture, he congratulates himself because his method had proved useful to George Bellows and Robert Henri, whose popularity and ability to command the high prices which he finds impressive are due chiefly to the obvious and appealing subjects!

It is by the fruits of "dynamic symmetry" that we may know it. Miss Herter, in making use of it, "felt no embarrassment at any stage of the painting." Which of us does feel any embarrassment in repeating the multiplication-table? But the climax of absurdity comes in the fact that the method has been useful to George Bellows and Robert Henri, painters of pictures which reveal in every lineament a complete dearth of personal vision, of imaginative originality, whose chief stock in trade consists in the use of other men's ideas and methods. It is not surprising that the method should be commended by such men, or by the critic of *The New York Times*, in a review quoted by Mr. Hambidge, in which every sentence throbs with pleasure at the sight of little children obeying authority and never making any choices of their own except between Tweedledum and Tweedledee. "The mischievous notion of 'art for art's sake' is disposed of by this clear, precise method." Surely this sentence would more precisely express the critic's meaning if the phrase "for art's sake" were dropped out of it, for art in any form is abhorrent to newspaper critics.

In brief, it is quite obvious that Mr. Hambidge was a man who had no real esthetic sensitiveness, and no idea what an understanding of art could possibly mean. In the art of the past he missed all that is virile and distinctive—all which is not consecrated by authority and easily included in his formula. Even in the field from which he says his theory is drawn—that of Greek sculpture—he misses the significance of the great archaic period. His esthetic theory, as his quotations from Denman Ross show, was a set of platitudes, some of them true, some false, but none of them really grasped. His ideal was the cooked-up picture, in which threadbare devices are feebly reshuffled for the delectation of the half-educated. It is represented by such a painter as Leon Kroll, whose "youth and freshness" are entirely a matter of attractive subjects, and whose work is plastically trite and stale in the last degree, an imitation of the mannerisms of other men's art. For the production of such painting "dynamic symmetry" represents a useful tool, a means of reducing still farther anything like individual perception. It is like an adding-machine, serviceable when mechanical problems are in question, without significance for genuine thought or creation, and when used as a substitute for them actually pernicious. It is a method to construct a skeleton and leaves entirely out of account the content that makes a work of art a living expression of an individual mind and soul.

The secret of Mr. Hambidge's mind and personality is revealed in the pleasure he took in the prices paid for pictures constructed in accordance with his method. Success of this sort means success in giving the public what it wants, in conforming to the standards generally accepted. These standards, which find the boundary of their authority at the point where art begins, Mr. Hambidge never seriously questioned. Essentially he was a Rotarian instructing Rotarians. He desired to think and feel like the crowd, only more conspicuously so, in order to be the crowd's leader. To those who have discovered the husk of art but not its kernel, he offered a recipe for making chaff look like wheat. His method corresponds to the devices for memory-training, for strengthening the will, for cultivating personality, which we see advertised in the magazines. The complimentary letters published in his book on

Dynamic Symmetry in Composition are chiefly sug-
gestive of testimonials to patent medicines; if we refrain from characterizing them as bad taste, it is only
because Mr. Hambidge was too naïve to be judged by
other standards than those which we apply to children.
For the same reason it would be ungracious to call his
system charlatanry—his first imposition was upon himself.   There is nothing in his system that deals with
the grasp of essentials in a subject and their presentation in that individual form which is characteristic of
all true expression, of all that is entitled to be considered as art.   By a flagrant abuse of the meaning of
"logic" and a transfer of the values of mathematics to
a field where they have no real significance, Mr. Hambidge built up an elaborate system of mechanics that
enables people with no imagination and no esthetic
feeling to produce works of counterfeit art that win
prizes and sell for high prices.   The psychological
principle at work is precisely the one of hypnosis:[3] and
that is always possible when art and science are couched
in high-sounding formulas and their prestige-value
brought to bear upon people in whom sentimentalism,
emotionalism and lack of individuality function as
substitutes for individual experience and intelligent
thinking.   The system is, therefore, not a matter for
the consideration of artists and estheticians, but for
the sociologist who deals with questions of economic
waste occasioned by ignorance of the first principles of
rational thinking and of personal and significant experience.   The existence and vogue of such a system shows
the imperative need for a more popular grasp of the
rudiments of educational theory and practice which
have been current in informed circles for more than
twenty years.

   [3] The slogan "dynamic symmetry" is the equivalent in art of the
hypnotic word, "Mesopotamia."

PROBLEMS ENCOUNTERED IN ART EDUCATION[1]

Mary Mullen

The experience gained in carrying out the educational program of The Barnes Foundation has been sufficiently interesting and instructive to warrant a statement of some of its significant details. Before we obtained a charter as an educational institution, the larger part of our present staff had been engaged in a practical experiment that had two main features: first, a linking-up of the modern conceptions of psychology and esthetics with a first-hand observation of old and modern paintings; second, through the experience thus gained, an application of modern educational methods in a class of students of diverse degrees of culture and social rank. The experiment covered a period of ten years and the results, when analyzed by educational authorities, were considered of sufficient importance to justify the extension of the plan to universities, colleges, schools and, particularly, to groups of people who had never had the advantages of a college education or the opportunity to study good paintings.

Within a few months of the announcement of the Foundation as an educational institution there appeared about a score of articles in various American and European magazines written by men well-known in art and educational circles. As a result of this unsought-for publicity, we were overwhelmed with applications from institutions and individuals who desired to avail themselves of what we had to offer. The corre-

[1] Adapted from Mary Mullen's essay, *Learning to See*, Journal of The Barnes Foundation, January, 1926.

spondence yielded a wealth of leads which, under suitable circumstances, could be made extremely valuable material for further educational experiments in the paths which we had already followed for more than a decade. We found oceans of enthusiasm which would have been of inestimable power if it had been accompanied with sufficient intelligence to meet the first requisite of any serious educational movement. This disbalance was manifested in quarters of considerable eminence in the educational world, and almost invariably the plea for admission presented by such applicants was that of prestige. After we had eliminated triflers and would-be exploiters from serious consideration, there was sufficient promising material to occupy our buildings every day with classes of adult students enrolled for systematic study. The present article will deal particularly with a few of the chief difficulties encountered.

We were handicapped at the start by the fact that a majority of the students had dabbled in art in college courses, art academies, public lectures, etc. This necessitated attempts to change the superstitions that painting represents either a pattern, a set of fixed rules for the use of color, line and space, or a (unsuspected) confusion of narrative, historical or moral values suffused with a mystical glow. In each of these cases of mistaken identity the outstanding common factor was the demonstrable *inability to see*. How almost universal is that defect is not suspected until specific tests of esthetic vision are made. How difficult it is to convince even mature painters that they never get anywhere because they never learn to see, cannot be realized except by a teacher familiar with modern educational methods who has made experiments tending to remove the obstacle. This learning to see is so vitally important that it merits the detailed consideration given it in the following recital of some of the observations made in reference to the initial experiment carried out in our classes.

Several of the professors of the Pennsylvania Academy of the Fine Arts, who were granted permission to bring their students to our gallery, became so much interested that they asked to attend the regular talks given by our educational staff in front of the paintings. At one of these sessions the subject was the analysis of space as an element in plastic form, and its characteristics and significance were demonstrated in paintings that covered the period from the Florentines to the moderns. In the work of a contemporary, it was pointed out that it was his skilled use of space, more than of any other means, that gave the painting its esthetic value. Thereupon, one of the Academy teachers volunteered the statement that until that moment he had never liked that painter's work and never seen the subtle spatial relations which, after they had been pointed out, converted his dislike into pleasure. A different aspect of this inability to see was exemplified in the case of another member of this group of Academy teachers, a painter who had been influenced by the work of Matisse. This individual failed to see that, while the decorative element in Matisse's painting is strongly in evidence, sufficient grasp of the significant features of experience is revealed to change the character of the painting from mere decoration to personal expression in balanced plastic form. As a result of this teacher's inability to see, his own painting presented a thin version of Matisse's decorative character and nothing of the expressiveness that constitutes personal insight into reality.

One of the most striking cases of utter blindness in people who are supposed to know something about art was represented by an instructor at the Corcoran Art Gallery, Washington, D. C. His blindness was evidenced by his remarks about two of our paintings, which analyses in plastic terms reveal as among the most important achievements in contemporary art. The *Three Sisters* (The Barnes Foundation, No. 25) by Matisse is, he said, "so slight that it is not entitled to serious consideration." Pascin's *Seated Figure* (The Barnes Foundation, No. 229) was condemned because the drawing did not fit into the formula which he recited as the recipe for art. This type of intellectual disorder is duplicated a dozen times in the record of our observations, in the presence of paintings, of men and women who teach art in universities, colleges, schools, public galleries and art academies throughout America. It was this state of affairs that led us to study the psychological principles which explained the condition, and to adapt educational methods to overcome it.

Although the manifestations of this inability to see are so varied, its cause is to be found in a failure to grasp certain simple fundamental principles of psychology which no well-informed person would dispute. *To see* means to perceive, to bring to consciousness; recognition of what constitutes perception and consciousness is, therefore, indispensable. Another truism is that since perception and consciousness are inseparably connected with appreciation, which is a mental state, it follows that mind is the chief factor to be considered. The connecting links between seeing in the sense of perception, in the sense of consciousness and in the sense of mind are most clearly and convincingly presented in Professor Dewey's book, *Experience and Nature*.[2] What he

[2] Open Court Publishing Co., Chicago, Ill., 1925.

writes not only explains the inability to see but points the way to supplant the blindness with the experience which constitutes genuine art appreciation. A word of vital importance in the building of this new structure is "meaning." In each of the above-mentioned instances of blindness in relation to painting, there is a clear perversion of the rational conception of the word "meaning." To be specific: one of the Academy members failed to recognize the meaning of space in the construction of an artist's creation; another did not see that his own preoccupation with decorative qualities prevented him from grasping the meaning of Matisse's message; the instructor at the Corcoran Art Gallery applied the meaning of an outworn academic rule to Matisse's and Pascin's individual variations of the great traditions of painting as a means of embodying their personal reactions to the world. However, if art is a fragment of life presented to us enriched in feeling by means of the creative spirit of the artist, it is irrational to believe that mathematics, formulas, mere pattern or decoration, etc., would supply means adequate to the extraordinarily complex manifestations of the human spirit. More rational, indeed demonstrable, is the belief that the artist's work is an expression of an experience which he has undergone, and that the meaning of the painting *is* that experience.

This conception of meaning as synonymous with experience, is one of the fundamentals upon which Dewey builds those conceptions of consciousness and mind which have revolutionized educational practice and enabled people to understand and enjoy their own experiences in all the activities of life. Dewey writes that "consciousness denotes the perception of meanings," that is, the "awareness of the heres and nows;" and that "mind denotes the whole system of meanings

as they are embodied in the workings of organic life."
If we submit these definitions to the test of concrete
situations in any phase of life, including the study of
paintings, there is a convincing adequacy to the meanings of our own experience. Fixed rules give way to
the boundless field which human beings, whether they
be the creators or the appreciators of art, must have
if their spirit is to be free and unhampered. In short,
art is a record of experience, and education in art
consists in an application of method that takes into
account the human attributes of both the artist and the
student. Fortunately, experiments in educational
science have developed methods which have records of
proved value obtained through actual experience.

It is the above-noted conceptions of perception, consciousness, mind, art, that we have tried to weld with
modern educational methods, in order to remedy the
widespread inability to see, and to replace it by the experience without which art is devoid of meaning and
becomes a superstition. The recognition of consciousness as the "awareness of the meanings of the heres
and nows" points the way to all the goals, but it will
lead to none until those present meanings become alive
and significant in relation to that whole system of
meanings, which constitutes mind; in other words,
mind contains the luminosity that gives color, quality,
precision, to the "heres and nows." For example, if
we look in a painting for a story or a moral, our mind
holds the meaning that a painting is the record of a
story, not of an experience presented through the
creative use of line, color and space. If we like Titian
and do not like Renoir, we have failed to see the meaning of the "heres and nows" in the case of each artist;
that is, from the organized meanings which constitute
our mind there is missing that meaning which makes

the work of the two artists closely akin. If we like both men, our minds contain the meaning that the "here and now" in each painter is the use of line, color and space in a similar manner to create something which is independent of subject-value. In this case, another meaning in our mind is that art is not imitation but creation; and how can we differentiate between imitation and creation unless we have in our mind a clear grasp—that is, the meaning—of the tradition as it is represented in Titian; and the consciousness—that is, the perception of the "here and now"—that Renoir modified the Titian tradition to his own ends and by so doing created something new by the same plastic means used by Titian?

It thus becomes apparent that a thing is seen only when its significance is perceived in the light shed by the organized meanings which is mind. To thus see, means that there is, as it were, "a series of flashes of varying intensities" (perception, consciousness), thrown intermittently upon that persistent, substantial structure of meanings which is mind. Experience is possible only when that duplex action takes place, and it is valuable only when both factors in the situation are constantly alive to the finer shades of meanings which this interplay reveals. The absence of that interplay explains the blindness of the painters and educators above referred to and their unsuitability to act as guides to younger people who seek help in expressing themselves or in learning to appreciate the artistic expressions of others. It is the development of that interplay which is the goal of all modern educational science.

Educators complain incessantly that the most difficult of their tasks is to get rid of the set of fixed forms which, especially in adults, masquerade as thinking and prevent the process of learning by experience. That difficulty has been ours and, because of the prevalence of outworn and irrational methods in teaching art, progress has been even slower than in those other fields where the objective features of experience are more susceptible to verifiable observation than in the field of art.

From the start we have kept in mind the essentially experimental character of our venture, and for material we have drawn upon various sources, such as young painters, school and college students and teachers, writers, people in the ordinary walks of life. Large numbers of students from the Pennsylvania Academy of the Fine Arts were admitted several days a week accompanied by their own teachers. We made no attempt at instruction but spent our time in observing the behavior and noting the remarks of both the teachers and the students. After about four months of this experiment, it was clear to everybody, including the intelligent minority of the students, that nothing of educational value came of their repeated visits. Their teachers never having been taught to see, either confined their remarks to unimportant matters of painting technique or spread the kind of diffuse, free-floating emotion that characterizes the behavior of those in whom superstition functions in the place of relevant ideas and intelligent method brought to bear on paintings. In fact, from the educational standpoint, these Academy instructors and their students got hardly more out of their visits than did the group of bankers, lawyers and college professors who had also been frequently admitted to the gallery. We learned from this and similar experiences that aimless wandering in a gallery is about on a par with the daydreaming furnished by attendance at the movies. To the most intelligent member of the faculty of the Pennsylvania Academy of the Fine Arts, we finally suggested that we coöperate in an effort to work out a plan by which their students could be guided toward an intelligent approach to the study of art. This suggestion yielded a group of about a score of painters and students of painting who enrolled in our classes for a systematic study of the arts.

What is the meaning of "systematic study" of paintings? The books published by members of our educational staff state the plan from the three indispensable standpoints, psychology, esthetics and educational method.[3] What we seek to do here is to state a few general educational principles upon which the method is based. For example, we start with John Dewey's conception that education is another name for meeting the practical problems of life, one of which is the significance of art. It results from an interaction between an individual and his environment, and in our case that problem is to establish an interaction between the qualities common to all human beings, and a collection of works of old and modern art. We accept the modern conception that mind is not something in itself, but a course of action in which aims, ends, selection of means to attain ends, are intelligently directed. We find that the individual and the world are engaged in a constantly developing situation. This, and this only, results in experience—an environment which affects the individual and which in turn is affected by him. From experience arises culture, that is, the constant expansion of the range and accuracy of the perceptions which

---

[3] In general, the point of view of these books is explained in Section I of this Volume, with some illustrations of the results yielded when particular problems are considered in its light.

the individual obtains from the varied contacts with
life. Education, thus carried out, develops initiative, inventiveness and the ability to readapt
one's self to the constantly changing situation
which is life. We have found it an adventure, as much
fun as playing a game, and enjoyable for the same
reason.

All these principles are indispensable parts of
modern educational science; they seem so much matters
of common sense that it is almost incredible that any-
body should balk at accepting them as the intelligent
way to approach the study of paintings. And yet,
when various educational institutions applied for the
privilege of "studying" our paintings and we asked
them to furnish evidence that their courses in art showed
that their students had had preliminary training according to those principles, they were stunned at what
they considered our effrontery but were unable to
satisfy our request.

A great number of our students have also come from
various categories of people whose vocations or avoca-
tions indicate a genuine inclination toward the esthetic
aspects of life. Many of them, laymen and teachers,
are interested in music or literature; others are engaged
in the professional occupation of law or medicine, or
in public movements in the line of civic culture. With
many of these students, just as with most of the
painters, art teachers, college and university professors, admitted to our classes, we met with the same
inertia, the same pious wish for knowledge, the same
daydreaming as they wander through our galleries, the
same desire merely to be allowed the thrill of basking
in the mystical aura of art—in short, the desire to get

something for nothing. They are "practical" people, they say, and have no time for any sort of "book-stuff"—a remark amusingly ironic to us, since the records show that The Barnes Foundation collection, its buildings and surrounding park, and its Arboretum, all owe their existence essentially to the fact that "book-stuff" had been applied to the problems of everyday life, to the intelligent carrying on of both business and leisure, work and play. Indeed, the principal objective in our class program is to integrate with life itself, those values to be found in the work of the great thinkers, the great artists, of all times, and we make the manifestation of *interest* the price of identification with our project. In order to avoid wasting time and energy on the part of all concerned, we make it clear that by "interest" we mean—in the words of John Dewey—"an anxiety concerning future consequences which impels the individual to do something to obtain better consequences and avoid worse ones." The plan has for years worked out well. Classes held in our gallery are continuously filled to capacity. The most encouraging result of our effort is the growing evidence that students trained by the Foundation's staff are successfully applying the basic principles of scientific educational procedure to their own work in art or in teaching, and to the "practical" affairs of daily life.

What this article in essence maintains is that the problem of *learning to see* is basic to education in art. This may seem paradoxical; that is, everyone, not physically blind, is likely to suppose that he already knows how to see. However, when reflection brings to light the fact that perception of the external world is truly such only in proportion as the mind illuminates such perception, seeing becomes but another name for experience, for education and for culture. Seeing is then something individual, whether the person seeing is an artist or simply an ordinary person who has entered into the heritage of art. Our problem, the problem of The Barnes Foundation, is to restore continuity to what confused and inept educational methods have pulled asunder.

ART ACADEMIES: A STUDY IN FUTILITY

Violette de Mazia

In 1922, when The Barnes Foundation was chartered as an educational institution, throngs of students and teachers in art academies all over the United States clamored for permission to view its collection of paintings and sculpture. In the beginning, and for some time thereafter, permission was freely accorded them. Coöperation with existing institutions was an integral part of the Foundation's plans, and all possible steps were taken to make it fruitful, though we had been well aware that prevailing systems of education in art had serious imperfections. How tragically inept that education was, however, or how complacent those who controlled it in their ignorance of both esthetic principles and the methods of modern scientific education, we realized only after the results of the experiment described in the article *Problems Encountered in Art Education*[1] were recorded. The comments of the visiting painters and students, as well as their general behavior, made it all too apparent that they had no idea what the objective realities are that make a painting a significant work of art, or how to look for them. Plastic qualities and relationships lay entirely outside their ken, and they never dreamed of distinguishing between emotional reverie and enjoyment of values specifically esthetic. When it had become certain beyond any shadow of doubt that study of plastic art by people so entirely without the necessary qualifications was foredoomed to futility, teachers in art academies were denied permission to bring their students to our gallery.

[1] Page 251 of present Volume.

Reluctant, as we were, to close the door of our collection to students whose native endowment might have survived bungling instruction, we offered to provide teachers from our staff to coöperate with the faculties of neighboring institutions—most notably those of the Pennsylvania Academy of the Fine Arts in Philadelphia, and the Art Students' League in New York. The suggestions were ignored, obviously because the authorities in these schools either were incapable of grasping their own incompetence, no matter how clearly demonstrated, or had complete confidence in the invincible ignorance of their clientele.

All the long-established and well-known art academies have in common the fact that their boards of directors and administrative heads are drawn from conservative financial, social and intellectual circles, with a long record of opposition to innovation of any sort. These Bourbons of the world of art have in common with their confreres in other fields the fact that they learn nothing and forget nothing. Change has always been anathema to them, and when compelled to accept it they make use of it only to bludgeon all subsequent change: just as in the past, when Courbet was a club against the Impressionists; the Impressionists, against Cézanne; Cézanne, against his own legitimate successors. To cling to the old out of fear of the new has always been the policy of entrenched power, and it has made the very word "academic" a symbol for oppression of creative originality. In the art academies the authorities exert very great power: they award fellowships and prizes, control exhibitions of pictures, and subject students of independent mind to an incessant fire of disapproval and ridicule. Most important of all, the methods they inculcate do furnish the key to financial success. Almost all the painters whose work commands high prices from magazines, advertisers, and the more benighted but vastly larger part of the general public, bear the typical academic hall mark. As a result of this deep-rooted confusion of values, the impulse to create is corrupted or aborted by the very forces that ought to nourish it.

This indictment is proved valid by the actual results of academic training, as weighed in the scales of history. Since the Pennsylvania Academy of the Fine Arts was established in 1806, the painters it has graduated who were also creative artists of real distinction can be counted on the fingers of one hand. Nearly all the pictures that have left an abiding influence have been the work of men independently trained, or students whose subsequent work showed that they had been immune to the corrupting effects of their teachers. This record of futility is as characteristic of the *Ecole des Beaux-Arts* in Paris as it is of the Art Students' League of New York or the Chicago Art Institute. The final and conclusive proof of the educational bankruptcy of art academies is furnished by the bleakly stereotyped paintings hung at their exhibitions, which tell their unmistakable tale of sterility to all who have eyes to see.

It would be worth little to point out this unchanging futility without a diagnosis of the cause. All academic instruction is based on the assumption that a student can be taught a technique and at the same time left free to use it or not as he sees fit. Nothing could be more misleading. Usually the technique or style taught is an imitation, an academic banality formulated in total ignorance of the fact that what an artist has to say involves his whole manner of envisaging his subject and displaying its relationships; and this is the essence of his art. What the painter sees and the way

he puts it down are inseparably united: what distinguished Leonardo's technique, for example, from
Giorgione's, Renoir's from Cézanne's, is integral with
the bent, cast or color of the man's entire artistic
personality. This is why inculcation of a particular
type of technique or style is fixation of a habit of
perception: once this is done, the painter's enchain-
ment is accomplished.

An obvious example of this fatal mistake is the use
of classical sculpture to provide models for draughtsmanship. This procedure diverts the student's mind
from the true purpose of drawing, which is to *draw
out* the individual character of the subject treated,
and, instead, implants the error that standardized
models exist to which conformity is a duty. It makes
imitation of linear contour, combined with precise
copying of light and shadow, the backbone of drawing,
and paralyzes the artist's own conception of ideas and
their means of realization. When, as is usually the
case in academic practice, the models chosen are late
Greek or Roman, the result is likely to be an enfeebled
version of late Italian eclecticism—and this cannot
possibly be something which the student has found for
himself, but something he has been forced to adopt as a
crutch.

It is true that there are academies which plume
themselves on respecting the learner's freedom: pre-
senting him with models, they do not compel him to
follow them. This can be no more than pretense,
offering the shadow of freedom, but withholding the
substance. The fact that they are furnished these
stereotyped models by teachers whose prestige is impressive and whose power to award prizes and scholar-
ships is universally known and feared, is an almost
sure preventive of freedom of expression. As we have
just seen, a habit of copying establishes a habit of

seeing through the eyes of another. In a sense, of course, there must always be a model: nobody could learn either to see or to do by the exercise of some unaided spontaneity of his own, springing miraculously from nowhere. He might as sensibly attempt to invent a new language for himself. But between a model freely chosen from possible alternatives, a traditional procedure consciously elected as a result of deliberation, and a model authoritatively prescribed, or hit upon *faute de mieux*, because no other is presented as possible or conceivable, lies the difference between liberty and either despotism or anarchy. Under intelligent guidance, a student can be led to see the possibilities inherent in a wide range of methods of execution, provided with an understanding of the conditions under which any of them may advantageously be employed, and thus given an opportunity for meaningful choice. If he is taught one, and *only one* method of doing anything, he does it as significantly as a parrot speaks English.

On a larger scale, the blunder illustrated in courses in drawing is repeated in courses in perspective and anatomy. Ostensibly designed to acquaint the student with scientific knowledge about the construction of the human body and the laws of perspective, they treat descriptions of natural phenomena not as a fund of suggestions for design but as norms or prescriptions, departure from which constitutes error. This is a reversion to the hoariest of esthetic superstitions — art conceived as imitation. An identical bias is manifested in courses on composition, in which what *might* profitably be investigated — the manifold ways in which painters of all ages have organized their material to suit their individual purposes—is never even mentioned; instead, balance and symmetry are prescribed in terms appropriate to a fixed set of arbitrary rules, with never a whisper that ancient China and India, modern Japan, and primitive peoples all over the globe have developed their own modes of plastic organization, which have furnished rich sources of material to many of our most distinguished contemporaries. Especially in the field of decoration, the art of the primitive peoples has supplied an apparently inexhaustible mine of treasure to European art—which the typical academician has turned his back upon, doubtless because it threatens to play havoc with the set of formulas to which, since they support and justify his power and prestige, he is irrevocably committed.

A candid examination of the academic curriculum as a whole reveals much that is superfluous, more that is noxious, and nothing that is indispensable, or even fundamentally valuable, to an artist. In part, this is undoubtedly due to the absence of intelligently guided courses in the study of the traditions of painting from the earliest times to the present. Since it is by looking at what others have to show us that we learn to see with our own eyes, the neglect of proper study of paintings by the great masters of the past and present makes education in art almost impossible. However, an even more important part of the cause is to be found in the very indifferent quality of academic personnel. The leavening of reasonably competent technicians in their faculties cannot compensate for the practically total absence of vigorous intelligence or real artistic eminence. All the better universities, all the outstanding professional schools, have on their staffs scholars who have either made important contributions to the advance of knowledge, or who have demonstrated their possession of a ripe, humane and broadly balanced cultural heritage. Set beside them, the teachers in any typical school of art present a shocking contrast. Pedants, sentimentalists and disguised (or undisguised) practitioners of commercialism predominate over-whelmingly, and the tiny fraction of "progressive" painters, recruited to mitigate the blight of total re-action, are practically all as ignorant of the painting of the past as their colleagues are of the significant painting of the present.

Even from the most narrowly academic point of view—that is to say, when judged by the standards of ordinary competence in teaching—the staffs of the art academies offer a sorry spectacle. Almost destitute, as a rule, of general culture, practically none of them have been given any training in modern educational methodology, their knowledge of psychology is nil, and they have not the slightest idea how to bring esthetic insight into fruitful interaction with the other processes of a comprehensive personal development. They thus remain little islands of obscurantism, almost totally isolated from the far-reaching illumination that in recent years has brought new life and vigor to the American educational world.

All academic teaching, in summary, contravenes the fundamental truth of esthetics, that seeing and doing are indissolubly united. We see—in order to discover ways and means to execute the purposes which con-stitute our individual vision, the essence of our esthetic personality. *Unless* our ways of seeing and doing are thus correlated, they are mere bad habits—automatisms usurping the functions of intelligent thought and action. This truth, forever hidden from academic eyes, explains the futility of all academic teaching, explains why the typical academic product is permanently numbered among the lame, the halt and the blind, explains why the doors of The Barnes Foundation are forever closed to the use of our collection for the extension of the academic blight.

SABOTAGE OF PUBLIC EDUCATION IN PHILADELPHIA[1]

Albert C. Barnes

For years Philadelphians who have their city's welfare at heart have been uneasy about conditions in the city's public schools. Rumors have been rife that the authorities who administer its educational system have lagged so far behind in the march of progress that their objectives, methods and teaching personnel are hopelessly antiquated. Frequently the rumors emanate from sources within the system itself, from teachers whose tenure would be jeopardized or lost if they allowed themselves to be quoted. Aware that their city's name has been a byword for municipal maladministration and political corruption for decades, public-spirited citizens cannot dismiss such reports lightly; yet occasions are rare when they are presented with indisputable evidence of what is going on behind the scenes at the Philadelphia Board of Public Education. The present is such an occasion.

In 1944 the Board published a brochure entitled *Invitation to the Arts*. In an official Foreword, Alexander J. Stoddard, Superintendent of Schools, wrote: "It is our responsibility to attempt to shape the program of education so as to pass on to each student those discoveries of former times that have helped men to live abundantly. One of these discoveries is that the greatest progress of the individual or race comes with a balanced integration of thought and feeling. . . . It is to assist us in such consideration that a copy of this brochure is being given to every member of the professional personnel of the Philadelphia Public Schools."

[1] October, 1945.

270

If these words leave any doubt as to the authoritative character of the brochure, an introductory statement by Mr. C. Leslie Cushman, Associate Superintendent of Public Schools, puts its status beyond dispute. Not only is the author of the brochure a graduate of the Philadelphia school system and at present a member of its staff; but plans for the brochure were laid by its Art Director, Mr. Earl B. Milliette, and by Mr. Cushman himself, in conjunction with the actual writer. Mr. Cushman lists five supervisors with whom conferences were held during preparation of the text, as well as an unspecified number of others who supplied written comments. All five officials have stated that they "fully agree with the major thesis of the brochure," so that it can be taken as fully representative of the spirit and point of view of the Division of Fine and Industrial Art, and the Division of Music, in the Philadelphia Public Schools. For the Philadelphia School System, in brief, *Invitation to the Arts* is the equivalent of a Papal Encyclical, and no individual, but the system as a whole, must stand or fall by it. The unauthorized use in the brochure of the name of The Barnes Foundation has led the unwary to suppose that the institution thus exploited supports or endorses the ideas, form or spirit of the brochure. Nothing can be further from the truth.

The brochure opens with some bromidic comment on the impoverishment of life in an industrial civilization, and the desirability of esthetic expression for everyone. Then follows an account of the Summer Workshop, a vacation school maintained by the Philadelphia Board of Education to provide an opportunity for such expression. In it the beginner, symbolized by a hypothetical Miss Meek, finds the courage to start painting when her instructor tells her that there is only one thing to be feared—that thirty canvases by thirty people should come to look alike. A vase of flowers serves as a model: the instructor, "instead of explaining how to blend colors, raves about the flowers." "The zest and eagerness for expressing is allowed to go unhindered, come what may." Is Miss Meek worried about her technique? She must be reassured. "Technique is important. Nobody should be without it. Nobody is. Technique is simply the manner of doing something."

This, of course, will be recognized instantly by every well-informed reader as the familiar "free-expression" program, which was demolished by John Dewey in the Journal of The Barnes Foundation nearly twenty years ago. There, Mr. Dewey wrote that the basis of this program is a psychological blunder, the assumption, namely, that the individual, told or incited to "create," can produce by spontaneous germination from his own inner consciousness suggestions of things to be done. No such source exists; and if the teacher is forbidden to make suggestions, they will be gotten, Mr. Dewey points out, "from the home or street or from what some more vigorous fellow-pupil is doing." (He might have added the advertisements and the comic-strips.) From such haphazard sources nothing valuable can be expected to come: it can only come, Mr. Dewey concludes, "from a sympathetic and discriminating knowledge of what has been done in the past, and how it has been done."

Starting thus from an exploded fallacy, the brochure continues by triumphantly overthrowing such men of straw as the view that talent is identical with ability to draw a straight line or a perfect circle, and by demonstrating that talent sometimes develops late in life, and that you never know whether you have it until you try to use it. *Invitation to the Arts* then goes on to deny, for the ten-thousandth time, that art is imitation, incidentally repeating the popular myth that this was Aristotle's view, and gratuitously substituting the absurdity that most contemporary art is "non-representative expression." Next, the reader is pontifically informed that in matters of taste differences of opinion exist, that no critic can claim infallibility, and that therefore everyone ought to have the courage to stand up for his own convictions; but at the same time he is told that some critics have more experience than others, hence can recognize a hierarchy of intrinsic merit in works of art, and consequently are entitled to receive more consideration for their judgments than less experienced critics. Finally, the reader learns that art gives to everyone "new eyes, new ears," and makes us all more aware of our kinship with all men and all times.

These threadbare commonplaces are set forth to the accompaniment of an unceasing barrage of great names, so that an unwary reader, not in the habit of looking for evidence of firsthand experience—of which, from the first page to the last, there is not an iota—could hardly fail to get the impression that the author of *Invitation to the Arts* is truly, in the words of Plato, "the spectator of all time and of all existence." Allied to this intellectual pretentiousness is a strain of emotional exhibitionism, never content with a statement in simple terms if more high-flown or more fervid terms can be found. Thus what might be phrased as "adversity broadens human sympathies" becomes "the great wisdom of Christ came from under the shadow of the Cross;" and "it is desirable to live as fully and richly as possible" becomes "Whatever helps us to open what is locked inside, whatever helps us to release that which is chained in every heart, that thing is good. It is good by all the standards ever devised by decency and love. Whoever and whatever gave us life ordained that we should live."

What, in summary, Mr. Stoddard offers to his teaching staff as a contribution to the "balanced integration of thought and feeling" that promises "the greatest progress of the individual and the race" turns out upon analysis to be a rehash of discarded panaceas, banalities in the guise of daring innovations, abundance of sound and fury, with significance at the vanishing point. That the teachers and the tax-paying public should be invited to swallow this unappetizing mess might seem beyond belief. It is entirely credible, however, to those familiar with the history of the Philadelphia Board of Public Education that in this its latest exploit the Board is merely illustrating afresh the maxim, "The more it changes, the more it stays the same thing."

In 1925, under the title *The Shame in the Public Schools of Philadelphia*, the Journal of The Barnes Foundation reported the results of a survey of the teaching of art in the Philadelphia public schools. The survey revealed that the policy-making authorities of the school system were oblivious of all the discoveries, in the field of esthetics, psychology and scientific method, which had ushered in a new era of education in art; that they lacked even a rudimentary understanding of the principles and methods by which works of art could be fruitfully studied and made a living reality in the student's experience; that the teachers were themselves uninstructed in these principles and methods, and in large measure lacking in firsthand acquaintance with the subject-matter they were expected to teach. In consequence, the work of the pupils showed either a lifeless conformity to prescribed models, or a spirit nakedly commercial—it was art in the manner of *The Saturday Evening Post*. The ultimate responsibility, it was disclosed, lay at the door of the authorities, who not only furnished no guidance to the teachers, but who stifled criticism, repressed initiative, intimidated the bolder members of the staff, and did all in their power to maintain the conditions that had earned for Philadelphia its reputation as "a depressing intellectual slum."

Another Philadelphia institution, not officially a part of the Board of Education but closely allied to it in administrative policy and with a conjoined program of education in art, is the Philadelphia Museum of Art, and this too has done its share in dragging the reputation of Philadelphia in the dirt. The Museum officials, having made their city the laughing-stock of the nation by buying for the Museum at a high price a Cézanne painting which the French government subsequently announced "had been abandoned by Cézanne unfinished," held in 1937 a "Forms of Art" exhibition, arranged and directed by Mr. E. M. Benson. Its purpose, widely publicized by posters and circulars, was to offer the public "a fresh understanding of the art of the past and present."

Hardly had the exhibition opened when a flood of protests began to pour in upon the authorities, pointing out the unacknowledged source of the central idea of the exhibition in a widely-known book published thirteen years earlier, an idea basic in an educational program actively operating in the Philadelphia community for many years. Organizations as well as individuals branded the exhibition a fraud, and John Dewey, in a formal public statement denouncing the imposture, wrote: "The exhibition itself not only fails to carry out the borrowed idea, as expressed in the circular, but so completely contradicts it as to show that Mr. Benson never got the idea, but only some verbal expressions of it." Mr. Dewey went on to bring a further indictment against the Museum officials for "virtual endorsement of meaningless language" and for lending institutional prestige to the propagation of confusion. The Board of Trustees, with powerful political, financial and social connections, succeeded in hushing up the scandal, but memories of it linger on in the nickname that has clung to the institution ever since—"the house of artistic and educational prostitution on the Parkway."

In his latest affront to informed public opinion Mr. Stoddard is thus following faithfully in the footsteps of his predecessors. He and the Board of Public Education, of which he is the responsible head, poison the wells of public enlightenment by maintaining pseudo-modern educational projects that nullify everything which the leaders of modern scientific education have striven for and accomplished; in doing lip-service to spontaneity and liberty they condemn their deluded followers to frustration and futility; like Mr. Benson, they try to pass off as their own the contributions of others, and misunderstanding these they leave confusion twice confounded. Exposed as mountebanks and educational illiterates, they refuse the public the explanations to which it is entitled and take refuge in silence, with their political barricades assuring them continued access to the public funds. Mr. Stoddard's speeches and other public activities make capital of the prestige of high educational office, sometimes for causes opposed to the basic principles of American democracy. His advocacy of government subsidies for private denominational colleges, for example, was detrimental to Philadelphia's standing in the world of culture and civilization.

The Board of Education's sponsorship of the puerile and pretentious chatter of *Invitation to the Arts* puts a fitting climax upon a long career of educational sabotage.

Section III

COMPARATIVE STUDIES
Renoir, Cézanne, Matisse, Stravinsky

BIOGRAPHICAL SKETCH OF RENOIR[1]

Albert C. Barnes and Violette de Mazia

Renoir's life was comparatively uneventful, and a brief account of it reads like little more than a bare record of dates. He was born in Limoges on February 23, 1841, and when he was about four years old his family moved to Paris. In 1854 he went to work in a porcelain factory as a painter of ornamental designs, and subsequently made his living by decorating fans and window shades. Upon these he frequently reproduced pictures by the Old Masters, especially by the French painters of the Eighteenth Century, for whom he acquired a great admiration. The clear and transparent tones of all his mature work were also probably a survival of his porcelain-painting. When he was seventeen he entered the studio of Gleyre, where he made the acquaintance of Monet, Bazille and Sisley. His first exhibition at the *Salon* was in 1863, and about the same time he met Pissarro and Cézanne. The year following he was rejected at the *Salon*, but exhibited instead at the *Salon des Refusés*. Between 1865 and 1868 he frequently visited the Forest of Fontainebleau, where he met Diaz, and in 1865 and 1867 his work was again shown at the *Salon*.

Early in the war with Prussia he enlisted in the cavalry, but saw no active service and returned to Paris in 1871. Two years later he met Durand-Ruel, the first dealer to sponsor his work, and in 1874 and 1877 he participated in the general exhibitions of the

---

[1] From Albert C. Barnes and Violette de Mazia, *The Art of Renoir*, The Barnes Foundation Press, Merion, Pa., 1944.

Impressionists. In the seventies and early eighties his previous acquaintance with Cézanne, whom he had always admired, became more intimate. Between 1879 and 1881 he traveled frequently, going to Algiers for six weeks in 1879 and again in 1881, to Guernsey in 1880 and repeatedly thereafter, and to Italy in 1880–1881. He was married in 1880 and his first son, Pierre, was born in 1885.

During the eighties he continued to sketch in the country and after 1885 went regularly each summer to the village of Essoyes in Champagne. He painted with Cézanne at La Roche Guyon in 1886, at Les Martigues and L'Estaque in 1887, and at Aix-en-Provence on frequent occasions between 1886 and 1893. From 1890 to 1893 he spent his summers in Pont-Aven, and in 1895 he made a trip to Spain. His second son, Jean, was born in 1894. In 1899 he had his first attack of rheumatoid arthritis, a malady which eventually crippled him. Claude Renoir, his third son, was born in 1901. Shortly after 1900 he began to go regularly to the Midi, spending one year at Le Cannet and three at Magagnosc, and in 1907 he settled down finally at Cagnes. In 1911 he lost the use of his limbs almost entirely. He died on December 3, 1919.

The dearth of incident in Renoir's actual existence is in striking contrast to the wealth, variety and audacity of his inner life. Except at the time, just before and after 1880, when the resources that had previously sufficed him seemed to be petering out, he had no need to wander afield for material; it is typical of him that when told of Gauguin's departure for Tahiti, his comment was "one can paint so well at Batignolles." His surroundings were those of a *petit bourgeois*; when he finally went to live in the south of France it was for his health's sake; but in the most commonplace scene he could find an inexhaustible source of interest and delight. Even when his success enabled him to live in greater comfort, he was satisfied with the barest of rooms and the simplest of furnishings; the color and light, the grouping of objects, which he cared for above everything, could be found everywhere. When he went to a reception, it is said, he was so absorbed in the burst of color in a flower, the light playing across a face, that he forgot to listen to what was said to him.

He was equally interested in putting upon canvas whatever moved him, and he did it without effort and so far as possible, without interruption. Except under compulsion, he never missed a day's painting in his whole life; in the hospital, awaiting an operation, he propped up a canvas on the bed before him and painted the flowers which had been sent him; and the day his son, who had been wounded, returned to the front, he could find consolation only in painting. He even said *"c'est avec mon pinceau que . . . j'aime."* He had the utmost admiration for the great painters of the past, who knew their craft so thoroughly, and he expressed his esteem by saying that "the instruction of the museum is the only thing valuable to a painter." He called himself a painter, not an artist, and despised the need for unusual conditions or emotional "inspiration" which condemned other painters to long periods of inactivity. Though he enjoyed music and literature, he gave them up when they threatened to compete with his own work, and though he took pleasure in the companionship of other painters, he had not the slightest interest in theories about art: indeed, he professed to be dismayed when some one suggested entitling one of his pictures *La Pensée.* His nature was extraordinarily spontaneous, averse to what he considered formal or pretentious, whether in persons or works of art, as well as to everything somber or painful; but he was transported by intense color or brilliant light, and wished his pictures to be full of charm and delight. This *joie de vivre* never left him; it survived through the infirmity of his later years, and the canvases painted with a brush he could not hold unaided were as filled with it as those of his early youth. His life and his art were completely one; there was nothing in himself which he could not put on canvas, and nothing on his canvases which was not completely himself.

CEZANNE'S LIFE AND PERSONALITY[1]

ALBERT C. BARNES and VIOLETTE DE MAZIA

PAUL CÉZANNE was born in Aix-en-Provence on January 19, 1839. His father, though of humble origin, had made of himself a prosperous banker, and Paul received, at the *Collège Bourbon* in Aix, the classical education customary for members of well-to-do families in his day. He showed an early fondness for poetry and literature, learned Latin so thoroughly that fifty years later he could repeat from memory whole pages of Virgil and Lucretius, and himself composed verses in Latin as well as French. While at school, he made the acquaintance of Emile Zola, with whom he quickly formed an intimacy that lasted many years, and profoundly influenced Zola as well as himself. With many common interests and ambitions, the two mapped out their future together, planned a joint career that should revolutionize both literature and painting, and probably did much to confirm one another's vocation. Cézanne's interest in art had declared itself when he was very young, and he had begun the study of drawing while still a schoolboy. He continued as a pupil in the Academy at Aix, where he succeeded in winning a prize; however, conformity to academic rules was distasteful to him even at that early age, and he never took this particular success seriously.

After his graduation from college, Cézanne wished to go to Paris, where Zola had preceded him, to fit himself for a career in art. His father, to whom such

[1] From Albert C. Barnes and Violette de Mazia, *The Art of Cézanne*, Harcourt, Brace & Co., New York, N. Y., 1939.

an ambition was unintelligible, wanted him either to enter the paternal bank or to undertake the profession of law. A compromise was reached: Cézanne agreed to attempt the study of law, while his father fitted up a studio for him in Aix and allowed him to paint in his leisure hours. The study of law progressed slowly and laboriously, though at the end of two years he passed his preliminary examinations. All his real interest was in painting, but the museum in Aix, and such guidance and companionship as he could find in a small provincial city, were totally inadequate to his needs. At the same time he was constantly receiving letters from Zola, describing the opportunities that Paris offered and urging him to come there and begin the career on which he had set his heart. Finally, in April, 1861, his father relented, assured him of the necessary financial support, and Cézanne took up his residence in Paris.

Here disillusionment followed quickly. He entered the *Atelier Suisse*, a free studio where models were provided, but neither instruction nor criticism. This had the merit of leaving him to paint as he wished, but offered nothing else of the slightest value. Zola had his hands full to keep himself alive, and could be of little service to him. For the conventional *vie de Bohême* Cézanne had as little taste as he had for any other form of conventionality; his self-distrust made him morbidly fearful of any associations that might develop into entanglements; the confusion of Paris so bewildered and distressed him that he became doubtful of his vocation; and after four months, in spite of Zola's vehement protests, he confessed himself defeated and returned to Aix. Convinced that he had no future as a lawyer, he entered his father's bank; but a second revulsion of feeling took place almost immediately.

He found finance as repugnant to him as the law; he could not put the memory of Paris out of his mind; and when he attempted to paint in his own studio he became acutely conscious of his isolation from the masterpieces of the Louvre, in which he had at hand the traditions of painting that he needed for the nourishment of his growing mind. After a year in Aix, he persuaded his father to allow him to abandon business as he had already abandoned his legal career, and he made his second venture in Paris.

This time there was no vacillation or thought of again retracing his steps. A few months after his arrival the famous *Salon des Refusés* was held, where he saw and immensely admired Manet's *Luncheon on the Grass* and other paintings belonging to the new "realistic" movement. He saw, perhaps for the first time, that he was not alone in rejecting and despising the moribund tradition of David and Ingres, which still dominated official art and the academies, and before long he made the acquaintance of Pissarro, Guillaumin, and a number of the other young painters who were later to become known as the Impressionists. Later on in the sixties, he met Manet, and also Monet, Sisley and Renoir; he came to be on intimate terms with all of them except Manet, who was an older man, fond of the sort of society in which Cézanne was ill at ease and toward which he felt contemptuous. Cézanne, indeed, though his relations with the other painters as individuals were cordial, was never really a member of any group. He was always afraid that others would, as he expressed it, get their *"grappin"* (hooks) into him; furthermore, Manet, Monet and Pissarro were disposed to be revolutionaries in principle, and Cézanne, though he bitterly disliked the traditions of painting that happened to be in power at the moment, was far from objecting to authority as an idea or ideal. He had applied for admission to the *Beaux-Arts* and been rejected; later on, he sent his pictures to the annual *Salon* year after year, and year after year saw them refused; but he never questioned the propriety of an official school or salon as an institution. This was one of the contradictions of his nature, as were also his political conservatism and his Roman Catholicism. When it was a question of submitting his own perceptions and judgments, in a field in which he had first-hand experience, to the judgment of others, he rebelled at once; in most matters, however, feeling himself feeble, he craved something stronger than himself to lean upon, and for such support authority was indispensable.

In 1866 the jury of the official *Salon* rejected many, and in 1867 all but one, of the works of the younger painters with whom Cézanne was associated, and Zola came to their defense on each occasion with a series of articles in which the insurgents, especially Manet, were eulogized and the official tradition caustically attacked and ridiculed. These articles produced no change in official policy, but did much to rally enlightened opinion to the side of the new movement. Unfortunately, Cézanne individually profited little from the change. Zola, whose perceptions in the field of plastic art were at bottom conventional, did not really care for his work and scarcely alluded to it; furthermore, Cézanne himself was still far from having discovered his distinctive vein. He had not yet learned to abandon entirely the literary strain in his painting; the influence of Delacroix upon him was not altogether outgrown; he had still to catch up with his own contemporaries. This was the period of his melodramatic narrative pictures, some of them patterned very closely after

Manet as well as Delacroix. His development was slow: he had not yet acquired even the limited mastery of paint to which he later attained, and the critics who charged him with crudity, however blind they may have been to the personal force and distinction always present in his work, were not wholly wrong. He himself was perfectly aware that he had not completed his apprenticeship, and though his steadfastness did not really falter he was the victim of constantly recurring fits of uncertainty and depression.

During the rest of the 1860's Cézanne continued to work steadily, producing pictures of the same general sort, spending part of his time in Paris, part in Provence. This alternation between the north and the south of France continued for nearly all the remainder of his life, or at least until failing health kept him permanently in Aix. He preferred nature as it was in the Midi, but his need for contact with the masterpieces of art in the museums attached him to Paris. He required long periods of retirement, but sometimes found the society of his family more oppressive than the crowds in the city. During the Franco-Prussian war he remained continuously in Aix and its vicinity, but afterward rejoined his friends and resumed his former way of life in Paris. At this period he formed an association with Hortense Fiquet, whom he eventually married. Their liaison had little or no direct effect upon his work, but indirectly it was the cause of an experience which was of great value to his development. Since he was still in complete financial dependence upon his father, who would have refused to sanction either an irregular union or a marriage with a dowerless girl, Cézanne could not visit Aix in the summer of 1872, especially as a son had been born to them the winter before. Accordingly he went to Auvers-sur-

Oise, near Pontoise, where Pissarro lived. The two
men began to work together constantly, and Cézanne
doing for the first time most of his painting in the open
air, really assimilated the Impressionists' technique, or
as much of it as he needed for his purposes. Pissarro
was the strongest of the Impressionists, and by far the
most congenial to Cézanne in the particular bent of
his mind; he was never so preoccupied with immediate
light-effects as Monet; and in addition to what he
actually communicated to Cézanne, he helped him form
the habit of painting his landscapes directly from
nature. The association continued until 1874, and in
its course Cézanne became more and more conscious
of "the magnificent colorfulness of nature," which was
to set the standard for his painting in all his later years;
he also began to modify the very heavy, lumpy im-
pasto of his first period, and to apply pigment in the
smaller regular brushstrokes which are characteristic ot
his mature work.

By this time, Cézanne was definitely on the way to
his own distinctive achievements. Popular recognition,
however, was still a long way off. He had pictures in
the Impressionists' exhibitions of 1874 and 1877, but
the official attitude toward the members of the group
was unchanged, and it was especially hostile to him as
an individual. He did not prevail over the indifference
even of those whose attitude toward Manet, Monet,
Pissarro and Renoir had become genuinely apprecia-
tive. For years thereafter he exhibited nothing pub-
licly and it was not until 1895 that the first extensive
showing of his pictures was held in France. He continued to send regularly to the *Salon* paintings which
were returned with equal regularity. During the next
years he kept up his personal relations with Pissarro,
Monet, Renoir, Zola and a few other intimates, but

ceased to be regarded by the public as one of them, and gradually sank into deeper and deeper isolation and obscurity. Those of his old friends who were painters never wavered in their admiration for him, regarding him as one of the outstanding figures of his age, an artist of the same order as the great painters of the past; but the academic critics reviled and ridiculed him when they mentioned him at all, and most people forgot his existence.

As the years went by, he saw even his old friends less and less frequently, though occasionally he visited Zola, and Monet and Renoir came to see him in the Midi. In 1886 he was finally married to Hortense Fiquet, and shortly thereafter his father died. This left him wealthy, but he was indifferent to money, except as it assured his independence, and he had had that for a long time. In the same year occurred his break with Zola. The immediate occasion of this was the publication of Zola's *L'Œuvre*, the central figure of which, a painter whose career ended in failure, was generally regarded as modeled after Cézanne. Cézanne was wounded, but in fact the intimacy between the two men had been withering away for a long time, and not much was needed to bring it to an end. No actual quarrel took place, and there were no subsequent signs of animosity on either side, but their visits to each other and their correspondence came to an end.

In the late eighties and early nineties Cézanne became more and more isolated, and not long afterward the decline in his health began. He had always been a Catholic, but with the first intimation that his days were numbered his interest in religion became much more intense and he reverted to a closer communion with the Church. Badly as he needed its support, it was characteristic of him that he was extremely suspicious of the clergy and constantly on guard against what he imagined to be their intention to get their "hooks" into him. He had now achieved the full command of his powers, and much of his very best work was done during these years of loneliness. It brought him no tranquillity of spirit. He never outgrew his inability to work rapidly, and many of his paintings displeased him so much that he destroyed them before they were finished. At times he felt his isolation as exile: though he was incapable of sacrificing his integrity to secure recognition, the absence of the recognition was a source of pain and mortification. At other times, as on one visit to Paris during which he refused to speak to his oldest friends when he passed them on the street, the desire for solitude, for the opportunity to work without distraction from any quarter, made him almost completely a recluse.

However, the period of obscurity gradually came to an end. In 1894 the Caillebotte bequest of impressionist and post-impressionist pictures to the French Government drew some attention to him again, and in the same year Gustave Geffroy published an article on him full of enthusiastic appreciation. The next year marked the turning-point; Vollard arranged the first exhibition devoted wholly to his pictures. In the controversy which followed, his detractors were as much in evidence as usual, but an important body of public opinion made itself heard in his defense, and wealthy collectors, such as de Camondo and Pellerin, began to buy his pictures. At least a decade was still to pass before the immense vogue began which for a time made him the most discussed painter in the world, but a measure of recognition in many quarters came quickly. Other exhibitions in which his pictures appeared were held in 1899, 1900 and 1901, and in 1905 and 1906 the

Salon d'Automne opened its doors to him. In 1907, after his death, the same *Salon* had a retrospective exhibition in which appeared many examples of his work both in oil and water color, covering all the periods and types of his painting. In 1936, the comprehensive exhibition of his work at *L'Orangerie* in Paris revealed to the public for the first time what a monumental figure Cézanne is in the history of painting.

After 1900, whether or not because of the increasing recognition accorded him, Cézanne became less a recluse, and began to establish cordial relationships with a number of his younger contemporaries. None of his characteristics—his aversion to associations which threatened to compromise his independence, his intolerance of opposition, his sense of "feebleness in life"—disappeared, but his suspicions were less easily called forth, his attacks of rage were less frequent, and he was more willing to believe in the good will and esteem of others for him. After his long years of loneliness, he enjoyed greatly the companionship of a number of younger writers and painters who admired his work and wished a better understanding of it. Though his mother, to whom he had always been deeply attached, died in 1897, his grief was alleviated by the fact that his son had already relieved him of the direction of his finances, his negotiations with picture-dealers, and the other practical affairs to which he felt himself unequal. On the whole, the last decade of his life was probably the most peaceful and cheerful that he ever had.

After 1904, Cézanne's diabetes, with which he had long been afflicted, grew rapidly worse and hastened the oncoming of the other infirmities of old age. It seemed to him that he was only then attaining the full maturity of his powers as a painter, but that his bodily weakness had reached a point at which he could no

longer control his brush as he wished. In the summer
of 1906 the approach of the end was unmistakable; he
suffered constant discomfort and frequent attacks of
severe pain; but the increasing exhaustion of his energies brought no enfeeblement of his will and he refused
to sink into the passiveness of senility. In October,
1906, while painting in the open country, he was caught
in a heavy storm, suffered a chill, and was brought
home unconscious. The next day he rose early and
attempted to go on with his work, but he collapsed
almost at once, and died before his wife and son could
reach him from Paris.

Although Cézanne's painting received a measure of
recognition before his death, no observer who viewed
his career wholly from the outside could have judged
it to be, in the conventional sense of the word, a success. A few enlightened critics had in the end acclaimed
him, but the public as a whole knew little of his work
and cared nothing for it; his hoped-for conquest of the
authorities had certainly never been made. Though
he had repeatedly announced himself to be "the only
painter," and no doubt on occasions felt the fullest
assurance that this was the truth, his unceasing suspicion of others, his terror of the "hooks," would long
since have been laid to rest if he had been able to feel
certain about himself. The contrast with Renoir in
this respect is illuminating. Renoir knew his own
mind perfectly and could carry out his intentions with
consummate mastery. His designs seem to have taken
form in his mind with little or no inner conflict, and
they were no sooner conceived than executed. Almost
from the start he enjoyed a command of technique
which Cézanne, after years of toil, never equaled or
even really approached. Renoir was unperturbed by

hostile criticism because no sense of failure, of inadequacy within himself, responded to it or corroborated it: the academicians were in his eyes too obviously unimportant to be given a second thought. Cézanne, on the contrary, wished to "make the officials blush with rage and despair," and in one of his late letters to his son he proclaimed that all his compatriots were dirt compared to him. These are the attitudes and expressions of a man whose conflicts were never solved, who never succeeded in being at peace with himself.

Nevertheless, Cézanne's claims on his own behalf cannot be dismissed as neurotic delusions of grandeur, and the measure of their validity must ultimately be judged by an analysis of his work itself. Their psychological grounds, however, lie within Cézanne's own experience, and these must be understood in the light of his personal history, the environment in which he grew up, the influences to which he was subjected, the goal which he set for himself, and the success of his efforts to reach it. In its broad general outlines, Cézanne's life was far from unique; it was a typical adventure in romanticism; and it can be made intelligible and judged only with the aid of a psychological account of romanticism in general.

The romanticist may be defined as one who lives only partly in the real world which we all share, the world of eating and sleeping, of making money, keeping engagements, and paying bills. Another part of his life, the part he is likely to regard as the more real and important, goes on in a world far more responsive to human wish and aspiration, a world from which boredom, defeat and disillusionment have been banished—in brief, a more glamorous world. Because he is more imaginative than the average man, the romanticist usually seems to the average man a visionary, and only too often it is his tragedy that the average man is right, that he *is* a visionary, that his ascent into his more glamorous world is a mere flight from reality. If the romanticist's intelligence is crippled, he becomes the dreamer too absorbed in his dreams to make them real; if it is entirely paralyzed, he becomes the lunatic for whom dreams are the only realities.

Romanticism and realism or naturalism are often regarded as opposites. The truth is that romanticism can only justify itself, can only prove itself valid, by having its nucleus in the realistic or naturalistic, a nucleus which is expanded by the imagination until it embraces the world of reality itself, and becomes a part of universally verifiable experience. This process constitutes the essence of artistic creation. What is fundamentally opposed to romanticism and realism alike is passive acceptance of convention. To conceive a world more rational than that habitually taken for granted, capable of arousing more vivid interests and yielding more profound satisfactions, is not an indulgence in illusion if the dream or vision is used as an instrument for the discovery of realities here and now. Subject to this control, the art of the romanticist becomes analogous to the art of the scientist, a process of exploring the environment and bringing to light in it things to which the conventionally minded are permanently blind. When the romanticist has proved his case, established the reality of his own conceptions, the stigma of illusion rests not upon him but on the follower of authority. Now that the insurgents of the 1860's and 1870's have made their ways of seeing things a matter of common perception, it is Cabanel, Meissonier and Bouguereau—the painters acclaimed in their day as "sane," "sensible," "normal"—who are felt to be unreal. The conceptions of the artist, in a word, are verified in the same manner as those of the scientist

—by experiment, by the production of objective facts which vindicate their standing in the real world.

Cézanne's original romantic bent is incontestable. He grew up in a provincial Philistine environment, in a family in which the only comprehensible ambition was that for financial success and a substantial bourgeois position in society. Nothing which the natural course of events in that society offered him could conceivably have engaged his interests and energies. His mind fed naturally upon the images of art and literature, and at his most impressionable age he was brought into constant and intimate association with Zola, a youth of boundless ambition, immense energy, unbridled imagination, and an intelligence greatly superior to any other that Cézanne was likely to encounter in Aix. Many men in their youth, of course, have been dissatisfied with their surroundings, formed vague aspirations, and remained mediocrities all their lives. Cézanne, however, had not only extraordinary potentialities as an artist, but an equally extraordinary degree of integrity and force of character. He owed much to Zola for personal stimulus and encouragement, as also of course for assistance in practical affairs, but probably nothing in his actual career as a painter. Perhaps even less than nothing, for Zola may well have been largely responsible for the literary preoccupation which distracted Cézanne's properly plastic perceptions for years before he could entirely rid himself of it.

As we have seen again and again in the analysis of his painting,[2] Cézanne was anything but precocious; he went through a long period of trial and error, studying the work of various painters and even copying from them for the purpose of trying out possible lines of advance, before he discovered the form in which he

[2] See Albert C. Barnes and Violette de Mazia, *The Art of Cézanne*, Harcourt, Brace & Co., New York, N.Y., 1939.

could embody what he himself and only he was able to perceive. Had he ever rested content with another painter's perceptions, he might justly be charged with a fixation, an arrest in development, but he was always aware that his ventures into imitation were temporary exercises, incidents in his own personal quest for reality. He was perpetually in search of the objective facts from which alone his mind could draw its sustenance.

Thus Cézanne's romanticism, his fidelity to his own inner vision, if it was the cause of his tribulations, was also the sustaining force which drove him on to his ultimate victory. When at last he found the kind of objective fact that his individuality could make its own—the colorfulness of nature as a revelation of its form and architecture—his romanticism was fully transformed into a grasp of essential substance. The interaction between his mind and his environment became cumulative, and his growth, the enrichment of his background, was thereafter assured. The interpretation of objects in terms of color-planes, and of total situations in terms of dynamically interacting color-volumes, offered unlimited potentialities, to the exploration of which the rest of his life was devoted. In his letters and conversations he commented constantly on the varied aspects—he called them motifs—of nature at various times, as he observed them in the light of his varying interests and perpetually expanding experience. It was the constancy and continuity of his own growth that enabled him to treat the same subject over and over without monotony, and notwithstanding his limited repertoire of plastic means, to create individualized forms of great variety.

To his romanticism, and the unremitting effort required to bring it to plastic fruition, Cézanne owed also the power which is the outstanding trait of all his char-

acteristic painting. In order to pass from the superficial literary romanticism of his early period to the
profound grasp of nature which he ultimately achieved,
he was compelled to make a thoroughgoing reconstruction of his whole artistic personality. Not only were
the paintings of his apprenticeship crudely executed,
but their plastic structure was loose, and their force
constantly degenerated into flamboyance and melodrama; and although, beneath all this crudity and literary romanticism, the feeling of power emerges, the
perceptions, the forms of organization embodied in his
mature work were present only in germ. Cézanne
himself, recognizing as he did the unsatisfactory result
of his efforts, was conscious only in part of his underlying purpose, and though he used his awareness for
guidance as best he could, it was mainly the systematic
push of his unconscious that furnished the drive toward
his ultimate goal.

This unconscious, refusing to be deflected, overrode
every obstacle that came in its way. It was manifested
in his concentration of purpose, his capacity to undergo
endless labor and hardship, his self-imposed isolation,
his renunciation of every interest that could have
detracted from his singleness of mind. These were the
qualities involved in his ability to transform and give
substance to his romanticism; they are also the qualities
which, psychologically, constitute power; and ultimately, therefore, Cézanne's romanticism was the
source of the power which makes his work unique in the
whole history of art. Because of the power in himself,
he had an incomparable eye for power in nature, for
the qualities which can make the simplest material
object seem massive, immovable and immutable. Because of it, he discarded in his work all the aspects of
things which are accidental, superficial or fugitive —
the play of light as it changes from hour to hour or

from season to season, the expression of transient emotion on a human face, as well as all preoccupation with incident or narrative. Only what was permanent and essential, basic structure unaffected by momentary circumstances, finally found a place in his mind and work; the search for that generated his strength, and his strength in turn made the search successful. That Cézanne's strength was inherent in him, and likewise his responsiveness to the same quality in the world about him, is evidenced by the fact that in his early treatment of romantic subjects, inspired by the forms of Delacroix or Rubens, his paintings have a new and strange feeling of power, not even hinted at in the prototypes.

This power governed not only his choice of aspects for emphasis, but also the mode of organization in which they were arranged. The composition of all his characteristic painting is, as we have seen,[3] highly architectonic. They are intensely dynamic and full of drama, but in his successful work the operative forces are always brought into equilibrium, and the drama is that of thrust met and stabilized by counterthrust, not that of energy unleashed and set in motion. The deep space, the solid weighty masses, the strongly emphasized lines linking the masses together and lending them support and rigidity—all these are the characteristics of architecture conceived on an epic scale and executed with conviction and power. They appear not only in his large landscapes and figure-compositions, but in his small still-lifes, which, irrespective of their physical dimensions, have all of Cézanne's typical scope of conception and vigor of execution. The strangeness, the departure from conventions, the distortions in Cézanne's painting are, psychologically, akin to his be-

[3] In Albert C. Barnes and Violette de Mazia, *The Art of Cézanne*, Harcourt, Brace & Co., New York; N.Y., 1939.

havior in social life; what his whole career, no less than his work, proclaimed to the world, might justly be given expression in these words: "I won't conform, I'll interpret imaginatively, my hand will put down what my eye, experience and feelings, all working together, say is real, sincere, myself." The point here is that the strangeness of his work is part and parcel of a self, an original self: his deformations of naturalistic appearances are akin to the brusque remarks made by Cézanne which, when sociability is the rule, project new interpretations upon conventionally accepted ideas, or redirect traditional feelings into new channels. The significant fact is that when he made these remarks, or dressed badly, or secluded himself, the members of the Batignolles group—Renoir or Monet, for example—thought Cézanne's conduct strange, yet did not utterly condemn it; but when he put into painting the psychological equivalent of this social strangeness, they admired it, saw in it a personality doing and revealing something new, individual, fundamentally significant, with the very subjects, technique, independent spirit, honesty, sincerity, which they looked upon as their very own. They prized it so much that persecution by either critics or public never swerved them.

Cézanne, like every other artist, had the defects of his qualities. The concentration of energies out of which his power arose entailed also many renunciations; indeed, a greater number of them than would have been necessary for a man less at war with his surroundings and hence less compelled to find self-possession by exclusion. Titian and Renoir, to take only two examples, show in their unlimited mastery of their medium, their capacity to realize an intended effect, a kind of power less accentuated, less intense, than Cézanne's, but in its own way not less real. At the same time, their more comprehensive interests enabled them to incorporate in their work a whole world of values, human and decorative as well as plastic, that are not even suggested in Cézanne's. The glow of diffused light bathing and transfiguring an entire landscape, the warmth of human flesh, the textural quality of silk or velvet, of flowers or jewels, have a reality of their own, a legitimate esthetic appeal that is not necessarily and under all circumstances inconsistent with the expression of power. Cézanne, however, because he felt himself "feeble in life," because he could not sufficiently control his human emotions to be indifferent to the "hooks," was obliged to shut out from his work innumerable qualities which more fortunate painters were able to admit without detriment to the balance of their feelings or the integrity of their minds.

Cézanne's vision, to sum up, because of the inherent character of his personality and the experiences involved in its successful growth, was extraordinarily penetrating. "The magnificent richness of color which animates nature," in so far as it can be used to build up solid masses and to organize them in space, was assimilated and made a part of his own mind with extraordinary completeness and with supreme power. In this sense his judgment upon himself—"I am the only painter"—is anything but an unqualified overcompensation, or a delusion of megalomania: it approaches closely to the literal truth. Little qualified as he was to do justice to painters who had other interests than his, he was not mistaken about himself. As regards sensitiveness to the specific form of reality in which Cézanne was interested above all others, and the ability to give it plastic realization, no other painter has ever equaled him. Whatever his difficulties, frustrations and doubts about himself, Cézanne did in essentials bring his romanticism to fruition, make his dreams a part of nature itself.

CEZANNE AND RENOIR[1]

ALBERT C. BARNES and VIOLETTE DE MAZIA

THE characteristics on which Cézanne's real greatness depends, and those which limit his greatness and make him an easy prey for imitators, are thrown into clear relief by a comparison between him and Renoir. Both men were artists of the first rank, both had their essential origin in the Venetians, both took impressionism as their point of departure, both made color the fundamental means of all their plastic effects. These resemblances were accompanied by differences almost as basic. Renoir's natural endowment in the matter of craftsmanship was of the same magnitude as Rembrandt's or Velásquez': by the early 1870's he was able to paint whatever he wished without any visible sign of effort. His ability to take for granted the means of execution left his energies free thereafter for the work of broadening and deepening his perceptions themselves, and this growth in artistic stature proceeded uninterruptedly his whole life long. What he had once mastered became his permanent possession; Cézanne, in contrast, was perpetually confronted with the necessity of solving the same problems over again. This struggle seems to have left him with little opportunity for more fundamental development. He did outgrow the literary preoccupations of his earliest period—Renoir's sense for the authentically plastic seems to have been innate, for he had no corresponding literary period to outgrow—but once Cézanne had

[1] From Albert C. Barnes and Violette de Mazia, *The Art of Cézanne*, Harcourt, Brace & Co., New York, N. Y., 1939.

found the form natural to him he never made any further advance in essentials. His *Bathers at Rest* (The Barnes Foundation, No. 906) of 1877 is as original and powerful as his *Nudes in Landscape* (The Barnes Foundation, No. 934) of 1890–1906. The later picture is conceived on a more monumental scale, it has a much greater range of values, it is far more effectively executed; but there is no fundamental difference in kind between the two.

The contrast with Renoir could hardly be more striking.[2] Starting his career under the influence of Courbet and Manet, he quickly assimilated the technique and characteristic effects of Impressionism, added to them a fluid, rhythmic, expressive drawing all his own, and in a short time painted pictures that were plastically more varied, richer, more powerful, and especially more colorful than any of Manet's, Monet's or Pissarro's. No sooner was this form mastered than, in the late 1870's and early 1880's, he went on to diversify his palette, vary his technique, intensify his light, and give to his color more comprehensive plastic functions, both decorative and expressive. In the middle 1880's he developed a new form which in many respects differed notably from that of his previous work, and marked his assimilation of the Eighteenth Century French tradition. The delicacy and grace characteristic of him from the start were endowed in these years with additional picturesqueness and charm; a sculptural quality developed in his drawing, modeling and textural effects; contours grew sharp, and reminiscences of Italian frescoes and the classical tradition in art made their appearance. In this period of active experimenta-

[2] For a detailed account of Renoir's development, see Albert C. Barnes and Violette de Mazia, *The Art of Renoir*, pp. 47–160, The Barnes Foundation Press, Merion, Pa., 1944.

tion and research, Renoir was exploring the traditions for new material; the form thus developed was, for him, comparatively exotic, and many aspects of it were subsequently discarded; but the added resources remained as an essential part of his working capital, to be utilized in all his later work.

In the 1890's, and still more in the years following 1900, Renoir made his own, more completely than any other modern painter, the qualities that set apart the Venetian tradition as the most important in the whole history of painting. Discarding the sharp linear contours which had for a while been the instrument of his sculptural effects, he drew everything with a constantly increasing fluidity. To his grace and charm, the exquisite quality he had always possessed, he added the solidity, depth, dignity and majesty characteristic of the Venetians at their best. More and more he eliminated the inessential and adventitious; and coincidentally he made color more and more completely the substance and integrating principle of his form. No other painter ever excelled him in the use of color to build up masses, draw space and organize composition. In his latest pictures everything is color: actual line practically disappears, light loses its separate identity and becomes a sparkle or glow of suffused color, the constantly changing yet always harmonious fabric of color binds together every area of the canvas.

Not only did Renoir show a capacity for growth that Cézanne lacked almost entirely, but he was able to diversify his methods and use them to draw out the significant character of any sort of material whatever. As we have so often observed, Cézanne's subjects are all conceived in much the same terms and his compositions are put together in the same general fashion. There are differences, of course, between the flesh in his figures and the pieces of fruit or napkins in his still-lifes, but the solidity, the weight, stands out with such intense conviction in both that the distinguishing qualities seem unimportant. Likewise with Cézanne's frequently recurring general types of composition: they are significantly varied by modifications of detail, but Renoir's inexhaustible ability to organize a picture about any one of a number of focal points, and to produce different schemes of organization in endless profusion, finds no parallel in them. In his figure-painting, Renoir was able to catch the pose, the gesture, the exact shade of facial expression which make human action and character convincing; except in his early work, and then often badly, Cézanne scarcely even attempted any such psychological characterization. His figures are dignified and real, but it is primarily as plastic or architectural units that they engage the observer's interest.

Cézanne's technical means are as limited in range as his pictorial effects. Pattern of brushstrokes and color-patches, flattened planes intersecting at definite angles to build up geometrical solid masses, general accentuation of line as a means of modeling and rendering perspective—these are the instruments on which he relies in all his characteristic pictures. As a result of his work in water color he was occasionally able to introduce a measure of fluidity and even of color-suffusion, but the rigid angular framework of the composition and the patterned technique are never really changed in essentials. Renoir was never compelled to rely on any single manner of execution: he could use very obvious and definitely patterned technique when he wished, or dispense with it altogether. Sharp line or loose line, linear perspective or aërial perspective, flattened planes or continuously rounded surfaces together with textural effects of every sort, were all at his disposal. It was this infinitely varied command of plastic resources that enabled Renoir to achieve the art that conceals art, to make technique so completely instrumental to form, that we are unconscious of its existence except when, for purposes of analysis, we deliberately seek it out.

In the light of these differences between the two men, Cézanne's much greater influence upon his successors, and especially upon academic critics and painters, becomes readily comprehensible. Not only is his most characteristic effect, that of extreme dynamic power, overwhelming in its impact upon the observer's senses, but the means employed to secure it are comparatively few in number, obvious, and easy to stereotype. Hence the innumerable imitative pictures with patterning planes, blocklike volumes and arbitrary distortions; hence also the theories of "significant form," which have not the slightest foundation in modern psychology or scientific method, and which when applied reduce plastic form to decorative pattern. Those who see in distinction of form only idiosyncrasy of mannerism can find in Cézanne much to imitate, in Renoir, little or nothing. In neither, of course, can they see the qualities that constitute real greatness; Cézanne's color-power, especially, is entirely beyond them; but his general color-scheme and superficial peculiarities of technique can be reproduced in unlimited quantity. Renoir's form, complex, subtle and infinitely varied in the manner of its execution, offers no comparable opportunity to the copyist or to the theorist with an axe to grind.

The foregoing comparison may have seemed unqualifiedly favorable to Renoir, and certainly his greater control of his medium, capacity for growth, and variety of effect are incontestable. Cézanne's relative lack of these advantages, however, does not compromise his standing as an artist of the highest rank. Lacking Renoir's natural endowment as a craftsman and his openness of mind toward new experience, Cézanne made of his limitations themselves a source of added strength. The struggle against immense odds to realize the effects of power and order in which his whole personality, conscious and subconscious, found its only natural expression, developed in him a degree of single-mindedness, of resolution, of fortitude, which immeasurably increased his sense of power itself. He achieved the full realization of his designs only on rare occasions, but when he did the result was of monumental quality which makes comparison futile and indeed impossible. There is no such thing as a choice between Renoir and Cézanne: far from competing with one another, they are both indispensable to a fully rounded contemporary esthetic experience. Both, in short, are so valuable as to be invaluable.

STRAVINSKY AND MATISSE[1]

VIOLETTE DE MAZIA

THE characteristic forms of Matisse's paintings provide an interesting parallel to those of Stravinsky's musical compositions, especially the scores which he wrote specifically for ballet, rather than those which he wrote in the formal symphonic style. Indeed, the vibrancy of Stravinsky's orchestral color, the compulsive patterning beat of his rhythms, and the dramatic transitions of his bold contrasts, may be said to disclose too obvious a kinship with the outstanding features of Matisse's paintings to require pointing out in detail. Nonetheless, we believe it will be fruitful to examine the amazingly ingenious use which each artist makes of the traditions to produce the striking innovations characteristic of their respective compositions.

In his first contact with the works of either of these artists, the untrained observer, or anyone not familiar with their compositions, is likely to be taken aback or even shocked by the impact of their unusual sensuous quality, as well as by the daring relationships in which the elements of their forms are set. Precisely because of the frequent pungency of their color, their daring palettes—of sound as of color—may well appear to be at sharp variance with what we have learned to expect in the work of other artists; but, beneath the disconcerting strangeness, we discover a wealth of firmly structural material. The obvious decorative emphasis, conspicuous in the work of both artists, and their frequent use of primitive and exotic traditions, are further fac-

[1] Adapted from Albert C. Barnes and Violette de Mazia, *Matisse and Stravinsky*, The Art of Henri-Matisse, Charles Scribner's Sons, New York, London, 1933.

tors which contribute to the marked similarity observable in their compositions. One is repeatedly surprised, even disturbed, by what seems at first like sheer audacity on the part of these artists; but their onslaughts upon our sensibilities are a challenge to probe into their past, and into the sources from which their boldly conceived novelties proceed.

Stravinsky shares with Matisse the rare talent for reorganizing into a highly individual form the essence of a great variety of traditions; but, measured against Matisse from this point of view, Stravinsky's assimilation of borrowed material is, on the whole, not so thorough. While for this reason, Stravinsky is on occasion less removed from eclecticism, he displays remarkable discernment in his ability to integrate a large number of thematic ideas and melodic phrases, drawn from widely diverse sources, into entities as new and personal as are the best of Matisse's paintings.

Like Matisse, Stravinsky has at his command a broad range of traditional resources, and he, too, follows his predecessors with varying degrees of fidelity. In Stravinsky's counterpoint and thematic development, for example, the influences of Bach, Haydn and Mozart are not so readily identifiable objectively, but are felt rather as pervasive qualities—in solution, so to speak;[2] but on occasion there are more definite though fleeting reminders of Bach's highly-figured themes and of Mozart's delicate touch and singing crispness. Usually, these characteristics are contrasted with some heavier rhythm or series of dissonant chords in exotic instrumental color, derived from totally dissimilar sources—most likely those of Russian composers—with which Stravinsky successfully integrates them.

[2] An exception to this is Stravinsky's recent opera, *The Rake's Progress*, which is based essentially on 18th Century music.

The influence of Beethoven can be detected in the occasionally rich expressiveness and bursts of weighty orchestral color. These borrowings, as a rule, are overlaid with, and thus transformed by, novel relationships in rhythms and motifs, and they are still further modified by sounds of instruments which either did not exist in Beethoven's day or were not used by him. Stravinsky is also indebted to Wagner and to Strauss for what might be described as their voluminous harmonies; and a certain affinity to César Franck may be felt in Stravinsky's tone-color, in the character of his orchestral warmth, and more specifically in overtones of mysticism, a dreamy ambiance that connects in the mind with the haunting, wailing, unrhythmically meandering improvisation of Oriental chant. Incidentally, one may note in passing that the finale of *L'Oiseau de Feu*, with its powerful unrelenting piling up of one climactic effect after another, brings to mind César Franck's not dissimilar build-up to a climax at the end of his *Symphony in D Minor*.

These selective derivations from the great European tradition quite frequently merge in Stravinsky's ballets with themes borrowed from folk melodies of all sorts, most often those of Russian, Chinese and African origin. At times, both of these styles—the traditional and the folk-music genre—are played off against each other: *e.g.*, a passage comparatively close to the traditional style is played against a background of strongly rhythmic monotone, and in such instances they are more clearly identifiable than when they merge completely with each other and relinquish the distinctiveness of their respective identities. While resort to folk music has not been uncommon, especially among those Russian composers to whom Stravinsky owes a great deal—Rimsky-Korsakov, Moussorgsky, Glinka, Borodin, Balakirev—it is doubtful whether it has ever involved the variety of primitive elements which are present in some of Stravinsky's music for the ballet. In fact, it is precisely this handling of elements from primitive or folk music which is responsible for so much of the dramatic and exotic piquancy which Stravinsky imparts to many traditionally conceived passages. A parallel to this appears in the canvases of Matisse in which features selected from early Byzantine mosaics (the broad patterning outlines, the patchwork of color-areas) and from primitive sculpture of India and Africa (the circumscribing grooves, the mask effect) are masterfully re-organized into exotic pictorial conceptions which embody characteristics representative of European traditional forms, such as those of the Venetians and Cézanne.

Still other composers to whom Stravinsky is obviously indebted are his contemporaries, Ravel and Debussy, who, in turn, were to some extent influenced by him. In general, we may say that Stravinsky's ballet music stands in relation to their work much as Matisse's paintings do in reference to Manet's and Cézanne's, although here the counter-influence noted above could not, of course, have taken place in the case of Manet, and did not take place in the case of Cézanne. Just as Matisse has many times availed himself freely of compositional forms and technical procedures of Manet and Cézanne, modifying them in characteristic ways, without, however, concealing their origin from anyone with an eye for plastic values, just so did Stravinsky, in similar fashion, weld organically into his own distinctive form, with attending modifications and without disguising his sources, the orchestral color of Ravel, the long-drawn-out fluctuating line of Debussy, with the expectancy it engenders, and the characteristic pictorial effects which are found in the works of both.

The suavity and elegance of Debussy are superseded in Stravinsky by bolder contrasts, jagged rhythmic outlines, dramatic blares of weird combinations of sounds, and a dynamic pushing forward and on by the propelling pulse of the sharply punctuated rhythmic pattern. Again, the analogy to Matisse in relation to Cézanne is clear: *e.g.*, however powerful the impact of Cézanne may be, there is never the shock, the assault on our sensibilities by sheer sensuous quality of color or bizarre pattern, which is so constant a feature in our experience with the work of Matisse.

As mentioned at the start, one of the most outstanding points of similarity in the works of Stravinsky and Matisse is their obvious emphasis upon decoration. Only infrequently does either artist attempt to render with any degree of fulness or depth of expressiveness some of the major human values. In this respect, nothing in their works corresponds to either Beethoven's *Eroica Symphony* or the *Credo* in Bach's *Mass in B Minor* — or to Giorgione's *Concert Champêtre*, or Renoir's or Cézanne's major figure-pieces or landscapes. When Stravinsky builds up a phrase or some brief passage in the style of Beethoven, it usually functions in the manner of those relatively isolated tile-like units noted in Matisse, *i.e.*, as an episode in itself — not imitative of superficial characteristics, but skillfully rendered in its essentials and well-woven into the fabric of the form — providing, in this way, a note of contrast, a refreshing element of surprise in a totality dominated by a type of conception or style of execution very dissimilar to it. When, on occasion, Matisse and Stravinsky attempt full-bodied expressions of broad human values, they are usually unable to move far from their sources; similarly, when they make use of easily-acceptable color of intrinsically sensuous appeal (warm, gentle or mellow), they are least themselves, closest to their predecessors.[3]   On the other hand, both artists have an exceptional flair for converting sounds or colors, which by themselves might appear harsh, strident, or devoid of immediate sensuous appeal, into strangely satisfying harmonious constituents of their emphatically assertive patterns.   The character of Stravinsky's pattern, in some of its phases, is a direct result of his use of the primitive traditions, *e.g.*, the complex rhythmic forms and the tom-tom beat of African tribal chants and music, which are in fact the predominant features of the throbbing rhythm in the greater part of *Les Noces* and *Le Sacre du Printemps*.   In the latter, the primacy of intricate decoration is the outstanding characteristic; the music to the dance is so crowded with complex and intricately intertwining rhythms—in this instance, an intensification of one of his habitual characteristics— that no human body could possibly move or gesture in correspondence to every nuance of rhythm in the score. That is, there are decorative features in the music to which no commensurate expressive aspects can be found to correspond.   In Stravinsky's adaptation of primitive themes, the qualities which he emphasizes may appear to be bizarre or startling, but there is no sustained temper of the eerie, the ominous, or the tragic.   Like Matisse, he is more concerned with the picturesque, and again as in the paintings of Matisse, the ballets of Stravinsky are replete with those effects which we have termed "transferred values."   Drawn from all categories of human experience, they enliven and enrich both the expressive and the decorative aspects of his compositions, always injecting characteristic touches of piquant illustrative allusions, without any of the literal

[3] *E. g.*, Matisse's *Still-Life with Peaches* (Formerly, Collection Sacha Guitry, Paris) and Stravinsky's ballet *Apollon Musagète*.

anecdotal imitation which makes inferior program-music so objectionably vapid. In other words, the descriptive in Stravinsky is never overstressed at the expense of intrinsic musical values. Correspondingly in Matisse, subjects and transferred values are selected and used for what their factual nature can supply of intrinsically plastic interest along the line of his major concerns.

Stravinsky's resources for achieving transferred values are as broad and varied as Matisse's, and his use of them is at all times as spirited and imaginative. Evidence of this crops up everywhere, particularly in those of Stravinsky's ballets in which whimsy or fantasy predominates. For this reason, it is not altogether satisfactory to limit the illustrations to only a few examples; but among the infinite variety he rings on these transferred effects, there are, in particular abundance, echoes and reverberations of such things as a military parade, a county fair, a milling crowd; spiralling flames and crackling fireworks; flashes of lightning, shrieks and leaps, a plaintive shepherd's pipe, brisk rumblings and thundering roars that carry the feeling of a rushing train or of a storm—the examples are endless. The tom-tom beat, noted earlier in a different context, is still another instance of Stravinsky's ingenious use of transferred values. In *Les Noces* and in *Le Sacre*, it lends its compelling pushing-forward character to the insistent background-pattern of the former, and to the weighty pounding rhythm of the latter. In *Petrouchka*, on the other hand, the rhythmic theme carries the joyous sprightliness of an out-door festival, which is reinforced by the frequent recurrence of a sing-song motif of the sort one associates with the sound of a hurdy-gurdy. Both of these motifs, the festival and the hurdy-gurdy, play into, emerge from, and revolve around snatches of melodies—a profusion of them—mostly in the spirit of Slavic peasant music, and are intermittently slowed down in their gay cavorting by those long and fluid swaying lines that recall Debussy's. The inventive ingenuity of this richly decorative organization, constantly "on-the-go" in the unceasing intertwining of its main motifs, is a close counterpart to that of Matisse's organization when he, too, selects one main motif as the general organizing factor, the rosette, for example, and proceeds to establish a constantly-varied interplay between its own constituents and those of contrasting secondary themes, that, among others, of the stripes and bands.

Both the composer and the painter excel, to an extraordinary degree, in their ability to combine into compositions that are new and distinctively their own, elements or effects of radically different nature, like musical passages or color-themes in daringly clashing keys or moods. Thus, in Stravinsky, a sequence of such seemingly disparate pieces as a gentle lullaby following a lively, abruptly-patterned primitive motif, or consecutive melodies in contrasting tempos, is analogous to Matisse's frequent dramatic interlocking of two distinct and sharply-contrasting sets of color: one of them light, delicate and tranquil; the other vivid, intense and more emphatically patterned. No less amazing than the mental agility of the two men which enables them to achieve those striking combinations of material borrowed from sharply contrasting traditions is the versatility they display in their development of single, simple themes: *i.e.*, by resolving a theme into its components, re-combining these, and varying their relationships to the context, Matisse and Stravinsky succeed in creating an extraordinary, ever-renewed sense of freshness and novelty.

Both Matisse and Stravinsky are very much alive to the complex and many-faceted civilization of our times. Both have at hand resources of a diversity never paralleled before in the fields of painting and music. While it is a fact that in their long careers of noteworthy achievements, the two artists have worked within a relatively narrow range of interest, they never closed their minds to any potential source of fresh material on which their fertile imaginations might feed, not even disdaining at times to draw on the material of artists whose work they neither admired nor considered significant. Examples of this may be found in one of Stravinsky's most recent pieces, his *Septet* composed in 1953, in which for the first time he uses the twelve-tone system of Schönberg—as well as in Matisse's late and novel "découpages" which were inspired in some measure by the early Cubists' experimenting with "papiers collés." In other words, they have, over the years and to the present day, exhibited an amazing capacity for increasing their working capital and for continually renewing themselves. In fact, the dramatic variety of constituents within a totally distinctive entity, which is a constant feature in practically any one of their compositions, is also an outstanding characteristic of their respective careers considered as a whole; *i.e.*, in each new work of Matisse and Stravinsky, as at each step in any single work, the dazzling novelties which they introduce keep those who experience them at a sustained pitch of excitation, on the *qui vive* for the expected unexpectedness which we have accustomed ourselves to look for in their works, and the dominant traits of their unique personalities carry through unmistakably in all the successive stages of their developments.

Both have adventurous minds, but having grasped fully the significance of traditional material in creative work and having assimilated thoroughly the essentials of other artists' achievements, they were able to wander far from conventional forms, which they have done successfully even in their boldest experimenting without losing their roots in the solid substance contributed by their predecessors and contemporaries. The results of their wanderings may make their own contributions seem strange to the novice and at times even wilfully obscure. To the inquiring and interested mind, however, the very strangeness of their forms is a challenge and an incentive to examine them more closely, and to put them to the test of an objective analysis of their observable features. As soon as the key to the novel sets of relationships is found in the fundamental intent—the design—of either the musical or the pictorial construction, an unusually rich store of new esthetic experiences is made possible, and bewilderment gives way to understanding and an ever-increasing sense of rare and profound satisfaction.